Electronic Performance
Support Systems

How and why
to remake the workplace
through
the strategic application of
technology

by Gloria J. Gery

Gery Performance Press

ELECTRONIC PERFORMANCE SUPPORT SYSTEMS
How and why to remake the workplace through
the strategic application of technology

by Gloria J. Gery

© Copyright 1991 Gery Performance Press
Gery Associates
108 South Trail
Tolland MA 01034-9403
(413) 258-4693

Library of Congress Catalog Card Number: 91:66425
ISBN 0-9617966-1-2
Printed in the United States of America

First Edition
Fourth Printing, 1995

To my parents, Agnes and Felix Sposito. Thank you
for always being there with unconditional love.
And to my sisters, Marie Cerino and Carol Gutter,
for their love, support, and friendship.

Table of Contents

Acknowledgments

The emergence of a new discipline such as electronic performance support often starts when a few people are frustrated with the mismatch between their needs and traditional approaches to filling them. Conversations heat up. People push away from the table and start drawing models and making lists on flip charts. Exactly that happened in mid-1989 when Alan Cohen, Gerry Puterbaugh, Bob Sofman, Marc Rosenberg, Bill Luithle, and Chris Most of AT&T were working with me on strategy for delivering electronic training. We rolled up the flip chart that included the paradigm comparison between conventional training and what we then called *knowledge support systems* and a chart on competency development and went back to work on the conventional approaches. We gathered again, and again, and started to bring others into the fray. AT&T hosted a meeting of its trainers from around the country—and the concepts were developed further. We changed the labels and the term *electronic performance support systems* emerged. Dick Horn and his associates at Comware in Cincinnati, Ohio developed the first AT&T performance support tool, the *Training Test Consultant* (TTC), which is described in the case study in this book, and the train left the station. Dick Horn had been banging on doors with the concept for some time, but folks were having a hard time making the conceptual and emotional leap from *training* to *EPSS*. When we were able to actually demonstrate the TTC, we heard the whistle blow and folks boarded the train.

More people jumped on board, and for the past two years, I have been working on some exciting concept development and implementation prototypes and pilots with both clients and vendor associates. The chicken and egg cycle accelerated: as the concept evolved, so did development tools; and the availability of development tools fueled the concept. And now the EPSS train is steaming down the tracks and many organizations and vendors are both on board and stoking the engine.

I want to acknowledge and extend deep personal and professional thanks to the many people who have actively participated in idea development, EPSS system development, arguments, review of writings, and emotional support for me during this early period of framing what electronic performance support can be. And, of course, many have played an active part in the development of this book by contributing ideas and input, reviewing manuscripts, and providing exciting EPSS projects about which to write.

Thanks, of course, to the seminal AT&T group described above. Gerry Puterbaugh, now of AT&T Paradyne, and Marc Rosenberg continue to stimulate me with both intellectual depth and emotional support. Dick Scott and Jane Paulsen of IBM, through their exciting Data Modeling EPSS, provided the chance to explore EPSS applications to abstract analytical tasks. Jane and the project team's work (detailed in the case study) is one of the more exceptional examples of EPSS available.

Barry Raybould of Ariel Performance Systems, Inc., in Mountain View, California, started talking with me about this concept when he was with Prime Computer. After one phone call I knew that two kindred souls had found each other. Barry's contribution to my technical understanding, as well as his influence on my thinking about design, has been extraordinary. Dick Horn of Comware was on the EPSS road before I was. Dick, thanks for dragging me onto this more powerful path. The Ziff Technologies' *Word for Windows* product (see the case study) and the AT&T TTC were both developed by Comware staff. Carolyn Ladd and Annette Crossley provided enormous assistance in getting them represented well—and in reviewing the chapter on development. Steve Caldwell, President of Ziff Technologies, deserves thanks, as well as praise for imaginative thinking. The commercially available Word for Windows EPSS will be both a business success and create the marketplace for commercial EPSS products.

Rick Hill and Leah Rampy of American Express in New York got me involved in an interesting project to create a prototype of what a software system would look like if it were designed to support job task performance and learning, as well as data processing input and information retrieval. Karl Schmidt of Apple Computer, a good friend and creative thinker, paired with us and brought Mark Carpenter and his associates at Santa Fe Interactive into the project. What a wonderful time we had! The case study write-up explains the project. The friendships we developed aren't detailed, but I'm thankful for them. Mark Carpenter is one of the most brilliant designers around. He continually maintains a *user/learner* perspective—and keeps me honest in that regard. His extensive involvement in my idea development couldn't be appreciated more. I publicly apologize for all the tight deadlines I've requested on manuscript review—and thank Mark and his staff for their wonderful work. Thanks to Cathy Malloy of Santa Fe Interactive for all of the exhibits for the Steelcase, Dow Chemical, and American Express cases. And Mark introduced me to his work with C. L. Price and Randy Jensen of Dow Chemical. Their Total Quality Management EPSS in the case study section represents one of the finest implementations I've seen to date. It offers the promise of the construction of a shell that could be made available to be populated with task-specific content. Thanks for letting me demonstrate it in my presentations. I don't know how I could have communicated the concepts without it!

Karl Schmidt of Apple Computer is one of the leading visionaries about EPSS. He participated in the American Express, Steelcase, and Dow projects, among others. Karl, many thanks for the support and the ideas. And, of course, thanks to all of the Apple Computer people who have pushed the limits of thinking and design through the availability of the wonderful Macintosh computer and software such as *HyperCard*.

I've worked with Rich Schmieder of Amdahl for years in CBT. Our conversations are loud and animated. When Rich showed me his Customer Services—Field Engineering EPSS prototype and disclosed his strategy for sponsorship development at Amdahl, lights went on. The case study tells the story of the good work, including that of Mark Walus of Amdahl. The chapter on strategy benefited greatly from Rich's input. A word of advice to Rich: if you could just be a little more enthusiastic...

Ann Farley of Farley Associates developed an EPSS for American Reinsurance that helped me further crystalize ideas. Our twenty-year friendship and professional association has been an important part of my life. I met Louis Baca of Intel Corporation, Albuquerque, at a SALT conference in February of 1991. His description of an EPSS supporting a complex manufacturing process intrigued me. He brilliantly conceptualized and implemented it with his associates. I share it with you in the cases. Thanks, Louis. And thanks to Mark Lembersky of Innovis Technologies for the beautiful Innovis DesignCenter application, also described in the case studies section. Mark says, "If they need a manual, it wasn't designed right." I agree.

Daryl Conner's seminal work and elegant methodology and training on managing organizational change has carried me through many critical projects. Thanks to Daryl (ODR, Inc., of Atlanta) for both the empowering tools and the permission to incorporate the various illustrations and material on sponsorship and resistance in Chapter Six.

Thanks, of course, to all of the corporations who willingly gave me permission to write and publish the case studies in this book. Ziff Technologies, AT&T, Intel, IBM, Amdahl, American Express, Innovis Technologies, Steelcase, Dow Chemical, and Prime Computer. Visionary organizations all.

All of my friends and associates at Weingarten Publications deserve special words. Floyd Kemske, my editor, can make my writing sound more like me than I can. His gentle prodding moves me further in less time than anything else can. His critical review of my ideas and assistance in clarifying them were essential to getting this book done. Thanks also to Ken Foubert for his design and layout work. The book looks great! Anne Murray's cover design managed to capture one of the fundamental points of the book: that the principles of EPSS are timeless. This is a millennial concept of human performance, it's not a technical fad. And thanks from all readers to Pat Brennan who indexed the book so carefully. What a wonderful job.

And, of course, special thanks to Nancy Weingarten, my dear friend and publisher. We've walked the professional road together for over ten years. It's wonderful when a friend of the road also becomes a friend of the heart. With love and appreciation for your confidence in me—and your contributions to all of us involved in the fields in which Weingarten Publications publishes and provides forums for our meeting and learning. You've made an enormous difference to the world.

Finally, special thanks and love to my husband, Bob. Every day is better than the last. You keep me going...

Tolland, Massachusetts
September, 1991

CHAPTER

The Great Cover Up

Our business organizations
are extremely effective at
hiding the performance
crisis—from themselves as
well as everybody else.

Organizations substantially increase the effectiveness of human endeavor. It is, in fact, nearly impossible to imagine modern work outside the context of our large, complex organizations. Manufacturing, research, business and consumer services, military activity, education—all these things would be virtually unthinkable today without the power that comes from organizations: the multiplication of human talent, strength, and experience through sheer numbers. As a species, we pool our talents and strength to achieve grand objectives.

Unfortunately, however, our talents are not all constructive. Human beings, as everyone knows, have a large capacity for self-delusion. This peculiar talent is multiplied along with the others in the modern organization. While we are cooperating to achieve grand objectives, we are also (mostly without knowing it) cooperating to delude ourselves on a grand scale.

Consider the current crises in the American banking and automobile industries. No matter what the general public thinks, the Japanese did not simply start manufacturing high-quality automobiles at a reasonable price in the Fall of 1988. Commercial banks did not expand capacity beyond market needs one afternoon in 1990. There were, in fact, major and ongoing indications of problems in these industries, but the organizations in them channeled a great deal of energy and effort into hiding the problems from themselves. And why shouldn't they? The rest of us were there to encourage them in their cover-up efforts. The media, our politicians, and our citizenry in general wanted nothing to be wrong. We all pretended it was business as usual.

The cooperative national effort in the cause of self-delusion has left our country's largest manufacturing industry nearly paralyzed in the face of foreign competition. And it has allowed the banking industry to drift into chaos, such that public debate now seems to center on the ability of our bankrupt government to sustain our bankrupt banking system. Problems in these industries have had a generation to grow and ripen beneath the surface, sheltered and cultivated by those of us who preferred to think that they would never take root, which is to say nearly all of us.

The pattern of our collusion on the crisis in employee performance is similar. Each of us encounters evidence of incompetence every day, but our strategies for denying it are many and powerful. We use them at every level, but they are probably most damaging within our organizations, where the crisis is the most threatening as well.

What are some of these organizational strategies?

Denial or refusing to admit the truth, is the strongest and most common defense mechanism. Essentially, making believe nothing is

2

wrong or that problem indicators are not serious, is the means by which we avoid confrontation with something that is either inherently unacceptable to us or which, if acknowledged, might be beyond our capacity to deal with. Several mechanisms are employed that result in denial. Typically, they are unconscious. When these strategies are confronted, the proverbial shooting of the messenger often results. Contributing strategies to denial include:

- Selective perception
- Avoidance of information or circumstances depicting the problem
- Explaining data or problems away with a "yes, but..." response
- Deliberate cover-up of unacceptable information
- Superficial review of information without appropriate diligence.

Symptoms of the denial strategy include:

- "Good news only" meetings that rarely include active discussions of problems, performance deficits, symptoms, or negative consequences of the status quo
- Exclusion of people who are "negative" or pessimistic from key situations, positions, and discussions
- Minimization of negative information as "unrepresentative, inaccurate, incomplete, a temporary condition," or otherwise unimportant
- Conscious or unconscious unwillingness to bring difficult situations to the attention of the people in power.

Examples of denial are not difficult to find. A senior software publishing company executive found reported sales unacceptably low and product returns unacceptably high. He requested that the warehouse temporarily withhold reporting of returned product with the expectation that the situation would turn around within the quarter. It didn't, so he made the same request the next quarter, and so on. This action repeatedly occurred, with the warehouse manager's cooperation. Ultimately, the auditors identified more product returned (although unreported) than had been sold in the previous year.

In another situation, a financial analyst identified discrepancies in reported results and brought them to management attention. He was ordered to reevaluate his findings and, when he guaranteed that his report was valid, he was "promoted" and reassigned to another unit.

Denial can, of course, be combined with other strategies, such as hope. A software publisher wasn't selling enough software to achieve planned business results. Sales reps complained that the products weren't competitive. Product development complained that the sales reps didn't know how to sell. Management tried to appease both.

The company preannounced software and committed to delivery by a specified date. They described the (hoped-for) new product features and provided new incentives for the sales reps. They believed that the software developers would respond to the pressure of sales and speed up delivery. The enormous rewards to the sales reps produced sales. Everyone was pleased. The management exhorted development to finalize the product. They couldn't. The reckoning came. Management had to announce its inability to deliver the promised product.

Acceptance of the "inevitable" is a common defensive strategy. It removes the pressure of actually having to *do* something about a situation. When you resign yourself to the inevitable, others often join in and commiserate about the situation. Commiseration is yet another form of collusion—and both parties reinforce each others' perceptions and position. Contributing strategies to acceptance include:

- Lamentation: "isn't it awful?"
- Comparisons with worse situations
- Agreement about the problem, without agreement to do anything: "Yes, but..."
- Nostalgia about the past
- Sublimation
- Hope and prayer
- Fatalism.

Symptoms of the acceptance strategy include:

- Formal and informal discussions of how unfortunate the situation is
- The expressions "I guess we'll have to live with it," "I wish there were something that could be done," or "People used to like to work and used to be concerned about quality"
- Reduced expectations, formal and informal, for performance, growth, business results, people, or the future
- Offering the situation up to the higher good: "I guess someone has to hire these people..."
- Inadequate follow up on or attention to agreed upon problems
- Browbeating

- Inability to see alternatives to the current situation or way of recruiting, training, operating, and so on.

Examples of acceptance are everywhere. A manufacturing company did not achieve its revenue or profitability objectives. When discussing the reasons, the sales manager described the previously agreed-to objectives as "unreasonable to expect from a small company that is competing against Fortune 500 firms." He argued for more "realistic" goals for the next year.

An insurance company with high expense ratios explained its unacceptable results on the work force in their urban location. "There's nothing we can do but live with the situation since we can't relocate the company."

An operations manager concerned with error rates held ongoing meetings about the problem and formed task forces to address the situation. Task force recommendations were reported, discussed, but never acted upon. He saw the situation as hopeless. He didn't believe people would buy into the recommended solutions given their past history.

A company, facing a 40 percent turnover among telephone customer service representatives, interpreted the condition as negative but "not as bad as our competition."

Emotional Response can run high in reaction to problem conditions. This active response is often mistaken as productive. When it remains just an emotional reaction, rather than a catalyst for change, there is lots of activity, but no movement. Often those who employ emotional detractors confuse people's reaction to their outbursts as a portent of positive movement. Sometimes action actually occurs, but if it is not well thought out, it serves to compound, rather than solve the problem.

Symptoms of emotional response include:

- Anger
- Blaming others for the situation (women, minorities, the competition, the Japanese, the computer)
- Withdrawal from discussions, marketplaces, or locations
- Frustration
- Bargaining for improved results
- Optimistic proclamations and projections
- Sloganeering
- Applying pressure.

The emotional response is familiar to most of us. When customer engineering staff were exceeding call times to diagnose and repair customer equipment, the engineering manager would rant and rave, and employees would scatter. Their discomfort and fear led to promises that things would get better. After several cycles of the anger-fear-promise cycle, the staff began to shave time off call reports and balance their time-activity reports by allocating the shaved time to training.

A group of systems development managers whose software was often late and did not meet customer expectations or needs would frequently gather at a local watering hole. There they would express their frustration and anger with customers about the poor quality of their specifications and their limited involvement during the design phase. They also blamed personal computers for increasing customer expectations, since they had always been able to contain these in an exclusively mainframe environment.

The perennially optimistic administration manager would focus on cheering people up after difficulties were discussed. "Things will get better! Just you wait and see! We're really good people and this just can't continue."

These strategies are not always unhealthy—only when they prevent attention to problem solving, partly because they divert energy from any effort to deal with the problem and partly because they create an immunity to change. If you have a performance problem, perhaps the best place to focus your attention is on performance.

And what organization or industry does *not* have a performance problem? How did we get to this state of affairs, where competence seems to be the exception and collusion with incompetence the rule? That is the subject of the next chapter.

CHAPTER

Getting to the Performance Zone

The innumerable variables
of truly effective
performance are more than
most can master. But in
today's world, who has a
choice?

Adequate performance in an organization depends on the nature and size of your organization, the level of employee skill and motivation, whether the consequences of inadequate performance are critical, time and financial resources, management philosophy, and other factors. External realities, such as the education and abilities of applicant pools, legal requirements, customer expectations, and competition can also make a difference.

It wasn't always so complicated. Once upon a time, employees learned exclusively within actual job contexts—while doing real work, in other words. They started performing simple tasks and progressed along the proficiency curve with personal and individualized guidance by an expert. These first *expert systems* were analog: the master's voice. The Socratic dialogue was the unconscious instructional model: questions and answers from learner to teacher and from teacher to learner. The teacher would also intervene as appropriate with coaching, feedback, explanations, encouragement, and so forth.

Over time, these relationships grew from informal mentoring to formal on-the-job apprentice programs. They worked for a while—and still do in some disciplines. But as the modern workplace evolved, such relationships became impossible for many organizations. The numbers to be trained just grew too large. The focus of most jobs changed from craft to production and—later—to knowledge, making on-the-job productivity and production measures far more formal. In most cases, it became too inefficient to keep the masters in one-on-one relationships. Group training was developed as a way to leverage mastery across larger numbers and distances. Instructional systems design and training as an organizational function emerged as institutionalized, structured, and controlled versions of the skill transfer process. Today, of course, training is a major industry.

But some not-so-good things have happened in this process:

Training (and learning) was moved out of the actual job context. The discussions, explanations, and application of knowledge to whole job tasks were moved into less and less real situations. The coaching and feedback that occurred naturally over time during actual job performance became more scarce.

Training (but not job-learning) became an *event* conducted in a classroom with images on overhead transparencies representing reality. Or it became a computer program that represented reality on a screen. True job experts who had integrated the numerous knowledge and skill strands that produce results became instead *subject matter experts* to a professional trainer who knew little, if anything, about the job. Performance within a training event was reduced to *content* related to a job. And the powerful individualized Socratic dialogue became the one-size-fits-all tutorial, with intermittent questions between teacher and learner, limited application of the knowledge to job task, and restricted opportunity for the practice of job behaviors. Training became an effort at information transfer, developing largely cognitive knowledge that (hopefully) prepared people to learn to actually do things quickly while on the job.

The experts were removed from the novices. In all but a very few situations, the experts were no longer coaching and mentoring. They were performing the more complex work, advising the MIS staff about systems development, reviewing content outlines and storyboards for trainers, or staffing help desks. All too often, they were promoted into management, where administration and politics became their work. The modern corporation has sensed the problem of the missing expert and has tried to compensate for it the way it tries to compensate for many problems, by bludgeoning it with technology. So today we have our organizations' experts monopolized by artificial intelligence specialists who are trying to replicate them through expert systems. The effort is laudable—and, in some cases, it makes an enormous difference—but it is being applied to only part of the problem.

Post-training support was reduced to manuals, an occasional job aid, and intermittent supervisory commentary. Expert mentoring has been replaced by peer coaching. Written manuals became larger and more numerous and, predictably, less integrated and up-to-date. The sheer logistics of manual creation, distribution, and maintenance has become a career. To simply locate the various product, process, systems, policy, and procedure information related to a given job activity requires the use of multiple manuals. And the learners for whom they were intended use them less and less due to frustration and limited payoff. Increasingly, asking the nearest person has become the norm. Unfortunately, the nearest person doesn't always know or have the time or interest to advise and coach. Enter the age of the organized help desk. Whether it's for systems, field service, or sales support, the help desk or various institutionalized forms of tiered support are among the fastest-growing units in organizations. There is even a national conference for help desk staff that attracted over 750 participants in 1991. In some cases, the help desks need help, so expert systems for the support of help desk functions have begun to appear. Where will it end?

When the span of control was five to seven employees, supervisory coaching and other controls compensated to some degree. When supervisors *actually know* the work, depending on them works. But recently, flatter organizations and wider span of control are being pursued. The concept of *self-managed teams* is being advocated. The modern supervisor is expert in interpersonal skills, administration, and politics—everything but the work. Unfortunately, people who don't

9

know the work and who don't have time to spend with an employee simply *can't* develop the competence of others through direct involvement. And while pushing the work to peers (who are either new themselves or to whom the work or information itself is new) will produce short-term supervisory relief, it won't *result in* employee competence.

UNCONTROLLED DEVELOPMENT

All of this has left us in a situation in which the development of competence is taking place in an increasingly uncontrolled environment—at the very time competency curves must be accelerated. The reasons by now are familiar to nearly everyone: many jobs today have become more complex, involve more variables, and require more analysis, synthesis, and interpretation in increasingly diverse contexts. Even entry-level jobs.

The environment is worse than uncontrolled. It is complex, and it is chaotic. Look at some representative threads of expertise the average white-collar employee must master and integrate.

First, there is the thread of the employee's position or profession (secretarial, financial, sales, whatever). There is the thread of the computer system or systems the employee actually uses to do the work. Then there are the threads of the company's procedures, products, and services. Then there are the threads of the interpersonal skill needed to move anything through an organization. Those four threads alone make the modern workplace a daunting experience.

Yet there are still more threads: company policy, situational analysis, pricing, updates on new products, legal implications, software updates, the competition, complex methodologies and processes, new lines of business, mergers and acquisitions, and the resulting relationships. For many jobs, the list can be extended indefinitely.

Different parts of the organization spin out their threads and the associated training, but the employee is expected to weave them together. There is no master weaver helping to construct an integrated pattern. It's as if we were teaching employees to dance by giving them individual steps but never showing them how the steps go together. And, in most organizations, they can't hear the music—and we keep changing their partners with reorganizations and reassignments!

Little time is allocated to develop the learner's weaving skills in current training programs. More and more, sheer content must be presented due to the volume and instability of job-related information. And those transferring the information are increasingly specialized in that information, not the job. Many, in fact, have never even seen the actual job context within which learners work, never mind being able to understand or perform it. More disconnected dance steps. More threads, no loom.

INCOMPETENCE, COMPETENCE, PROFICIENCY, MASTERY

An employee's performance can be more or less competent on individual tasks—or in a job. Frankly, when someone can't do something without external support—or when he does it inadequately or incompletely, that particular performance is incompetent. And few organizations today can afford incompetence at any level, in any task.

Competent is usually defined as "having suitable or sufficient skill, knowledge, experience, etc. for some purpose" (*Random House Dictionary of the English Language,* second edition). Competence is enough for an organization when competition and time urgency is low and when customers have only basic expectations for performance. Low customer expectations, however, are a thing of the past in all but economically desperate societies.

Organizations need something beyond competence. They need proficiency. The proficient organization is in a comfortable state, particularly when competitors are merely competent. Even proficiency, however, can be an inadequate condition in highly competitive environments with rigid tolerances for product quality.

Today, many organizations find themselves with a need for performance beyond proficiency. They need mastery. The Malcolm Baldridge competition aside, *the consistently best* individuals or organizations perform at this level all the time. They set standards. They are admired and honored; they gain all the financial and psychic rewards associated with their mastery. Clearly, this is the goal of most organizations in the global marketplace of the new century. Currently, management slogans of "excellence" and "quality" program the goal. Organizations are *benchmarking* themselves. Large staff infrastructures are being built to help facilitate the outcome. But exhortation and facilitation are not enough. Much more must be done to systematically institutionalize the knowledge and skills necessary for success.

THE COSTS OF INCOMPETENCE

There are various and significant costs when people cannot do what is required on the job. "Managers overestimate the extent of the difference between what exemplars actually do on their jobs and what average performers do. But they underestimate the value of that difference," says Tom Gilbert, noted performance engineering consultant (*What Works at Work,* Minneapolis: Lakewood Publications, 1989).

When employees aren't sufficiently competent, there are business consequences. These consequences show up in *limited business results:* limited productivity, inadequate quality, high costs of doing business, and opportunity costs. Sometimes new products or new processes take so long to integrate because people are so unable to sell, support, or use them that they must be aborted as unsuccessful. In other situations, new systems or processes fail to achieve anticipated benefits because of partial implementation or inadequate utilization or acceptance. Frankly, the only alternative to employee competence is reduced business expectations and results.

The most insidious cost of incompetence, however, is the *high overhead support cost* associated with supporting those who can't function independently. This cost is buried, and it is enormous. And the consumption of resources attendant on paying for work that adds no value prevents organizational growth and survival. A large national consulting firm recently reported to an insurance company management that, in one strategic business unit (of 15) which contributes 65 percent of the company's profits, 60 percent of its employees were involved in non-value-adding work. They were

- Supervising other people at a 1:5 to 1:7 supervisor-to-employee ratio
- Controlling the work of others
- Reviewing the work of others
- Training others
- Answering questions at help desks or in other expert support functions
- Coaching and correcting others
- Reworking other people's inadequate work
- Compensating for others
- Supporting others by joint work activities when incompetents couldn't perform independently
- Following up on others
- Actually doing the work of others who could or would not perform
- Conducting damage control activities
- Facilitating relationship problems that resulted from inadequate skills and work results
- Recruiting, hiring, and orienting new people to replace those who left or were asked to leave because of incompetence
- And more.

This situation is not unique, it is endemic. Whether the number doing non-value-adding work is 20, 30, or 60 percent, or higher, the waste of organizational and human resources is both tragic and inevitably fatal to the individuals and organizations involved. Something must be done, done now, and done well. In short

- We've lost the luxury of time to develop competence. No more money is available to spend on it.

- The gap between required and actual employee competence has increased.

- Organizations are experiencing major performance and results problems.

- Pressure is increasing to solve these problems.

How can we solve them? Offering more and more training events is not the complete solution. Neither is automating the the old lecture model in a computer-based training (CBT) environment. Nor will the problem be solved by implementing patched solutions like expert systems, help desks, or on-line manuals. Much more is necessary to enter what I call the *performance zone.*

THE PERFORMANCE ZONE

The performance zone is the metaphorical area in which things come together. It is the place where people *get it,* where the right things happen, where the employee's response *exactly* matches the requirements of the situation. It is the place where employees put together all the individual dance steps that they have mastered. The dance, the dancers, and the music are one.

As the number, complexity, and interrelationships between the various threads of expertise increase, the chances of operating within the performance zone decrease. Unless, of course, something is done to guarantee it.

WHAT'S REQUIRED

What's required is the conscious and systematic design of electronic performance support systems that provide *on-demand access* to all of the resources individuals need to solve a problem, perform a task, or—someday—to do an entire job. In other words, individual employees and entire organizations can systematically work and achieve in the performance zone.

This book is about what's necessary to guarantee the performance zone. It is largely about successful and powerful electronic solutions to the range of problems every organization is faced with. Case study after case study demonstrates radically different—and very doable—approaches to supporting and generating employee performance and knowledge via new design concepts. Some require workstation technologies, but many can be implemented even with more basic computer installations if management, trainers, documentation and systems specialists, and all who support and develop the performance of others have the right mind-set.

It challenges you to confront *head-on* the enormous waste associated with the ineffective and insufficient training, reference, and support systems so prevalent today. And it offers new design models and frameworks within which to construct performance solutions for your organization. You will read about the organizational and sponsorship issues that must be addressed before progress can be made. And you will learn about the various technological and systems development elements fundamental to success.

And you will, I hope, be inspired to weave the threads, dance the steps, and live in the performance zone.

CHAPTER

Retooling Old Paradigms

We don't need new
technology, we just need
new thinking.

"As in manufacture, so in science—retooling is an extravagance to be reserved for the occasion that demands it. The significance of crises is the indication they provide that an occasion for retooling has arrived." The observation is from Thomas Kuhn in his acclaimed book, *The Structure of Scientific Revolutions* (University of Chicago Press, 1972). Kuhn further said that "the emergence of new theories is generally preceded by a period of pronounced professional insecurity. As one might expect, that insecurity is generated by the persistent failure of the puzzles of normal science to come out as they should. Failure of existing rules is the prelude to a search for new ones."

Kuhn called the set of rules a paradigm. The paradigm creates a world view or a mind-set for the people who follow its rules. It is a kind of lens through which the scientist sees the world. As long as the paradigm is successful in framing scientific problems, it dominates scientists' thinking. As more and more unsolvable problems emerge, however, the paradigm's rules come into question.

This search for new rules has also been referred to as "picking up the other end of the stick" (Herbert Butterfield, *The Origins of Modern Science, 1300-1800* [New York: Free Press, 1965]), a process that involves "handling the same bundle of data as before, but placing them in a new system of relations with one another by giving them a different framework."

Science is not the only activity that is periodically beset with crises. Business today is at a point where *what we are doing is no longer sufficient*. It is time to pick up the other end of the stick.

Most of us, of course, are not creating scientific revolutions or consciously developing new models or frameworks. Rather, we are faced with daily tasks and are proceeding along an evolutionary path developing systems, interactive training programs, on-line reference, or expert systems to try to complete these tasks. As technological alternatives emerge, and as techology becomes more accessible, we are working actively and hard to apply technology to established models and methodologies such as instructional systems design (ISD) or systems development. We are applying technology to our activities to produce deliverables that are more flexible, easier to use, maintainable, distributed, and interactive.

WHAT'S WRONG WITH THIS PICTURE?

We're developing computer-based training (CBT), interactive video training programs, or on-line documentation with improved search capabilities. We are making some of these sophisticated training and support tools available from applications software in context-sensitive modes. Advisory or expert systems are being developed to assist in problem structuring and decision support.

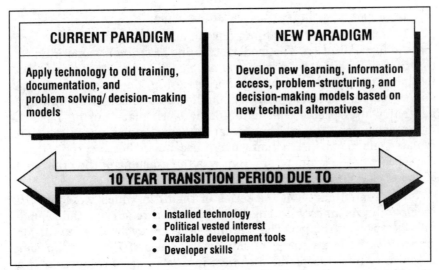

Figure 3.1

Each of these things is at least incrementally, if not substantially, improving our results. The reality is that, regardless of how much or how well we do, the problems we are attacking are accelerating at an even faster rate. Or our development efforts are simply taking too long.

What's wrong with this scenario is that we are applying radically different technological alternatives to old frameworks without reexamining their underlying assumptions and structures. In our pursuit of solutions, we have assumed that the future should be an extension of the past. We have not taken time to step back from the situation to reexamine whether the old approaches should or must be the best solutions. We apply sophisticated technology to an obsolete paradigm of human performance development. And as a result, we are not making the difference we should.

There are currently numerous independent training and support systems that exist in organizations to generate and sustain employee performance.

These systems include training programs, help desks, coaching, documentation, and job aid resources. Each is developed and implemented *independently* of any of the others—most often by independent functional departments which rarely, if ever, interact or cooperate. Each department applies its particular tool (training programs, manuals, help desks, job aids, and so on) to the performance problem. Very few have begun to look at the crisis from any perspective other than that created by their role (or hoped-for role) in solving it.

Let's look at training just as an example.

In many ways, the training paradigm is a byproduct of modern mass industrialization. The modern training *program* is something we constructed because the numbers of people we had to train simply got too large for the old methods: apprenticeship, one-to-one coaching, and so on. No one could possibly handle the number of apprentices and entry-level people that entered the work place during modern industrialization. The training program was the new paradigm that replaced one-to-one instruction when it became ineffective. In its time, the concept of the training program was the grasping of the other end of the stick.

We created an event (or series of them) in which we could *fill people up in advance* with enough information to survive (and hopefully prosper) on the job. The training program evolved as *initial job preparation* for large groups of employees or as *activities or situations* in which to introduce sudden *change* in a job (e.g., introduction of a new product, procedure, system, or philosophy).

During the early development of training, approaches to these training events evolved based on conscious or unconscious underlying assumptions that were either valid or necessary in order to proceed. For example, when a group of people are new to a particular job, it is necessary to assume that the group is homogeneous and that valid assumptions can be made about what they already know or don't know and what they need to be successful. We also hope that a single approach can be constructed to train them. Without the assumptions of homogeneity, chaos would result. When linear media were the only alternatives (i.e., sequential presentations to groups of learners via lecture, videotape, audiotape, or books), any approach to designing instruction *had* to involve determining content, presentation sequence, media, and related instructional strategy.

It was literally impossible to accommodate alternative approaches without extending training program time beyond available limits, resources, and budgets. A "training frame of reference" and related disciplines evolved in relation to the above conditions and assumptions.

There is a body of assumptions behind the training program paradigm (equivalent to Thomas Kuhn's "existing rules"). Whether or not these assumptions are based on reality, they affect outcome. When they were originally developed, they were close enough to reality that they worked. Today, they hold down our end of the stick. Here are some of the most important of them.

Training is an event with a beginning and an end. It occurs within a time and place. Only so much can be done within that time and place.

The audience can be defined and is relatively homogeneous.

Training must be consistent for all learners to assure they all "get" the same message.

Learners see a need to learn what the trainer sees as important. Learners trust the trainer's view implicitly and absorb the trainer's motivation to teach as their motivation to learn.

Learners require someone else who "knows better" to structure and sequence their learning experiences and to assess their learning. Without externally imposed structure, learners will be frustrated or incapable of learning; self-directed learning will be inefficient or inadequate.

People must "know" certain things before they can "do" anything (i.e., cognitive knowledge must precede experiential knowledge).

Teaching people "about" things will translate into their being able to "do" things on the job.

There will be adequate post-training support systems available on the job. What happens on the job is out of the trainer's control. Further knowledge and skill development becomes the supervisor's or employee's responsibility.

Instructional designers know better than individuals or groups of learners how those learners best learn (i.e., content sequence, instructional strategy, nature and amount of practice required, media, and so forth).

The job situation is static, or, if change does occur, there is either nothing more that must or can be done by instructional developers to maintain or enhance learner knowledge and skill in relation to the changes once training is completed.

When these assumptions are operating, trainers view their primary goal as imparting as much about a job component as they can in a usually predefined period of time (e.g., we must teach people as much as we can in "x" days). The time period is determined by logistical, economic, or political circumstances. The primary focus is on creating "the best" consistent program structure and sequence. Based on the assumption of learner motivation, instructional designers rely largely on the instructional design process—not on creating the motivation to learn—to achieve the required performance outcome.

"Performance" messages have left their mark among trainers, but there is a gap between what developers say and what they do. In fact, most developers *start* with a job or skill task analysis, but the resultant learning objectives fall short. While objectives are phrased in "behavioral" terms (e.g., "Be able to list the five product features," or "Be able to recognize a situation in which the product will apply"), these "behaviors" are still small, isolated *intellectual* or *cognitive* activities. Programs are typically characterized as "competency-based," but most are information-transfer oriented with the focus on content.

Another gap between words and actions relates to instructional strategies employed. For example, in conversation, most instructional designers will agree that people best learn by doing, but when faced with whether to throw inexperienced learners into a simulated experience without any prior training, they typically default into the "there are certain things people must know before they can do" mode. Instructional strategies employed are largely tutorial, whether electronic or instructor-led, passive or interactive. The emphasis is on exposition of terms, concepts, facts, and sub-tasks. There is limited establishment of the larger job context (or need to learn), higher order thinking skills, or transfer of learning outcomes into job performance.

HOW DOES REALITY COMPARE?

These assumptions and the behavior they produce are in stark contrast to the world as it has come to be. Today's world requires new assumptions around which to develop learning/support efforts:

Learning is a process, not an event. It occurs over time and with experience. Learning is an outcome of the nature and quality of experiences, regardless of the context they are in.

Groups of learners are rarely similar in entry knowledge, skill, learning style, motivation, or needs. Learning audiences cannot be accurately defined. Attempts to do that result in simplistic and inaccurate categorizations. Training developed from these audience definitions is always inadequate.

Learners control what they learn and retain. Trainers only control what is presented. Learners have a set of objectives when they enter a training program, and the learners' objectives prevail. Until you get learners to share your objectives, or you meet theirs, you are wasting your time delivering a training program.

When information about things is forced on people out of context, it is difficult to obtain and maintain their attention. Learners focus their attention on what they perceive they need and nothing else. When people are *doing* things, they are interested in information about the task, situation, related concepts, and variables that will help them to do what they think is required. They will inquire when ready. Only at that time will they internalize the cognitive components with a minimum of effort and repetition because it is presented to them in a meaningful context at the moment of need. Providing resources at the moment of *need* to learn is among the highest leverage activities that can be employed. In the absence of learner perception of need, trainers are reduced to "repetition as the mother of impression" or testing (with its related consequences) as the source of motivation. (Many of us learned to "take tests" in the first grade and to "press delete" when we left the test situation.)

Learners will learn in the most efficient and effective way for them personally. Learners need goals, such as a required proficiency level, and they need to see clear consequences of the lack of proficiency, and they need adequate informational and support mechanisms. When they have these things, they consciously or unconsciously execute their optimum learning strategy. Adult workers are fully capable of self-directed (which is far more than *self-paced*) learning.

In the context of a traditional training program, however, learners will both expect externally imposed structure and defer to it. They have learned to behave in acceptable ways while within the training program (not to be confused with learning while in the program). When learner control is increased during a traditional training event, learners will experience initial disorientation, but will quickly master and prefer self-directed learning. This does not mean that learners should be left to simply browse around a database. The appropriate structure must be developed and implemented, but the database permits a different structure (discussed further below).

When provided with a model or benchmark as a basis for comparison, learners can assess their own knowledge and skill without the involvement of others. They can compare performance, knowledge, and skill accurately, and they actively seek such comparisons as part of their learning and reinforcement process. Comparisons are frequent and intense when learners know that there are *consequences* to their not achieving the proficiency or knowledge outcome (e.g., results are visible, opportunities or rewards are based on achievement).

In order to become skilled or proficient at anything, people must have sufficient practice in actually doing the task—not talking about, listening to information about, or watching someone else do it, regardless of whether that someone else is live, on video in technicolor, stereophonic, or overlaid with sophisticated graphics. Knowledge without practice rarely, if ever, translates into skill or specific behavior.

Consistent training experiences produce inconsistent and unpredictable learning outcomes because of the diversity of the learning audience. The focus needs to be on consistent performance outcomes, not on a consistent training process.

Most post-training job support is unstructured, inconsistent, inadequate, or inaccessible. In most organizations, post-training learning is largely left to chance or to the learner's ability and will-

21

ingness to assure it happens. Knowledge degradation is inevitable in such situations.

The job situation is dynamic. Change is frequent; ongoing adaptation and learning is required. Unfortunately, however, once employees are *trained*, they are usually "on their own," even if the product or process has changed. In this situation, most employees reach a performance plateau and never get beyond it.

It's no wonder the outcomes of our training programs are inadequate. Far from being congruent, the training paradigm's operating assumptions hardly even overlap with reality.

THE TRAINER DEFENSE

Trainers actively defend the inadequacy of training programs. They explain that there is neither time nor resources to incorporate "enough" practice activities on any one skill component. They describe job requirements as very complex and cite the difficulty in developing true understanding of them. Instructional designers elaborate on media limitations or the pressures of time and money. They explain that their personal expertise is in instructional design (or media production or teaching) and leave the examination of actual performance to someone else. It is up to others to support on the job.

Trainers also complain that at times products or processes about which they are training have not been completely developed or are changing so often that it is impossible to ensure that the training matches the job context that ultimately results. They also say that they cannot get access to employees or monitor actual job performance after formal training occurs.

That all of the above and more might be true does not diminish the organizational consequences of our failure to develop employee competence.

Enter the computer, the videodisc, CD-ROM, multimedia, and expert systems. Uninformed optimism prevailed. Expectations for distributed, "just-in-time" or "desktop" learning, individualized instruction, rapid information access, and improved decision making increased. The good news is that these things are definitely possible. The bad news is that initial efforts at interactive training, on-line reference, and advisory systems have had limited impact. Efforts have been largely limited to automating the prevalent tutorial instructional approach and to putting manuals on-line.

CBT and Interactive Video (IVD) programs permit more questioning of learner knowledge. But answering test questions (i.e., knowledge) does not translate automatically into task or job performance. And yes, interactive programs can increase the number of practice exercises, but typically the practices are limited in scope, complexity, and number. Program individualization has largely been limited to *scheduling* use of a program and choosing which module to complete first. Sometimes programs don't require every learner to complete every module, but most programs are still highly structured and computer-controlled *programs* that all learners are expected to complete.

Often, organizational administrative processes that grew up around classroom instruction get in the way of using available CBT. For example, students must sometimes formally register for courses to take them. This requires supervisory approval and creates a delay. The *moment of need* may have passed by the time the approval process is complete. CBT and IVD offer the promise of effective refresher training. But when the programs are very structured, people may not be able to get to the specific point in the program that they need, if the registration policy allows them to take the course at all! The ideas that you should register for a course and take it only once stemmed from the days of scarce facilities and student enrollment resources. When the learning environment is electronic, however, limiting access is irrelevant, if not destructive. And yet these requirements remain—often because the training department is rewarded based on body counts or student-day measures.

Self-paced is often equated to self-directed learning, and they are not the same thing at all. In most currently available interactive training, alternative learning styles, diverse learner entry knowledge, and differing job needs are not really accommodated. In other words, we've put "wheels" under the old training, documentation, and problem-solving models: we've automated the past—invalid assumptions and all.

To date, CBT and IVD have resulted in only incremental improvements, mostly in terms of learning efficiency. Learners learn the same material and achieve the same (generally inadequate) learning outcome *faster*; at best, they are able skip certain unnecessary segments. Retention of facts and terms is improved, but those improvements have not increased their job proficiency or made them more effective.

In many cases, the efficiency gains alone are desirable and justify the effort and expense of creating and implementing interactive training programs. Employees, however, are typically still not competent to fully perform their jobs after they complete the programs.

On-line documentation systems have done little more than speed information searches. Most efforts to implement on-line documentation have simply implemented the paradigm of paper-based manuals. They have not addressed the critical need to integrate information with task performance, systems, training programs, and situations.

Expert systems have addressed problem-structuring and decision-support models for the new reality, but they are typically used by people lacking the knowledge or the information necessary to interact with them. When users can't get access to information to assist them in responding to an expert system query, advisory systems do little more than help people get to inadequate conclusions faster.

Some of these limited results have been due to hardware and software limitations, but I believe they are more directly a function of the mind-set of those involved in training, documentation, and systems development than they are a function of equipment. The paradigms of these three functions served us well in a world in the throes of industrialization. But that was a world geared to the assimilation of a large, homogeneous work force into a system of relatively few variables and highly standardized procedures and routines. In such a world, we were well advised to adopt assumptions that limited our imaginations and ambitions.

But in the electronic world, mass storage, random access, variable manipulation, conditional branching, multimedia and graphical interfaces, dynamic data exchange and object-oriented databases are available. And our limiting assumptions are restricting rather than helping us.

THE OTHER END OF THE STICK

Here and there, companies have begun to pick up the other end of the stick. IBM Corporation, for example, has looked at its education needs for the year 2000. The corporation has profiled its anticipated employee and customer populations. From these profiles, it developed attributes of required learning environments (see Table 3.1). When it compared what will be required in just a decade to the current way of doing business, it was clear that a new view, process, and outcome were necessary.

The traditional *training frame of reference* encompasses only the training-event part of the learning process. A *performance support system frame of reference* includes all of the activities and resources associated with the entire learning process. The performance support view is the view we must take to achieve the outcomes of accelerated performance. Table 3.2 compares the two frames of reference.

Nothing ever changes unless a number of prerequisite conditions exist. The first of these is *sufficient dissatisfaction with the status quo* on the part of people who can support the change, logistically, economically, and politically. Second, someone must have a *clear vision*

Table 3.1

IBM EDUCATION
IN THE YEAR 2000

Profile	Required Learning Environment
Diverse Student Base	Multi-Sensory, Transferable
Diverse Skill Base	Modular, Non-Linear
Changing Skill Requirements	Responsive, Distributed
Flexible Work Schedules	Distributed, Interruptible
Flexible Work Location	Portable, Distributed
Computer Mediation	Multi-Sensory, Distributed
Information Overload	Modular, Non-Linear

DEFINITIONS

Distributed. Self-directed and on-demand; accessible.

Modular. Addresses a single skill, in contrast to courses addressing multiple skills.

Multi-Sensory. Stimulates sight, sound, and touch in a variety of ways.

Portable. Easily moved with the employee.

Interruptible. Provides ability to stop and start easily.

Non-Linear. No fixed sequence of modules.

Transferable. Easy movement across languages and cultures.

Responsive. Short development cycle.

With permission from the IBM internal report, "A Vision of IBM Human Resource Performance in the Year 2000," IBM Corporate Education, 1990.

of an available, affordable alternative that addresses the insufficiencies of the status quo. This vision is the desired state.

Third, there must be a *critical mass of people* with the vision, skill, and commitment to change things—and there must be a sufficient installed technological infrastructure to support the vision. Finally, there have to be *adequate transition and implementation strategies to develop and implement the new alternatives.*

These conditions are discussed in detail below. When some, but not all, of the prerequisite conditions for change exist, there's lots of discussion and maybe even activity, but there is little change. Usually the forces for and against the change are in balance, so nothing happens. The man who developed this model of organizational change probably said it best. "Pain without alternatives produces ulcers, not change. Alternatives without pain produce task forces, study groups, and academically interesting reports," says Daryl Conner, President of ODR, Inc., an Atlanta-based consultancy in organizational change.

Table 3.2

THE FRAMES OF REFERENCE

Traditional Training	Performance Support
Event-oriented; not integrated with work environment or other performance support tools	Learning systematically integrated with work; learning and support provided at moment of need; includes, but not limited to, training
Responsibility on trainer or program to teach	Learner responsible for performance and required learning to achieve it
Defined, program-controlled objectives, sequences, processes	Job-, task-, or learner-defined objectives, sequences, processes
Measured on volume and learner satisfaction	Measured on competence of job task performance
Media-oriented	Includes learning systems, information systems, job aids, career systems, rewards and incentives, organization design, procedures, etc.

Recently, several conditions have developed and converged that permit new technological and design alternatives. These alternatives both permit and require a change in our assumptions about what we have previously accepted as inevitable (i.e., performance gaps, the slow rate of achieving competence, and so on). These new alternatives also bring into question our fundamental assumptions about training concepts and approaches (i.e., what is needed, how it must be structured, who must develop learning programs, and how they are offered).

Fast, inexpensive, large memory and networked hardware is available. It permits new types of software and sophisticated user interfaces. Integration of previously independent software components can now occur. Workstations are replacing PCs as the hardware of choice.

Historically, the biggest issues have been technical: limited, slow, inadequate hardware, or lack of software. It is now relatively simple to identify and acquire hardware and to buy or develop software. Existing hardware in place for other purposes can be used in combination with networks attached to minicomputers or mainframe systems. If required hardware is not installed, it is becoming less expensive and easier to justify. Software development tools are available for developing component elements (e.g., on-line reference development systems).

Those with a broad vision of what an electronic performance support system can be are structuring development platforms that permit both component development and integration. The software is either already installed (e.g., relational database management systems) or is moderately priced (e.g., expert system shells). The challenge and complexity now lies in understanding the actual job requirements and in structuring the information and access methods with an eye toward system power and ease of maintenance.

Large, fast, and inexpensive computer processors, including adequate portable computers, are becoming available. Today, you can buy a personal computer that incorporates the processing power of an IBM 3090 from 1985. And the power is spreading throughout our organizations. Workstations are the main growth area in computer sales today. Even laptops are typically configured with a 386 chip and a hard disk.

Inexpensive electronic mass storage devices are being introduced. CD-ROM is one such technology, but even hard disks themselves are getting larger and larger. It is not uncommon to find machines with hundreds of megabytes of storage on people's desks. Enthusiast computer magazines have learned to use the term "gigabyte."

Data communications networks are becoming ubiquitous.

New software development tools are announced almost daily. Hypermedia, expert systems, on-line reference systems, image processing software, and relational database management systems for text, images, and audio data are more and more readily available.

These new technologies are giving birth to new mind-sets. We are in a period of explosive creativity and a related paradigm shift. Many people are picking up the other end of the stick and reorganizing the data they see into new frameworks. The change in our thinking is even more important than the changes in technology. Here are some of the new ideas.

- "Mass Customization" (See Stanley Davis, *Future Perfect*, Reading, Massachusetts: Addison-Wesley, 1987), or the ability to tailor products and services to individual customers or users in a timeframe that is virtually immediate

- Expectations of consumers, individual employees, and managers to have their particular needs met while obtaining the economic and logistical benefits of mass production and distribution systems

- "Intelligent workstations" that offer integrated packages of previously independent resources (e.g., documentation, training,

27

software, support, information access) without involvement of intermediaries

- Redefinition of how training can occur once integrated performance support systems are available

- "Disintermediation," or the elimination of unnecessary intermediaries in any process (e.g., in the same way ATMs took tellers out of much of the banking process, learner-defined access to available databases can eliminate trainers or help desk staff from the learning process).

THE MISSING CONDITIONS

Currently, there are two critical conditions missing for the widespread establishment of the new paradigm of human performance. *There is not yet a critical mass of people* who understand these technologies and how they can be used, and *there are few strategies and transition tactics in place to exploit them.* When new approaches are being implemented (e.g., on-line information access or interactive training), they are typically being developed in functional vacuums by people with singular views (such as the technical documentation or CBT units). As a result, only *components* of a performance support system are being constructed.

The overall vision of how the range of technological alternatives can be merged into an integrated performance support system is still lacking—or the vision is being constructed at too low a level in the organization to mobilize the economic, logistical, and political resources necessary. People are applying new technology to old models rather than reorienting themselves to the possibilities and alternatives that new technologies will permit. Gains in efficiency are likely, but the overall potential and possibilities that new technologies bring are being overlooked. Without a new view, the net effect on performance problems will be marginal.

AN EXAMPLE

Here is an example of how our mental models prevent us from fully exploiting technology. An integrated performance support system was developed by an R&D group at a leading communications company. The system was integrated with complex applications software and eliminated the need for all conventional training and documentation associated with the applications software. It reduced learning from weeks to hours. And it permitted system users to learn "instantly" on the job when presented with a new set of tasks.

Over 300 staff and management personnel viewed demonstrations of the prototype during a twelve-month period. All were impressed, but they couldn't see where it "fit" into their current organization. They couldn't understand (or preferred not to act on) the idea that new organizational forms and development processes would be required to develop and implement such systems. For example, if a performance support system were to support an applications software package, the on-line reference materials and learning materials would have to be developed in parallel with the system itself. The previously separate technical writing and training staffs would have to become active members of the development team. They would have to participate in system design and would have to complete their components of the system as part of the overall development effort. Historically, those activities are performed in other departments *following* systems development. And interestingly, while many documentation and training units complain about involvement that is "too late," few functional managers are willing to give up their staff to become members of the team and have their work become part of another larger effort.

It's easy to understand why. People in organizations are usually rewarded for independent effort and results, not teamwork and collective results. Tom Gilbert, the noted Performance Engineering consultant, says that "people at all levels of an organization are rewarded for unproductively increasing the time allotted to training." (*What Works at Work*, Minneapolis: Lakewood Publications, 1989).

The importance of managers is increased by having more, not fewer, staff. Manuals, training courses, and "student days" are counted and are the measures against which rewards are distributed. If, for example, development of a performance support system increased system usability and decreased needs for manuals or training, the perceived importance of the training and documentation managers would decrease. And so, the forces operate to maintain the status quo even when affordable, available alternatives have the potential to dramatically accelerate performance among employees at less cost. Logic is not, in the end, the basis for much decision making.

MOVING FORWARD

Throwing on more traditional training events, regardless of whether they are interactive or not, will not result in the required performance. The outcomes of traditional training are simply inadequate. Simply putting documentation on-line and improving search capabilities is inadequate as well. And inadequate is now (and probably always was) insufficient. We have the technological means to develop and implement alternatives, but in order to accomplish the results we need, our view must shift from training to learning and then to performance; from documentation to knowledge, and then to its application.

The focus must shift from rigidly defined content and training program structure created by an instructional designer, to truly individualized learning experiences created by the learner. We must get out of our historical mind-set and organizational boxes and take the broader and longer view. We must stop applying technology to old models and paradigms. We must develop new learning, information-access, problem-structuring, and decision-support models based on new technological alternatives. Yes, there will be a long transition period with coexisting mind-sets during at least the next decade, but the visioning and implementation has begun. The future requires it.

CHAPTER

What Is Electronic Performance Support?

As hardware issues inevitably move into the background, the technology of EPSS becomes the technology of information structures.

In previous chapters, we discussed the size and nature of the performance deficiency. Now it's time to get down to the level of the individual performer to find out what the performance deficiency looks and feels like in the trenches. The *goal* of an electronic performance support system is to enable people to perform, so we start with the performer's perspective. Only then can we begin to define and design what's necessary for performance support.

One way to understand what a performance support system must do is to recall a situation in which you were required to perform and lacked prior knowledge, experience, or training in the activity. You must be *very* specific about the task you have in mind. Then recall the strategies you employed to learn and do the task and the resources that were helpful in making progress. It's likely questions like these came to mind: What must I do? How do I do it? Am I doing it right? In addition to questions, you had requests you wanted to make of the people around you: Show me... Teach me... Tell me what to do...

While learning, novices often switch quickly from one question or request to another. Or they repeat requests as they seek to organize their understanding of the situation, the tasks, and what must be done. As control over the variables, processes, procedures, and information occurs, people may seek more understanding of the concepts, rules, principles, and relationships. The required sequence, depth, and repetition of information will vary for individuals. And an individual may not be internally consistent about the way he or she goes about this process of doing and learning—or learning and doing.

When one approach doesn't work, the novice tries another or makes the question or request more specific. The person helping the novice or learner will employ different strategies in responding, sometimes describing what to do, other times illustrating with a diagram affirming what the novice is already doing, or demonstrating a different or more efficient way to get to the same outcome.

Apprentices and masters communicate dynamically in relation to the situation and to the needs and to each others' capabilities. In the best situations, this process is fluid, complementary, and energizing. Learners maintain or increase their motivation as skill, knowledge, and confidence increase. Masters, teachers, or coaches increasingly understand what's necessary and what works—and they anticipate the needs of the learner and avoid unproductive paths. But that's the best situation. In the worst situation, communication between apprentice and master is frustrating, demoralizing and unproductive—and either or both of the participants withdraw from the process.

Table 4.1 summarizes the various questions and requests people have when faced with performing new or complex tasks. Table 4.1 also lists possible appropriate responses to those questions or needs.

Table 4.1
THE FACE OF A COMPLEX TASK

The Question or Need	Response of Performance Support System
Why do this?	Explanation Example and consequences
What is it?	Definitions Illustrations Descriptions
What's related to it?	Available links
How do I do it?	Procedure Interactive advisors Structured paths (flowcharts, step charts, job aids) Demonstration
How or why did this happen?	Explanation Example or demonstration
Show me an example...	Examples
Teach me...	Interactive training Practice activities with feedback Assessment or testing
Assist me...	Interactive Advisors
Advise me...	Structured paths, job aids, step charts, flow charts Monitoring systems with feedback
Let me try...	Practice activities Simulations
Watch me...	Monitoring systems
Evaluate me...	Assessments or tests
Understand me...	Feedback with scoring, judgment, or interpretation Monitoring systems tracking user actions or context
How does it work?	Explanations
Why does it work like that?	Examples
Compare this or these for me	Comparative explanations or descriptions
Predict for me...	Descriptions or demonstrations of consequences
Where am I?	Monitoring systems Navigation systems Views of context ("you are here...")
What next?	Directions, prompts, or coaching Lists of options or paths

The list is by no means exhaustive, but provides a departure point for creative thought and performance support system design. Remember, the number of learner questions or requests is finite. And the information associated with a given question or request can be reasonably defined. It's the *process* associated with the learning that varies so widely among and between individual learners. And the better the individual learner is supported in his or her *unique* process, the faster learning and performance occur. The reality is that most learning environments are more *hostile and unresponsive* than they are supportive to a particular learner: too much too soon, too little too late, an unclear response, a response that's inconsistent with what was previously communicated—or no response at all.

THE GOAL OF ELECTRONIC PERFORMANCE SUPPORT

The goal of an electronic performance support system is to provide whatever is necessary to generate performance and learning *at the moment of need*. This kind of support has always required human beings in the past. But we now have the means to model, represent, structure, and implement that support *electronically*—and to make it universally and consistently available *on demand* any time, any place, and regardless of situation, without unnecessary intermediaries involved in the process.

Of course, the concept can be operationalized in many and diverse ways, depending on requirements, available technology, developer skill, and available development resources. These systems can be more or less powerful, as we'll discuss. But the common denominator that differentiates an electronic performance support system from other types of systems or interactive resources is the degree to which it *integrates information, tools, and methodology* for the user. This integration clearly makes it different than, say, a powerful help system available from within software or a rich interactive on-line reference system, although either of these could be *part* of an electronic performance support system.

Most of the system responses summarized in Table 4.1 will look familiar to those knowledgeable in instructional systems design. In fact, these approaches are the building blocks of effective training programs—including computer-based training (CBT). Electronic performance support systems are distinctly *different* from CBT, however. Table 4.6 summarizes the differences between electronic performance support systems and conventional computer-based training. As you can see, the primary differences lie in the organization of the information and support for the learner, the degree to which learners can structure their own learning experience, and the availability of the support in an on-the-job context. Of course, as interactive training programs become more granular and more task-oriented and employ more hypermedia structure, they will begin to resemble performance support systems. The differentiating factors then become the interactive advisory systems, the ability of the system to accept and manipulate user data, and the task-monitoring activities.

THE CONTENT OF THE PERFORMANCE SUPPORT SYSTEM

Coining a term. There is yet no commonly accepted word to describe the content of an electronic performance support system. "Database" doesn't work very well, because a generation of use has given it connotations that simply do not apply to the performance support methodology. "Knowledge base" is more descriptive, but, unfortunately, the term is already taken and is in widespread use by the artificial intelligence community, where it describes the body of rules employed by an expert system. That is why I use the term "infobase." It might sound like technoslang, but it is reasonably serviceable, and it should help us maintain clarity in this discussion.

The infobase is the fund of information the employee will inquire against, access, or have presented to him or her to do the job. It can include a database (or several of them), and it could include a knowledge base (*a là* expert systems) as well. This infobase can and will be organized in varying ways based on the task, software, or jobs being supported and the nature of the information required to perform the defined tasks.

Decisions about what content should be included and in what detail must be directly related to findings of the audience and task analyses. Certainly, the infobase should provide minimum information to respond to user questions or requests. How much more than the minimum should be included is a function of at least:

- objectives (e.g., minimum performance? development of expertise?)

- available time and money

- storage limits

- user needs and profiles

- organizational philosophy.

Keep in mind, however, that one of the reasons people don't use traditional documentation is that it contains *too much* unnecessary or irrelevant information. Developers often include anything and everything anyone could possibly want to know—and it overwhelms users. With electronic media, it's possible to "layer" the information so interested users can pursue information in depth. But when money, time, and storage are limited—and when users are urgent about getting on with what they have to do, a good rule of thumb is to include every-thing that is *necessary* and *only* what is necessary.

Kinds of Information. There are various *kinds* of information, such as concepts, facts, examples, and procedures. Each kind of infor-mation can be organized and presented in various ways. For example, a procedure can be described using text narrative, a flowchart or decision tree structure or diagram, or by example or demonstration.

Different types of information can be expressed or represented in different ways or media.

The way the infobase is organized and internally and externally cross-referenced or linked, will be a function of need, technical envi-ronment, money and time available for development, and designer skills. The organizing of infobases is a discipline of its own. It will be generally discussed in the chapter on design and development.

Well developed schema for organizing and representing non-quantitative types of knowledge or information have been developed and employed extensively by those in the fields of documentation and training. The methodology taught in Information Mapping® semi-nars, for example, has been used as a basis for high performance communication for some time (this methodology is a product of Infor-mation Mapping, Inc. of Waltham, Massachusetts). Grounded in re-search in the areas of cognitive science, human factors engineering, task analysis, display technology, and effective writing techniques, the Information Mapping method provides structure, frameworks, process, and modes for the representation of information in either on paper or on-line. Table 4.2 lists and describes one aspect of Informa-tion Mapping's methodology—the categorization of information based on its purpose for the reader.

While Information Mapping's roots are in text, its concepts can be extended to other expressions or media such as audio, image, and sound. Other well-developed knowledge organization approaches certainly ex-ist. What's important is that an approach be articulated and adopted so that the infobase development and representation process is structured, comprehensive, and appropriate to user and task requirements.

Modes of Presentation. Information can be represented, and stored and presented, in the various media, including

• Text

• Fixed or animated graphics, including manipulable images

• Audio, including sounds, voice, and music

• Full-motion video sequences

• Still images, including photographic representation

Table 4.2

THE SEVEN BASIC TYPES OF INFORMATION, BASED ON INFORMATION MAPPING'S METHOD

INFORMATION TYPE	DEFINITION
Procedure	A set of steps performed by one person to obtain a specified outcome
Process	A series of events or phases which take place over time and have an identifiable purpose or result
Concept	A group of items which share a unique combination of critical attributes and can be referred to by the same generic name
Structure	A physical object which can be divided into parts and has boundaries
Principle	A statement which tells the reader what should or should not be done or what seems to be true in light of the evidence.
Fact	A statement that can be asserted without supporting evidence
Classification	A sorting of items into categories based on a sorting attribute

©1977 Robert E. Horn. Reprinted with permission

- Logic, including step charts, flow charts, formulas or scientific notation, and computer programs.

The various information types or categories can be expressed in one or more of the modes. "The wing must project at a 45 degree angle" could be written just that way, shown in a picture, or presented as some combination of words and pictures. "The rate of acceleration is X" can be described in words, a formula, the plot on a graph, or with an image of some sort. The most effective strategy is to match the presentation to the information itself. Consider the message: "the high-pitched chime indicates a SIMM problem." You could write it in words for the user, but how much better to attach the actual sound to the message file so that it plays when the sentence is displayed?

While not every information type can or should be expressed in alternative ways, many can be variously represented with an electronic performance support system so users can select or be presented with their preference in relation to the given situation. How information should be expressed is a function user needs, the nature of the information, the nature of the performance task, and available development and delivery technology. Again, available time, money, and developer skill are determinants. Assuming time and resources rarely permit every representation, designers should represent information in ways that leverage understanding.

Views of the Information. An infobase will often be developed for use by many, many people. Individual user situations and needs vary based on many factors, including location, expertise, responsibility, authorization or security levels, and so on. Table 4.3 lists criteria that could be individually or collectively considered in determining the possible views allowed to users in given situations. Essentially, infobase developers can "tag" or notate various knowledge types or modes based on analysis of their appropriateness for a given user population. When those users call upon the infobase, only the information that applies to them is presented.

Table 4.3
SAMPLE CRITERIA FOR INFORMATION VIEWS

Function
Location
Objective or purpose
Certification status
Expertise level
Job title
Experience
Need
Security Level
Role

For example, a company that sells different products in different states might choose to base a user's view of product information based on the user's state. (This might be particularly appropriate in industries with products that are regulated at the state level, such as insurance). Novices would typically require different information or more detailed coaching than experts in solving a given problem. Based on the system design, users might get a prompted version of an applications software system or advisor—or they might be able to fastpath through the system via keystrokes or direct information entry (see the American Express case study).

This kind of flexible view can be quite sophisticated, as in the *Bachman DB2 Product Set*, an application software package that, among other things, permits reverse engineering of DB2 databases that were not modeled prior to development. Users set the level of information, structure, and feedback they wish from the system for each task at four distinct levels of interaction and information. (See Exhibit 4.1). Novice users get lots of information and description on the right window of the screen. Experts basically act autonomously and get limited communication or control from the system. (See Exhibits 4.2 and 4.3). The users can set their level of interaction and communication by task as a system default or for each session when they work with the system. When they are within a session or task, they can adjust the level up or down based on their competence, confidence, or the risk they perceive in a given situation.

Technically, these differential views could be controlled by the system, by the user, or by both. Of course, individual users need not have their access limited. The amount of user flexibility must be determined during the design stage, based on need, available technology, money and time available, organizational philosophy, and developer skill.

This concept of *views* of the infobase or performance support system is best compared to the concepts in traditional data base design and development (see James Martin, *An End User's Guide to Data Base* (Englewood Cliffs: Prentice-Hall, 1981). Essentially, the infobase is the information equivalent of normalized data within a data base (i.e., a self-contained, standalone element that represents a complete chunk of information; the information cannot be further sub-divided and maintain meaning). There are various physical files stored in the computer. Based on the user's needs or inquiries or developer specifications, a *logical* view is constructed for each user or situation from that one set of physical files. This concept of differentiating between logical and physical *views* of the information is particularly important when diverse user populations will be using the same system. The goal of the designer is to construct the *most specific and appropriate* view of the infobase so that performance is efficient and effective. Whether users will or should have access to other parts of the infobase or system interfaces is, again, a design decision.

INFORMATION FILES

The types of files included in (or accessed by) an electronic performance support system correspond roughly to the modes of information:

- Text databases, including on-line reference, containing content in various structural forms. Content includes procedures, policy and

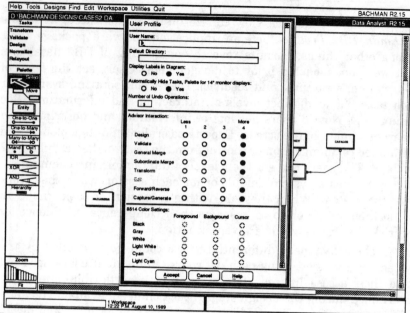

Exhibit 4.1

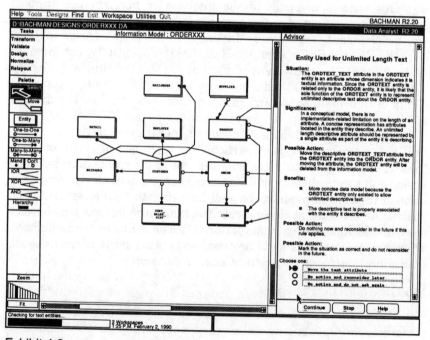

Exhibit 4.2

Courtesy Bachman Information Systems

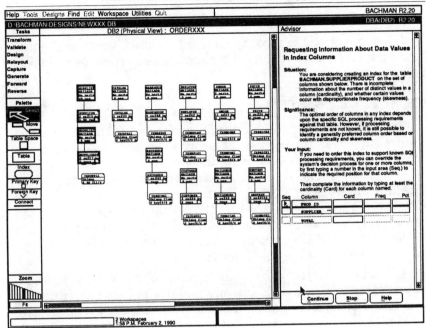

Exhibit 4.3
Courtesy Bachman Information Systems, Inc.

product information, concepts and explanations, specifications, business policy, glossaries, commands, and so on, as well as stored images of text relevant to the job (memos, reports, backgrounders). These text databases will be technically stored and organized in many ways: hypertext tools, on-line documentation software, text retrieval software, database management systems, and so on.

- Visual databases including libraries of pictures, schematics, diagrams, graphics, maps, and full-motion video, to provide information or to serve as models, representative images, reference points, and so forth. In these visual databases, video and images are viewed as data elements—both from a technical and a structural perspective. These visual databases will be stored and organized in several ways, including hyper-reference tools such as *HyperCard*™ and *Super-Card*™. Emerging database management systems, particularly object-oriented DBMSs are being designed to accept multimedia data. In the meantime, media-specific development tools will be used to organize, store, and represent multimedia information—and the information will be linked via hyper-reference tools or programming code to other elements of the performance support system.

- Audio databases with libraries of sounds, voice sequences, and music.

In addition to those three types of information, traditional quantitative data files can be available from within a performance support system.

THE SUPPORT SYSTEM

The other part of the electronic performance support system provides support to the user in achieving a performance objective. A performance objective is something that must be accomplished. Success is typically a function of the application of knowledge, process or procedure, and rules to a given situation within a given context. The individual must be able to structure the problem or task and bring to bear appropriate and complete knowledge and processes that are specific to the situation or context. Various parts of the support system will access or link to the infobase.

The support system can include a range of support mechanisms and software tools, including advisory systems to help in structuring or executing tasks and decision making, commercially available software programs, organization-specific applications software, special-purpose software utilities built expressly for use within the performance support system, and other interactive capabilities. The user will, of course, understand that there are various and alternative support mechanisms available, but the more tightly integrated the design and implementation of the mechanisms, the more invisible the distinctions to the user. Let's look at the possible types of software found in an EPSS in more detail.

Advisory or expert systems for problem structuring, decision support, analysis, or diagnosis will be a common component of an electronic performance support system because often the performance objective being supported is complex and difficult to perform. These advisory systems can exist in many forms and can be invoked by the user when needed. For example, The Source, an EPSS at Prime Computer (see the case study), allows sales reps to call up an advisor to assist in qualifying leads or in determining whether to continue working on a prospect. In an equipment troubleshooting EPSS, a technician might activate an advisor to assist in diagnostics (see the Amdahl case study). At one step beyond this type of interaction, however, the system might be programmed to activate an advisory system based on data input. In the troubleshooting case, for example, the advisor could recommend an action and coach the technician through a complex task when certain data is entered into the equipment log.

Self-activating advisors are particularly appropriate for software support, because the system has a kind of access to the user's thinking. Rules can be built into the EPSS to effectively monitor user performance with the software and, when those rules are activated, initiate interaction with the user in the form of explanations, other advisory dialogs, warnings, suggestions, or questions (e.g., "Would you like to know a simpler way to perform this task?"). (See the IBM case.)

Interactive productivity software including spreadsheets, text processors, and task-specific interactive job aids, can be integrated into the EPSS. For example, in the Dow Total Quality Management Performance Support Tool (see Dow Case Study), users who are working through the process of identifying and analyzing opportunities for improvement in their work group can call upon both embedded software utilities and tools, such as electronic flowcharters, graphing tools, prestructured surveys, voting systems, or diagrammers—or they can invoke full-blown software tools such as an installed word processor or graphics package.

Applications software to perform specific job tasks or functions (e.g., claims systems, rating, pricing, or estimating systems) is another component. Sometimes applications software is the primary environment for a user and the EPSS supports performance within the applications software.

Help systems can be constructed that are either user- or system-initiated, context-sensitive and inquiry-based, or intelligent. Help systems can include explanations, demonstrations, advice, and alternatives for operating within or using the software.

Interactive training sequences can be built in to permit self-directed or structured learning experiences that are task-related and flexible. Programs can be system- or user-initiated. Within a performance support environment, these are more typically granular sequences that are task-specific, but they may also be strung together and experienced as a more or less comprehensive traditional computer-based training program (with or without video).

Assessment systems will permit evaluation of knowledge or skill either before job task performance or in assessing employee competence. These assessment systems can be for user purposes only, or they can be tracked as a basis for certification, level of expertise, access to certain system functions, and so on based on design specifications and organizational philosophy.

Monitoring, assessment, and feedback systems that observe user activity can inform users about the appropriateness of their actions within software (e.g., error messages or conditions and related instructions) or track user activity to determine whether and when assistance or information is needed. These monitoring systems can be rule-based or simple tracking mechanisms that observe actions and prompt users based on context, activity, time factors, and so on.

In addition to the components I've described, an electronic performance support system can incorporate anything else that helps an employee do a job when the employee needs the help in a form the employee needs.

THE USER INTERFACE

The user interface may be the single most important element of a successful electronic performance support system. If it is inadequate, unclear, or too complex, the power of the underlying system is essentially irrelevant. The user interface should provide user-defined access to all the components in a straightforward and consistent way and that permits the integration of relevant components so that a meaningful and whole context is provided for the user to work in. The interface typically will make available options clear to the user and may include functions such as tracking previously accessed screens or displays to permit backward, as well as forward and lateral navigation. The means for individualizing the EPSS is typically available via the interface, although sometimes individualization can be accomplished by establishing system- or user-defined profiles prior to using the EPSS.

SUPPORT SYSTEM CONSTRUCTION

Exactly *how* a performance support system is structured, organized, and integrated is the developer's concern. Naturally, task performance requirements and technological options will drive design. Developers must determine, for example, the best way to construct an advisor from the alternatives such as decision trees, decision tables, rule-based systems which interact with the user via a dialog, and so forth. Developers must then determine how to *technically* construct the approach. For example, a decision-tree type advisor can be programmed, constructed using a hypertext system, or in other ways.

Developers must determine

- the types of support mechanisms and resources it contains such as application software, decision trees, dialog-based advisory systems, or knowledge bases

- whether it contains or accesses data from databases, applications software, or information services

- whether it accepts user data or input

- whether it manipulates or acts upon user or other data

- how the structures, infobase, and software tools or utilities are organized, stored, and interrelated, such as within hyper-reference tools, database management systems, expert systems shells, and so on

- the modes in which information is represented
- the system interface, navigation techniques, and information search mechanisms.

When the components are chosen and decisions are made on how they should be integrated, the development environment must be chosen. There are hundreds of development tools in the marketplace, ranging from CBT authoring system and hypertext tools to object-oriented programming languages. Development environments and tools are discussed in the chapter on technology and tools.

The design of the EPSS must, of course, be driven by the nature of the resources users need based on both the user population and the tasks at hand. This technical structure is determined following task, user, and technical analysis. Although there are hundreds of tools and development environments to choose from, in reality, the choices are often limited by the need. For example, some tasks would benefit enormously from audio databases of sounds that represent conditions such as mechanical problems or electronic signals. That *need* would require a sound database, and in order to provide adequate explanation of the sounds, the sound files would have to be relationally connected to explanatory text, voice, or possibly a graphic representation via a hypermedia link. Those two sets of needs would, therefore, require adequate hardware platforms, and the tools for software development requirements would include a hypertext platform, audio recording or production system, and graphics tools.

Clearly, there are many alternative design approaches to the EPSS Figures 4.1 and 4.2 indicate the range, which can be very broad. The cases throughout this book include similar diagrams of actual systems. These are high-level design plans. Much more detailed diagrammatic representation is necessary when specific functionality and relationships must be expressed.

SOURCES OF POWER

An EPSS will have more or less power to support task performance. Of course, the ideal is that everything and anything that someone wants or needs is available instantly in whatever form or expression is preferred at the time. In reality, however, there are tradeoffs that will be consciously or unconsciously made. Let's look at the variables that will dictate the power and effectiveness of an electronic performance support system?

- infobase quality, completeness, accuracy, clarity, and the number of ways and media within which knowledge is expressed

- the number of support functions it supplies, from help to consulting to data management or whatever else is needed

DIAGRAM OF BASIC EPSS

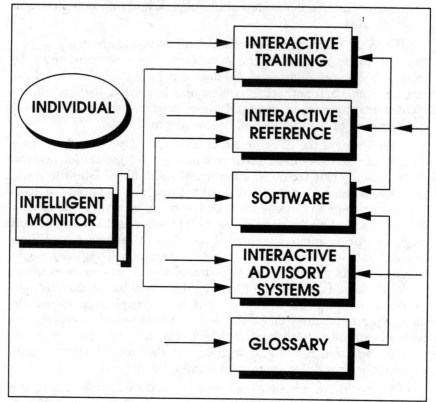

Figure 4.1

- the quality, completeness, and relevance of the functions to the job of the person using it

- the quality and degree of internal and external integration permitting users to make meaningful connections among and between the available information, support, data, and systems and their specific needs or situations

- the degree of intelligence the system brings to bear on analysis, decision-making, or diagnosis

- the quality and intuitiveness of the user interface and the transparency with which it provides access to functions.

- its context sensitivity in the specific and broadest sense, of being able to provide support and information at the point of need

DIAGRAM OF COMPLEX EPSS

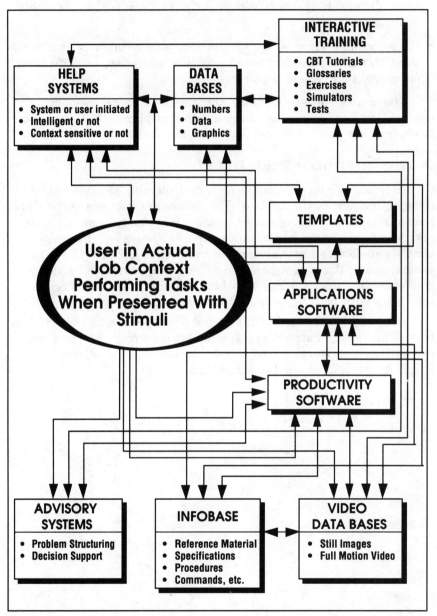

Figure 4.2

- the diversity of its forms of information, to meet the user's needs from different perspectives or orientations (sound, visuals, explanations)

- the customized views of the system available to tailor information, support, and tools to user need, location, expertise, security level, job responsibility, and preference.

The critical development is not any new technology, but the application of the technology from a different approach. Design considerations are covered in more detail in the chapter on development.

IS THIS JUST GLORIFIED HELP?

In trying to gain perspective on a new concept, it's often useful to compare the new to the familiar. The differences between *standalone* reference systems, CBT, or expert systems is typically clear, but initial reactions to electronic performance support systems is that they are simply well-designed help systems or interactive job aids. In the most general sense, this might be so, but there are differences which are delineated in Tables 4.4 and 4.5 which compare relevant EPSS characteristics with both job aids and help systems.

In reality, performance support is a hybrid concept: it selects the best of previously independent species—and through its combinatorial approach, produces a new breed that has familiar attributes but is inherently different at the same time.

Table 4.4

COMPARING EPSS TO TRADITIONAL HELP SYSTEMS

PERFORMANCE SUPPORT	HELP SYSTEMS
Support a broad range of tasks, whether or not software is involved.	Typically support only software related tasks and are usually confined to software rather than job task support.
Provide information, task structuring, interactive, conditionally branched advice, examples, and interactive training.	Provide passive information only.
Internally cross-referenced information or knowledge, which is also linked to other structures.	May or may not be internally cross-referenced. Typically context-sensitive to software applications and not linked to other resources.
Can support complex, interrelated tasks with conditional branching.	Usually provide limited descriptions or procedures and, sometimes, examples. Rarely deal in combined procedures or complex tasks.
Provide multiple means of access and alternative views of the content.	Typically accessed via structured menus (listing topics, alphabetical listings, commands, and so forth).
May accept user input or data.	Do not accept user input or data except as menu choices.
Can contain customized views of the information or support.	Could contain customized views of the information, but rarely do.

Table 4.5
COMPARISON OF PERFORMANCE SUPPORT SYSTEMS WITH JOB AIDS

PERFORMANCE SUPPORT	JOB AIDS
Can support simple or complex task performance; can address multi-pathed, conditionally branched, integrated *processes* via expert systems.	Typically support simple, linear sequential procedural tasks.
Can accept user input or data as a basis for situationally specific branching, advice, information presentation, etc.	Do not accept user input or data. Structuring occurs in advance of need and addresses limited situations.
Provide task structuring, advice, and related information.	Provide task structuring but not related information.
Can present customized views of the system to individual users.	Structured in advanced and do not accommodate individual user requirements.
Can incorporate multiple modes of information presentation (e.g., text, audio, images, animated sequences).	Typically paper-based with possibility of passive multiple modes (i.e., text and still images). When electronic, could incorporate multiple modes, but is mostly text and still images.
Can provide alternate access to the information (e.g., menus, alphabetical listings, context-sensitive to software or condition, hierarchical access through outlines, or relational access through hypermedia).	Typically provide predetermined and structured access. Because the infobase is not integrated, the path is usually linear.

Table 4.6
COMPARISON OF PERFORMANCE SUPPORT SYSTEMS WITH CONVENTIONAL COMPUTER-BASED TRAINING

PERFORMANCE SUPPORT	COMPUTER-BASED TRAINING
Contains an organized, interactive, hyper-reference infobase that can be accessed in multiple ways or pre-linked to other components of the system.	Contains an infobase that is typically structured within predetermined presentation sequences. When infobase in CBT is organized with hypermedia and linked to interactions or applications software, it is more similar to EPSS than traditional training.
Contains a broad range of support mechanisms, including interactive advisory or other problem structuring and decision support mechanisms to assist users with specific problems or situations.	May outline procedures or processes as part of information presentation, but rarely includes other interactive support mechanisms.
Can accept and manipulate user input or data.	Typically uses pre-established examples for task practice. Does not accept specific user input to address a given user problem, situation, or need.
Permits very flexible navigation and information access by users in nonlinear structure.	Typically structured in advance by developer to present optimal sequence and approach to communicating information and task practice. Can permit some learner flexibility in access and navigation, but most often control is limited to sequencing prestructured modules.
Available on demand, in context, on the job to provide information and support.	Most often organized as an event with the goal of teaching to be experienced prior to job performance. When available on-demand at the job site, CBT is typically designed to be experienced as a sequential training event, rather than as a reference or support environment.
Emphasis is on user construction of an individualized learning sequence.	Structured to present information and experiences as organized by the developer.
Multimedia possible.	Multimedia possible.
Can include monitoring of user performance in a task or system and provide context-sensitive advice, information, control, or various types of support.	Monitors and tracks user activity either to record user paths or performance on questions or exercises. When CBT is concurrent with applications software, it can "know" where users are and provide pre-linked instructional sequences or content.
Granular.	Modular.

Cases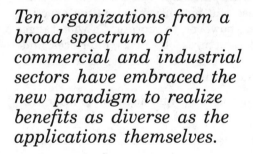

Ten organizations from a broad spectrum of commercial and industrial sectors have embraced the new paradigm to realize benefits as diverse as the applications themselves.

Exploring EPSS Design Through Case Studies

Describing electronic performance support systems design is a little like describing aliens from outer space: only a few people have seen them, and the descriptions range from wondrous or impossible to just plain unclear. It is also very early in the continuing development of this concept to generate definitive design principles as they relate to various tasks, processes, or jobs to be supported. Ten case studies representing a range of task applications, technological environments, and sophistication have been selected and described to help operationalize the design and structure considerations outlined in Chapter Four.

The purpose of these case studies is to make the EPSS concept tangible. They take *real* business problems—such as supporting a group of field engineers servicing an enormous and changing product mix (Amdahl)—and look at the needs with nontraditional support and learning alternatives in mind. Each case describes a particular situation in a particular company with particular technological alternatives. As such, no individual case will match your situation exactly. The cases were carefully selected, however, to represent a wide range of examples, applications, design structures, objectives, interfaces, and implementation platforms. Their diversity and the elegance of their designs should give you six kinds of help:

- Increase your understanding of the range and depth of EPSS in the workplace

- Give you *generalizable* problem descriptions and design structures

- Demonstrate the practicality of the EPSS concept with concrete examples developed by talented people in highly credible organizations under deadlines and with currently installed technology

- Stimulate your thinking about alternative approaches to your organization's learning and support needs

- Provide departure points for your own design

- Provide examples for use in explaining and proselytizing the EPSS concept with various groups within your organization.

Using the Case Studies

Study the cases in detail and use them as sources of inspiration for both application identification and EPSS design. Each demonstrates a unique user interface, alternative ways to orienting users, varying levels of interaction and user control, components, software, and power. Each could have been designed *very* differently and still have been effective. Their designs reflect designer creativity, client needs and priorities, technological platforms, and goals for the EPSS project itself. Clearly, a system intending to prototype a concept that doesn't have to be implemented (as in the American Express example) will result in a very different outcome than a system that must run on previously installed hardware (as at AT&T). A system that supports nontechnical users in a retail environment (the Innovis DesignCenter) will be different from one supporting technical staff who are experienced with computers (IBM's data modeling EPSS).

While each case study stands alone, they are best understood in the context of the frameworks explained in Chapter Four. When reviewing the cases, keep the following considerations and questions in mind:

- How does the problem or need description relate exactly to my organization's situation? If it doesn't, how can the *nature* of the problem or solution be generalized to fit?

- In my organization, would this approach be feasible? Politically practical? Technologically possible?

- How could I use this example in advocating the EPSS concept?

- What issues, questions, or barriers would it raise for me?

- What additional benefits would be possible in our situation?

- What required knowledge and skills currently exist in our organization? Which would have to be acquired, developed, or contracted?

Key Success Factors in EPSS Design

The primary things to keep in mind about EPSS design are to always

- hold paramount the meeting of performer or learner needs

- keep an open mind

- don't freeze prematurely on what electronic performance support is or what it should look like.

Success requires that you suspend the design of solutions until the performance problem is rotated before you several times and that you continually ask yourself a fundamental question. "What would someone learning or doing this new or complex task *want* or *need* in order to perform?" This means adding an additional step in the conventional development process. You must go beyond task and content analysis to *learner needs analysis*. This is a fairly straightforward activity, and the questions to consider are summarized in the table on page 33, "The Face of a Complex Task."

Use these case studies to help you *rotate your problem or need* and to provide additional fuel for acceleration of EPSS.

Software Support

Ziff Technologies

The Business Problem

Most organizations, large and small, rely on off-the-shelf software for basic office tasks: word processors for document production, spreadsheet software for organizing quantitative information, graphics software for creating images. These tools have the potential to improve work quality, speed up production, decrease dependence on technical professionals such as graphic artists, and enable the organization to perform at a higher level.

The two major disadvantages to installing this casual software are the training and support they impose on the organization. New users must be trained to use it, and even experienced users must be taught functions they are using for the first time. Even after they have learned, however, nearly all users require support in solving problems, performing complex tasks, or just acquiring confidence. This support increases organizational overhead, whether the organization recognizes it or not. And the support burden always grows. Help desks are among the fastest growing functions within organizations. Sometimes the help desk staff needs assistance to keep up with all of the software features, versions, functions, and relationships among and between software packages and hardware.

The nature of the software knowledge and skill transfer problem gets more complex as more users have access to powerful software that is designed for people grounded in conceptual frameworks such as those associated with video, graphics and sound production or in technical areas such as presentations, database design, accounting, or other fields. New users must not only learn the software, but a professional field as well. I learned more about audio-visual effects in trying to use presentation software than I ever wanted to know! Needless to say, my interest in learning the in-depth accounting knowledge presumed by my general ledger or tax preparation software, engages me even less. At least when creating a "glitter right" effect on a computer-generated slide, I see something pretty on a screen!

Most users bypass formal training programs and are likely to try to learn on their own or by asking a co-worker for help. Often motivation to learn new things deteriorates as people use trial-and-error strategies. Even when they are positively certain that the software permits certain tasks or has features that ease their burdens, the effort associated with learning always seems greater than the time available at the moment of need. When co-workers are willing to assist newer users, the costs of such support are high. Often two people, rather than one, attempt to figure things out. In other situations, peer experts spend enormous parts of their work day helping others with software, leaving them less time to do their expected job tasks. There is an enormous hidden computer support budget in every organization.

When users do attend classroom training or take structured computer-based training programs, the training usually concentrates on the basic features. Or they view the programs as too fast, too slow, too much or too little content, and not directly connected to the way they are using the software. Often the training is in advance of the need, so maintaining attention is difficult; or it covers previously known skills. Even advanced training often doesn't address the user's specific needs, experience level, or frame of reference. As diversity in user knowledge and skill increases, the structured classroom or CBT training solution deteriorates as a high impact alternative.

Manufacturers' technical manuals are often the last resort when a user needs information or help. Locating information in the manual isn't guaranteed, nor is understanding it once it's found. Failure to locate information results in declining motivation, inadequate or inefficient task performance, calling on human support, and work delays. The fact that the manuals are often missing or incomplete adds further complexity to the problem.

Few organizations have formal or systematic methods for communicating new techniques and "workarounds" for off-the-shelf software. Such information tends to be confined to the user who discovers it, small groups of co-workers, or people who read the PC technical magazines.

These problems exist for all types of software use, including organization-specific proprietary software.

The Performance Support Solution

Ziff Technologies of Medford, Massachusetts and Comware Inc. of Cincinnati, Ohio have developed a solution to the problem of supporting users for one of the most popular off-the-shelf packages, Microsoft's *Word for Windows*. The solution is an integrated support, reference, and training system that runs on a user's computer with *Word for Windows*. It's designed to integrate the knowledge, coaching, training, and other support people need to learn while they are doing—and get better while they are doing it! The product was developed in cooperation with Microsoft, so its information is current—even the tips. The Microsoft help line provided information on common problems that people typically call the support service to solve.

This performance support system runs side-by-side with *Word for Windows*. It monitors the user's context in the application and provides information and feedback to user questions or assists in problems the user encounters. It can also work independently of the software. Comware calls this type of system a "knowledge support system," or KSS.

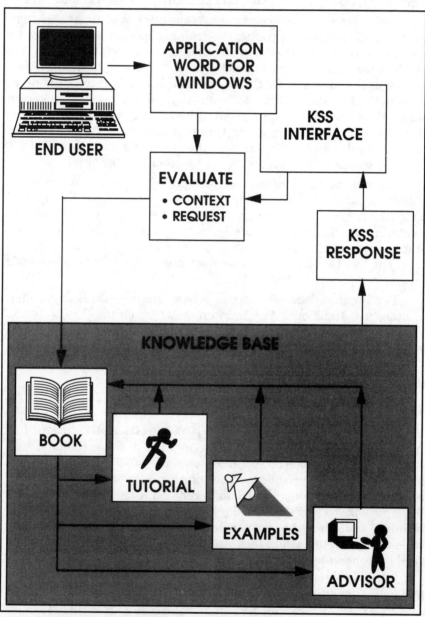

Figure 1. Diagram of the Word for Windows KSS.

Multiple resources are organized and cross-referenced in advance for the user. The resources include an infobase of the type we have been discussing (see the chapter, "What is Electronic Performance Support?"), examples with the opportunity to practice the task in a "safe" environment, and an Advisor (capable of helping to solve common problems or walking people through complex tasks without their learning how to do them in advance). Within the KSS, a user can ask for *exactly* what is needed when it is needed and, in many cases, get what is needed in several different forms (e.g., text description, example, practice, or structured coaching). Users can also access the information independently, so the KSS accommodates browsing as well. The product accommodates the primary learning strategies that people exercise: inquiry, trial and consequence (or variable manipulation), observation, and modeling and coaching.

The Book. The interactive infobase (called "the Book") is the central KSS resource. It contains more than 1600 pages of conceptual and task-oriented information. The topics are granular, so there's no wading through superfluous information to get to what's needed. Alternative means of accessing the information include context-sensitive retrieval, key word search, and access through menus.

Examples. The Example resource features common examples for the user to both observe and model against in an experimental mode without risking their *Word for Windows* files. Each example walks through the steps required to perform the task, with illustrations of various steps. At the user's request, the KSS makes sample documents available for a guided practice session with *Word for Windows.*

The Advisor. The Advisor resource helps solve problems commonly encountered with *Word for Windows,* such as getting documents to print the way they look on the screen. Each Advisor session asks the user a series of multiple-choice questions and recommends a course of action based on the user's response.

Sometimes, it even coaches the user through the task. For example, if a user must install a printer, the Advisor asks for certain information, such as printer type, and if the user wishes, it can actually step through the procedure. In effect, it permits a user to do something without ever having to commit it to memory. In the strictest sense, it automates the task performance. In a more general sense, it provides a model for the user to learn against while doing.

Implications for Software Designers

These concepts are important in that they effectively represent a new type of system interface that requires less knowledge and skill on the part of a user in order to perform complex, multi-variable or multi-step tasks. If system developers analyze what mechanisms are necessary to get users to perform with systems, they can incorporate them into their initial systems design, thereby decreasing external performance support system requirements. As they say, "it's all in the interface." And if you think about it, much of the training and support needed for software is really *compensatory* for badly designed user interfaces.

How the KSS Works

The KSS is a standard Windows application with Windows features such as a menu bar and dialog boxes. It can be configured to load automatically when the *Word* application is started. The KSS operates by monitoring the *Word* application. When the user asks for help (by clicking on the KSS icon or with a keystroke), the KSS searches the resources for information that matches the user's situation. It then displays the specific piece of information from the Book reference resource—or the Table of Contents, if it doesn't find a match. If other related resources, such as Examples, are available for the specific tasks, those options are presented to the user to choose at will from the "See Also" button on the control panel. Or the user can navigate *within* a given resource, such as the Book, to address additional questions or needs. Essentially, the user can access related information in multiple modes (i.e., Example, Book, and Advisor) and can work within a mode to explore additional information.

One strength of the KSS is the way in which it helps users find information. There are traditional methods available, such as browsing, hyperlinks (the ability to point at a word and jump to a corresponding page), and so on. The KSS, however, also has a Search button. Search finds information based on a question or statement typed by the user. The user need not worry about syntax or special command words, as the KSS is designed to handle open-ended user questions, just like the ones posed to hotlines or the person in the next office.

In addition, the user can choose from three different "resources" to find answers. Having identified a topic of interest (by searching, browsing, or whatever), a user can choose to see the answer from the "Book" resource, the "Example" resource, or the "Advisor" resource. Each resource gives the user a different way of assimilating the knowledge to perform the task.

Users can run the KSS in the Assist mode with *Word*. The Assist mode reduces the size of the KSS window and re-opens the *Word* window at the top of the screen. *Word* is restored at the user's current location.

Users can annotate their copies of the KSS by attaching "sticky notes" to any page in any resource. When the user has attached a note, a tiny icon appears at the appropriate point in the text; double-clicking on it displays the note. The user can also see a list of his or her notes in the current resource and use that list to move to annotated pages. Notes can be edited and deleted.

The vendor is contemplating an optional subscription service with the KSS. Subscribers would receive disk-based updates to the Book, Examples, and Advisor. Ziff Technologies is associated with the company that publishes several major PC magazines, such as *PC Week* and *PC Magazine,* so virtually all current information created and discovered by users and vendors is available to the KSS publisher to incorporate in the KSS.

Customization options are available to permit organizations to display their standard document formats, conventions, and so on. It is possible to limit the amount of information available so that users with limited requirements see only the relevant information. Customization of commercially available support systems combines the best of both worlds.

User Hardware Requirements

A variety of computer configurations will run the KSS. The typical hardware and software environment is:

- an IBM-compatible (286- or 386-based) PC

- MS-DOS Version 3.1 or later and Windows 3.0

- a hard disk, with 2 MB available for the KSS

- VGA or EGA monitor

- Microsoft *Word for Windows* application, if context-sensitive linking to the application is desired

- a Microsoft-compatible mouse is recommended.

A Day in the Life...

Barb, a new user, is writing a proposal with *Word for Windows.* She wants to add headers to it, but doesn't know how. *Word* is running and the KSS is loaded. As Barb pulls down a *Word* menu and locates the selector bar on the "Header/Footer" menu item, she stops and decides to find out how to perform the task through the KSS. She leaves her choice highlighted on the *Word* menu and clicks on the KSS icon.

Anticipating Needs. When the KSS appears, it presents the page from its on-line reference system (known as the on-line "Book") that

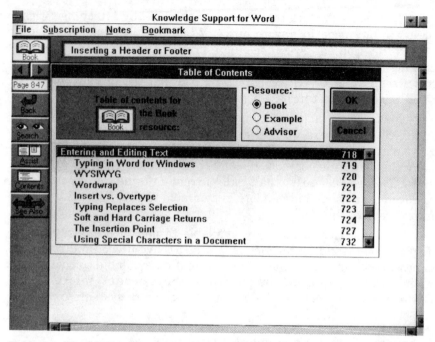

Exhibit 1. The KSS is a standard Windows application with Windows features such as a menu bar and dialog boxes.
Courtesy Ziff Technologies

describes the "Header/Footer" menu item. KSS anticipated Barb's needs by "reading" the *Word* screen, but it didn't assume that her needs ended there. Barb sees that someone in her department has attached a "sticky" note to the Header/Footer page because a Note button is present on the page (Exhibit 2). Barb presses the button to see its contents and finds that some sample headers are on the sales department's server. Although the description of the menu item and associated note are helpful, Barb needs to know *how* to perform the task herself.

Task-Based Access. There are a number of ways the KSS will help Barb find the description of the task. One way is that Barb could click the KSS's "Contents" button and search through the table of contents to find the task. The more direct route, however, is to just "ask" the KSS. She does this by clicking the Search button and typing the task she wants to perform—in her language, not the system's. She types "include a header" in the search dialogue box. The search locates several topics about including headers and footers in the Book resource of the KSS (Exhibit 3). Barb selects "Inserting a Header or Footer."

Multiple Response Styles. The KSS responds with the steps for the task from the on-line book (Exhibit 4) Barb reads the task and

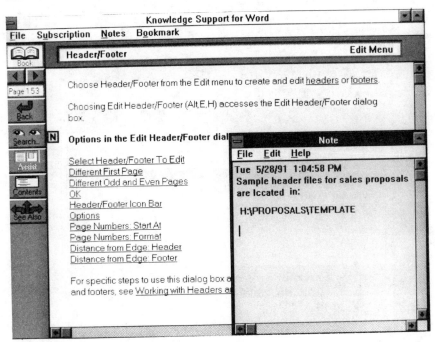

Exhibit 2. A note button indicates the presence of a "sticky note" attached by the user to a topic in the KSS.
Courtesy Ziff Technologies

decides that before she tries it with *her* document, she would like to practice with an example. She presses "See Also" and finds that there is an example available for this task. When she selects the example, the KSS temporarily puts her live document away and brings up an example document from its example library. Now Barb can practice the steps of inserting a header by following the steps located in the KSS window and using the example document in the *Word* window.

Results and Benefits

At this writing, the product is in final development and beta testing. Focus group results and beta tests on product prototypes indicate the following anticipated results:

- People can use it—and even users with no previous experience with *Windows* can use it with just limited orientation.

- Demands on Microsoft's hotline and company help desks will be reduced.

- Users become more independent, allowing employees to work at home or on the road with greater productivity.

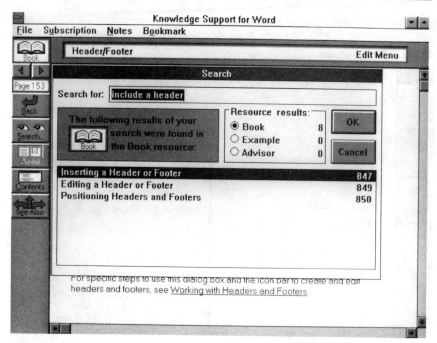

Exhibit 3. A search locates several topics about including headers and footers in the Book resource of the KSS.
Courtesy Ziff Technologies

- Training programs could be dramatically changed from their current rigid structure to teaching people how to use the KSS so they can operate independently on the job. Training programs could also be more like labs in which users bring their own documents and tasks and, following instruction in how to use the KSS, can work on their own work, employing the lab instructor primarily to help with further skill development in locating required resources in the KSS.

- Needs for formal training and external human support will be radically changed. Users will be more independent and their learning curve will be much steeper. Because information is available to them at the moment of need, users will be able to learn on an ongoing basis and will have the confidence to use *Word for Windows* more aggressively and extensively.

- The product accommodates an enormous range of knowledge and skill among its users.

- Work quality will be improved. Results associated with software utilization will be more consistent.

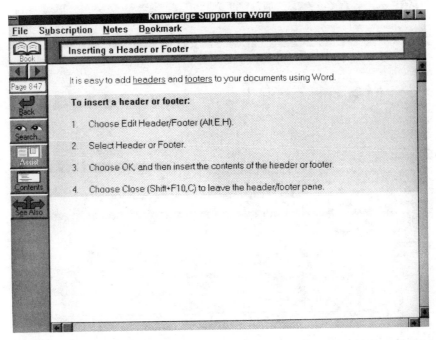

Exhibit 4. The KSS responds with the steps for the task from the on-line book.
Courtesy Ziff Technologies

Development Requirements

Development of the KSS employed Comware's *KSS Author* authoring system and other Comware proprietary software.

For More Information

For more information about the product, contact Ziff Technologies, 10 Presidents Landing, Medford, Massachusetts 02155 (617) 393-3069

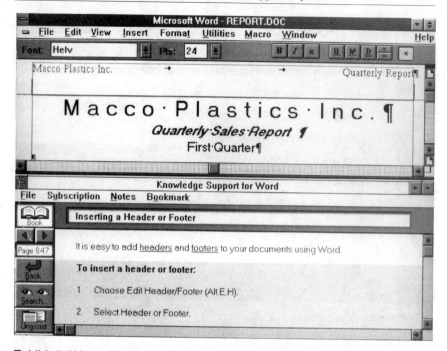

Exhibit 5. When the user selects the example, the KSS temporarily puts her live document away and brings up an example document from its example library

Courtesy Ziff Technologies

Point of Sale

Innovis DesignCenter®

The Business Problem

Homeowners like to design and build decks, shelving systems, and garages for their homes. Walking through a lumber yard generates lots of interest and motivation.

But many novice homeowners lack the knowledge and experience to design a structure that is safe and secure from an engineering perspective. Many also have difficulty visualizing their designs and developing detailed specifications on which to select required materials and price them. What types of posts, stairs, or railings should it have? How high off the ground should it go? Building codes complicate things further: the weather in Minneapolis requires different footings for a deck than are required in Florida. Of course, hiring an architect would solve the problem, but the cost associated with architectural plans is steep—and many architects don't want to bother with something simple like a deck. Contractors can help, but many of them find it time-consuming and unprofitable to work through the alternative design and redesign of home improvements. Their expertise is in construction, not necessarily in design.

Even when you can spend time in an old-fashioned lumber yard with a salesperson who is able to help with design and details, there are usually only one or two people who *can* help—and they aren't always available when you want them. The process of individual consultation takes hours.

Many of us now shop at the ubiquitous home center store chains. The good news part of these chain stores is that they provide one-stop shopping. The bad news is that they are often staffed with people inexperienced in construction. Frequently, the staff is made up of part-time students and retired folks who want something to keep busy. While intentions are positive, knowledge and skill is lacking. Order-takers cannot provide the required support. When you combine customer vagueness with sales representative inexperience, little gets built around the house.

The customer's confidence in his or her ability to build is critical to lumber sales. Owners of home center retail stores and lumber yards recognized the need to support their retail sales representatives in moving customers from dreaming to actually building. Given the staffing and turnover realities in retailing, there are built-in limits on their ability to train sales reps in design, related engineering concepts, product configuration, *and* sales techniques. The retail lumber business recognized that a radically different solution was necessary.

The Performance Support Solution

Enter the Innovis DesignCenter®: a custom computer that, based on consumer input, can design a deck in minutes and then display the design in color on a screen. The DesignCenter is an integrated proprietary hardware and software package installed in a kiosk that is placed on the store floor. Over 150 of the units are currently installed in lumber yards and retail home centers with over $250 million worth of decks designed on them to date.

The system can be learned within minutes and takes less than thirty minutes to master. Dr. Mark Lembersky, the president of Innovis, says, "If you need an instruction manual, we haven't designed it right."

The only visible equipment consists of a monitor and a trackball. The printers and processors are hidden from view. The goal is to focus on the ideas, not the technology. The trackball input device is used to control the interactive menus or input requests that are displayed on the screen (see Figure 4). Decisions include whether to attach the deck to the house or make it free-standing, types of wood, stairs, features, and so on. Essentially, the DesignCenter brings computer-aided design software capabilities directly to the consumer.

Exhibit 1. The DesignCenter was created with the salesperson in the loop.
Courtesy Innovis Interactive Technologies

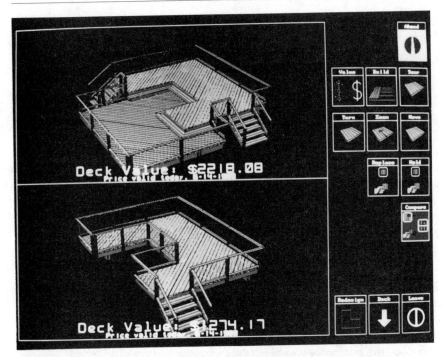

Exhibit 2. According to the DesignCenter's creator, "If you need an instruction manual, we haven't designed it right."
Courtesy Innovis Interactive Technologies

The system strives to be foolproof. If a two-level deck is called for, the software automatically draws in steps between the levels. The deck can be viewed from above, below or at angles, and a zoom feature gives closeup views of tricky joints and connections. The computer can also be used as a cost-control tool. One design that would have cost $3,966 with a Colonial-style railing with turned spindles was redrawn with two-inch square posts, reducing the total to $3,299.

One of the reasons that the DesignCenter is so effective is that it doesn't try to do everything. It can design a majority of the decks a homeowner would want, but there are limits. It cannot design anything over six feet off the ground or over 1000 square feet, due to varying building code requirements and the complexity for a do-it-yourselfer to build such a structure.

After the customer, the salesperson, and the computer work out the design (in an average of 6 minutes), the computer prepares a graphic representation of it (see Exhibit 3), a detailed blueprint with complete and clear specifications and diagrams (see Exhibit 4), and a materials list, including lumber, concrete, and hardware needed for the job (see Exhibit 5). General preprinted construction instructions are a part of the final package.

Deck Value: $1288.15

Exhibit 3. The DesignCenter is able to create a graphic representation of the deck the customer wants to build.
Courtesy Innovis Interactive Technologies

This point of sale performance support system was consciously designed with the salesperson in the loop. Consumers never use the DesignCenter alone, but are guided by a salesperson. The salesperson's guidance is to reduce the incidence of people using the machine for their own purposes, then leaving without ordering materials—but with a completed design and materials list in hand. The salesperson can determine how serious the customer is and then sell to the customer as necessary. Some stores charge a fee of up to $100 to buy the printouts from the DesignCenter. The fee can then be credited toward the purchase of materials. Many DesignCenter users are contractors who like to present the professional drawings, blueprints, and pricing costs for materials to their customers.

Results and Benefits

Benefits to retail stores, lumberyards, and the consumers themselves have been enormous. Economic and qualitative outcomes include:

- *Across the board increased sales volume.* One store sold 27 percent more board footage with the DesignCenter installed than during a comparable six-month period. The computer makes it easy to get a deck designed, and it increases customers' motivation when it presents their ideas to them in finished scale drawings. Over 50 percent of the customers using the machine ultimately make an order.

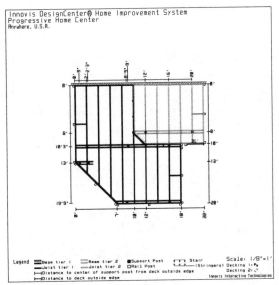

Exhibit 4. The DesignCenter draws a blueprint the customer can work from.
Courtesy Innovis Interactive Technologies

Independent market research results are described in the accompanying charts.

- *Increased confidence in materials lists and pricing.* The computer adds credibility and reduces uncertainty that something important has been overlooked or over-estimated.

- *Increased sales representative productivity.* The speed of the designing and costing processes permits sales reps to assist many more customers than if they had to work through them manually. Estimates take minutes, rather than hours.

- *Retailer employee satisfaction with the system and its impact.* See the accompanying charts for the results of independent market research on retailer employee satisfaction.

71

```
Innovis DesignCenter(R) Home Improvement System
Progressive Home Center
Anywhere, U.S.A.
```

DECK MATERIALS PACKAGE

Component	SKU	Quantity	Lumber
Tier 1			
Post	99-999-999	2	10' - 4x4 #2 & Btr Treated So.Y.Pine/DF
Post	99-999-999	1	16' - 4x4 #2 & Btr Treated So.Y.Pine/DF
Beam	99-999-999	2	10' - 2x10 #2 & Btr Treated So.Y.Pine/DF
Beam	99-999-999	4	12' - 2x10 #2 & Btr Treated So.Y.Pine/DF
Joist	99-999-999	5	10' - 2x8 #2 & Btr Treated So.Y.Pine/DF
Joist	99-999-999	3	12' - 2x8 #2 & Btr Treated So.Y.Pine/DF
Joist	99-999-999	2	16' - 2x8 #2 & Btr Treated So.Y.Pine/DF
End Joist	99-999-999	2	10' - 2x10 #2 & Btr Treated So.Y.Pine/DF
End Joist	99-999-999	1	12' - 2x10 #2 & Btr Treated So.Y.Pine/DF
End Joist	99-999-999	1	14' - 2x10 #2 & Btr Treated So.Y.Pine/DF
End Joist	99-999-999	1	16' - 2x10 #2 & Btr Treated So.Y.Pine/DF
Ledger	99-999-999	1	10' - 2x10 #2 & Btr Treated So.Y.Pine/DF
Decking	99-999-999	38	16' - 2x6 #2 & Btr Treated So.Y.Pine/DF
Blocking - Railing	99-999-999	1	8' - 2x8 #2 & Btr Treated So.Y.Pine/DF
Blocking - Joist	99-999-999	1	12' - 2x4 #2 & Btr Treated So.Y.Pine/DF
Tier 2			
Post	99-999-999	1	10' - 4x4 #2 & Btr Treated So.Y.Pine/DF
Beam	99-999-999	2	12' - 2x10 #2 & Btr Treated So.Y.Pine/DF
Joist	99-999-999	2	8' - 2x6 #2 & Btr Treated So.Y.Pine/DF
Joist	99-999-999	7	10' - 2x6 #2 & Btr Treated So.Y.Pine/DF
Ledger	99-999-999	1	12' - 2x6 #2 & Btr Treated So.Y.Pine/DF
Decking	99-999-999	17	16' - 2x6 #2 & Btr Treated So.Y.Pine/DF
Blocking - Railing	99-999-999	1	8' - 2x6 #2 & Btr Treated So.Y.Pine/DF
Stair Stringer	99-999-999	1	10' - 2x12 #2 & Btr Treated So.Y.Pine/DF
Stair Tread	99-999-999	4	8' - 2x6 #2 & Btr Treated So.Y.Pine/DF
Railing Post	99-999-999	10	8' - 4x4 #2 & Btr Treated So.Y.Pine/DF
Railing Top	99-999-999	5	16' - 2x4 #2 & Btr Treated So.Y.Pine/DF
Railing Bottom	99-999-999	5	16' - 2x4 #2 & Btr Treated So.Y.Pine/DF
Railing Baluster	99-999-999	107	2x2 #2 & Btr Treated So.Y.Pine/DF Baluster
Tier Stair Stringer	99-999-999	3	8' - 2x12 #2 & Btr Treated So.Y.Pine/DF
Tier Stair Riser	99-999-999	1	8' - 2x8 #2 & Btr Treated So.Y.Pine/DF
Tier Stair Riser	99-999-999	1	16' - 2x8 #2 & Btr Treated So.Y.Pine/DF
Tier Stair Tread	99-999-999	1	8' - 2x6 #2 & Btr Treated So.Y.Pine/DF
Tier Stair Tread	99-999-999	2	16' - 2x6 #2 & Btr Treated So.Y.Pine/DF

Component	SKU	Quantity	Other Materials
Foundation Concrete	99-999-999	3 bags	80lbs Premix Concrete
Beam Bolt	99-999-999	38	1/2"x8" Galv. Bolt, Washers & Nut
Joist Hanger	99-999-999	39	2x Galv. Joist Hanger
Joist Tie Strap	99-999-999	2	16 Gauge 1"x18" Galv. Tie Strap
Ledger Screw	99-999-999	24	1/2"x7" Galv. Lag Screw and Washer
Stair Strap	99-999-999	13	16 Gauge 1"x18" Galv. Tie Strap
Railing Bolt	99-999-999	38	1/2"x7" Galv. Bolt, Washers & Nut
Nails	99-999-999	18 lbs	16d Galv. Nails
Nails	99-999-999	25 lbs	12d Galv. Nails
Nails	99-999-999	3 lbs	8d Galv. Nails
Nails	99-999-999	6 lbs	Galv. Hanger Nails

Deck Value: $1288.15, plus tax

Exhibit 5. The DesignCenter prepares a materials list for the customer's project.
Courtesy Innovis Interactive Technologies

- *Increased quality of cost estimates.* Virtual elimination of materials, mathematical, and pricing errors.

- *Quicker turnaround in information to customers.* In traditional environments, sales reps would often have to defer giving costs and materials listings to customers because they had to wait on other customers. Hours, even days, would elapse before a customer got a call back from the sales rep with the needed information.

- *Significant "add-on sales" of deck-related furniture, equipment, and accessories.* Many stores have reorganized display areas around the DesignCenter so customers can look over barbecue equipment, deck furniture, lighting fixtures, and so on with the picture of the deck in hand. This encourages abstract visualization, but it also gives a customer a chance to measure furniture for fit and placement.

- *Increased image of professionalism for the store and the sales representative.* An independent market research firm found that of those customers who shopped at a DesignCenter store and at least one other store, 76 percent preferred the DesignCenter store and 100 percent said they would recommend the DesignCenter to a friend who is planning a project. Customers liked the time savings for project design and project design quality. They felt the DesignCenter design best matched their ideas, and they liked receiving a printed picture and a plan. Contractors who use the system feel it increases their professional image as well.

- *Continued motivation of do-it-yourselfers to build projects*—and to come back to the DesignCenter to plan free-standing garages, shelving systems, and storage units.

- *Leveraging of installed DesignCenter equipment across multiple types of building projects.*

- *Awards.* The DesignCenter received the ComputerWorld Smithsonian award for Innovative Use of Information Technology, and was cited among *Popular Science's* "Best of What's New." It is also on permanent display at the Boston Computer Museum.

Development Requirements

The special-purpose hardware for the system is strictly proprietary. The program is coded in C and operates under *Unix*.

Innovis Interactive Technologies, located in Tacoma, Washington, provides DesignCenters to the retail lumber industry and custom-development services to clients.

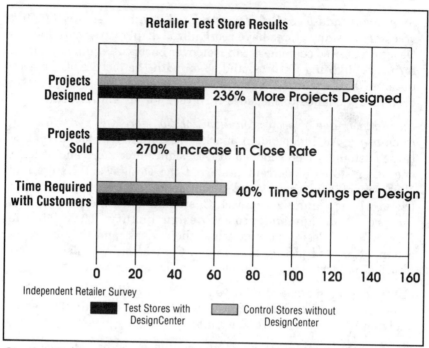

Chart 1. The DesignCenter has had a direct effect on the retail market.

Retailer Findings

Cumulative year one research shows the DesignCenter:

- Doubles the number of projects designed
- Enhances store image and builds loyalty with DIYers
- Helps retailers more than double their close rate
- Improves sales staff productivity by 40%
- Generates confidence in sales personnel

Chart 2. The DesignCenter benefits retailers who install it.

Chart 3. The DesignCenter shows evidence of providing employee empowerment.

Customer Services (Accounts)

American Express

The Business Problem

Providing timely, responsive support to cardmembers and service establishments that accept the American Express Card is a challenge. Callers present an enormous number and variety of situations to customer service representatives to resolve. They include the sorts of billing and payment questions you might expect, as well as requests for changes in accounts. The number of special promotions and programs is large and dynamic, as are the relationships between charge card companies, airlines, banks, stores, and other vendors. It is difficult, in this situation, just keeping representatives informed. Programs such as insuring purchases against loss or breakage when charged to the card are complex and subject to policies and conditions.

American Express also encourages cardmembers to rely on its representatives for help when traveling; most television viewers have seen the commercial in which the cardmember calls American Express for help after leaving his prescription at home. And cardmembers expect accurate, fast response. Conventional paper-based reference materials are voluminous, difficult to search, not integrated, and often neither current nor complete.

Representatives must access many conventional data processing applications to get information about an account, its billing, and so on. Observing a customer service representative flip through mainframe computer screens from several different systems to find a piece of data is like watching an experienced card dealer shuffle cards. Watching an inexperienced rep borders on the painful. Locating and integrating information that is spread among and between systems that were never designed for service support is an exercise in frustration.

The training and performance development problems are substantial due to:

- the large number of interrelated variables that representatives must locate and relate to a given business situation (e.g., data, business policy, product and program information, procedures)

- the range of both recurring and non-recurring customer needs and conditions

- problem complexity
- the number of applications software systems and tools required to support job performance
- growth in employment levels and staff turnover
- worldwide support requirements
- labor pools with limited or no experience in charge-card customer service activity
- high productivity requirements with limited time available for off-the-job training, programs, and information briefings
- increasingly high customer expectations for rapid, accurate response to questions or problem resolution.

Customer Service management cites six months or more to job proficiency. Staffing levels and business expectations typically assume an entirely proficient workforce.When employees cannot become competent quickly, productivity and customer service deteriorates and there is unacceptable overhead associated with several people involved in a single customer situation. This creates significant job stress for representatives, who are monitored for both quality and productivity. Stress further undermines performance, or people terminate from the job, which generates the need for more training. Turnover is often a significant issue.

Conventional training does not achieve job competence within a training program—and adding more time to formal training programs is increasingly unacceptable, due to productivity and customer service requirements. Computer-based training programs had some impact on the business situation, but they still required training in advance of need. And it was becoming increasingly difficult to maintain unstable content in programs developed with conventional authoring systems. Development lead times and costs were becoming increasingly unacceptable.

The business needs are to:

- accelerate competency curves and decrease time to competence
- reduce the average time per customer call
- assure sufficient, accurate, consistent, and rapid response to customer needs
- reduce time spent in system, product, and procedure training and increase time spent in training for customer service, listening, negotiating, and other personal skills

- support a diverse employee force
- leverage employee and supervisory expertise
- reduce overhead associated with problem-solving and response to customers
- reduce job stress.

The Performance Support Solution

American Express was looking for creative approaches to address the business needs. The Strategic Business Systems Group proposed a research and development project to structure a prototype of a system that would integrate knowledge, software tools, and problem solving methodology. The goals were:

- to provide an electronic environment within which the full range of employees, from novice to expert, could function on the job
- to enable novices to perform as experts
- to structure a systems environment that would reduce the amount of factual, product, procedure, and process training requirements and would permit more case-study or scenario-based training and increased training time on customer service and personal skills development
- reduce reliance on trial and error as the basis for on-the-job learning
- provide interactive, flexible communications and on-the-job training on new products, services, system capabilities, and procedures
- to provide up-to-date reference and training on-line and reduce requirements for paper-based information and help desks.
- to provide alternative access methods to information and resources to users.

Assuming successful development of this "proof of concept," the prototype would be used to sell the idea to business and systems development management and to receive funding to build a working prototype. In the long term, the goal is to institutionalize the interface and resource requirements into American Express's systems development standards and requirements.

The model was designed by Rick Hill, Director, Strategic Business Systems, American Express; Santa Fe Interactive, Santa Fe, New Mexico; and Karl Schmidt, Manager of Business Learning, Apple Computer; with input from the author of this book. It specifies a Macintosh platform, employing Silicon Beach's *SuperCard* development tool and MacroMind *Director*.

The System Interface

This is a prototype, but its capabilities have been reviewed against those of its various components, and there is no reason that such a system could not be fully developed. To simplify description, then, we describe it as if it were an operational system.

The system interface integrates multi-media data, information, training, and tiered coaching and prompting. It also permits immediate access to new and archived procedures, product and promotion information, and structured training sequences for the customer service position. It provides ready access to information needed for the job via context-sensitive access methods, alphabetical indices, selections from topically organized menus, and free-form information search.

A Day in the Life...

When signing on to the system, the employee is provided with news announcements, messages, and broadcast announcements via the messages window, and procedures changes and related tutorials via the procedures window (see Exhibit 1).

The news option includes ability to access full-motion video images of new television advertising, audio sequences of radio announcements, and copies of print advertisements and textual announcements. (See Exhibit 2). Anticipated questions and answers about the new information are included. Users can also access the libraries of promotional information if they wish to review other promotional information. Information will be maintained as "news" according to either company schedules, individual user access and review, or both.

The procedures section provides several views of a new procedure (see Exhibit 3). The new procedure can be read in a scrollable window or an interactive tutorial sequence that demonstrates implementation of the procedure in the system. In addition, the system could supply audio narrative in the language of the user, although that is not yet implemented. Practice activities on a new procedure could also be implemented. Certification testing could be required before active system work begins. From the screen in Exhibit 3, users have immediate access to the indexed procedures library.

On signing on to the production system, a user is presented with an array of options that include customer information fields on the top of the screen, reference and help systems, news, communications options (via the send button), and tools (such as calculator, software, and so on). Context-sensitive directions or coaching about both interaction with the system and job task performance are always visible on the screen. This integration of support, reference, and training for both system use *and* job task performance is a new and powerful concept. Historically, the focus has been on system support only.

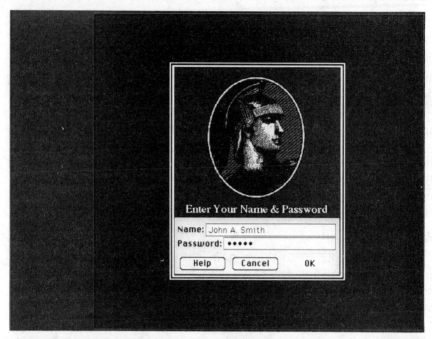

Exhibit 1. The user signs on to the system.

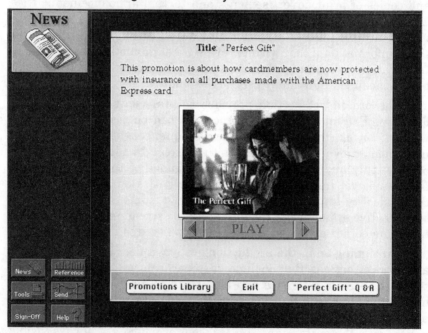

Exhibit 2. The news option includes the ability to view full-motion
video sequences of new television advertisements.
Courtesy American Express

When receiving a call, a user is prompted to obtain the account number and categorize the call according to one of the categories described on the left of the screen (see Exhibit 3a). Call categorization is a critical skill and one of the few that must be taught in advance. Once the the user enters the account number, the system automatically searches all databases, retrieves the relevant information, and displays it in a logical framework for the user in relation to the task being performed (see Exhibit 3b). In the conventional operating environment, the user would have to search, organize, and integrate the information based on a personal understanding of the situation. This individual "rule-based processing" is inconsistent and incomplete. This system avoids inconsistency and accesses, organizes, displays, and reorganizes information throughout the entire session without user intervention.

The goal of the system is to assure that a user gets into the correct problem-solving path so that only relevant options and coaching are available. Novices tend to view events as random; experienced staff have organizing principles and rules around which to structure task performance. One of the goals of the model was to rapidly get novices into the correct path and to institutionalize the rules and procedures that experts use within the system interface itself.

There are three modes of interaction with the system based on user knowledge, skill, and preference. Mode one is a fastpath option within which users can use key stroke combinations such as Option-K or Control-P. Mode two is via pull-down menus within given categories (see Exhibits 4a and 4b). Novices would typically choose the prompted interface (see Exhibit 5). That view of the system essentially displays task prompts and options (including system advice on how to handle something) throughout the task process. The system is actually working a user through a complex decision tree that presents new alternatives based on previous actions. Even experienced employees occasionally are faced with tasks not previously or frequently performed, so a user can change the degree of prompting offered by the system based on personal experience, confidence, or the risks associated with a given situation.

Available help options (see Exhibit 6) include system help, related system and job information, alphabetical listings of reference, and structured training sessions. Users always know whether they are in system, training, reference or help mode, based on the icons in the upper left corner of the active window.

Reference is available on demand (see Exhibit 7). So is structured training (at the "granular" level) that includes both system and job task training (see Exhibit 8). The training includes interactive audio role plays in which users must interact with both customers

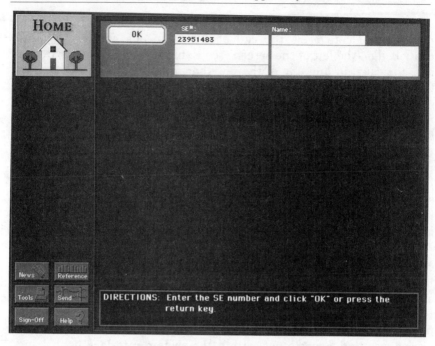

Exhibit 3a. The user fills in the account number.

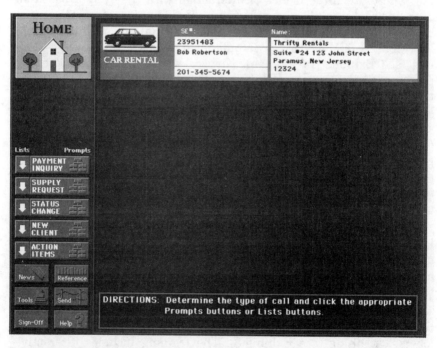

Exhibit 3b. The system responds with customer information.
Courtesy American Express

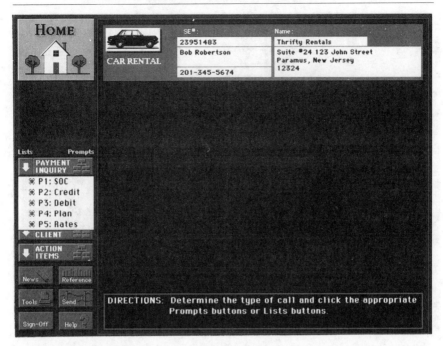

Exhibit 4a. A pull-down menu from the payment inquiry section shows keystroke options for accessing the information.

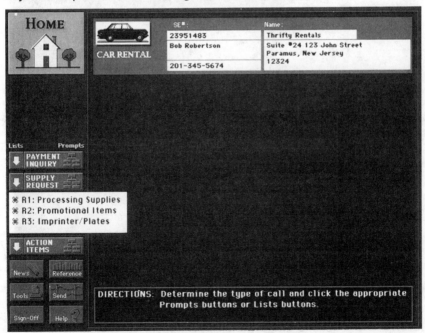

Exhibit 4b. A pull-down menu from supply request.
Courtesy American Express

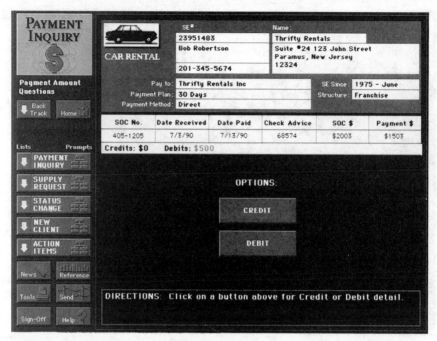

Exhibit 5. Novices would typically choose the prompted interface.

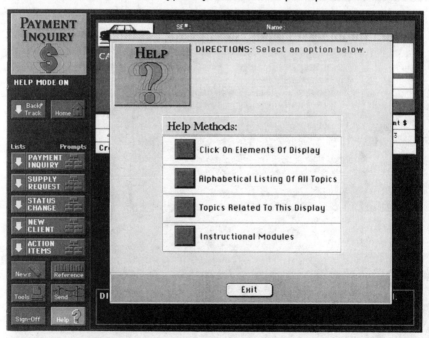

Exhibit 6. Help options range from context-sensitive explanations to structured training sessions.
Courtesy American Express

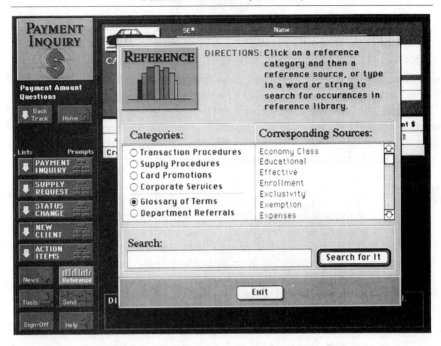

Exhibit 7. Reference is available on demand.

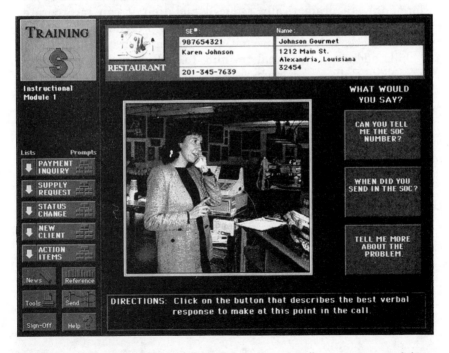

Exhibit 8. Training options include job-task as well as system training.
Courtesy American Express

and the system. Employees record their response into their headset microphone so the supervisor or trainer can replay and evaluate content, quality, and approach.

One of the more interesting features is the availability of an on-line catalog that includes images of supply options along with catalog and pricing information (see Exhibit 9). Note the script built into the catalog that integrates the sales script with the product information. One of the major goals of this model was to provide tightly integrated information with contexts so novices could perform as experts.

Results

Since the system is a prototype of the interface and is not operational, it is impossible to report on actual use or tests of it. But the prototype has been presented to systems developers, trainers, and management and has been acclaimed both within and outside American Express. The goal of the prototype was to redefine thinking and develop momentum around this alternative view of systems design. Funding has been secured to pursue this concept in a different functional area.

When you experience this system, even in a demonstration version, you clearly see that requirements for training in advance of job performance are dramatically reduced and that it can incorporate training that addresses only the systems and procedures aspects of job performance. This would permit a change in the mix of knowledge and skills addressed in formal training to include more comprehensive personal skills and customer service skills material. The benefits of expert performance by novices are obvious.

While there are no concrete results to report yet, the primary objectives for the design have been met. The model clearly operationalizes a vision of a new kind of system that incorporates and integrates software, information, and job task support and accommodates a broad range of user needs.

Demonstration Software Development

This demo was developed on a Macintosh II with eight megabytes of RAM using Silicon Beach's *SuperCard* and MacroMind *Director*.

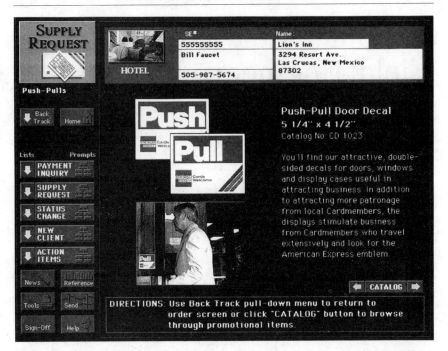

Exhibit 9. An on-line catalog can show product and pricing information.
Courtesy American Express

Customer Services (Field Engineering)

Amdahl Corporation

The Business Problem

Amdahl is a major supplier of powerful mainframe computers, data storage subsystems, data communications products, *Unix* system software, and educational and consulting services. With annual sales in excess of $2 billion, Amdahl products are sold in more than twenty-five countries worldwide.

Installing, configuring, and repairing complex and ever-changing electronic equipment requires skilled employees with knowledge of or access to product, defect, and procedural information. As any equipment vendor knows, maintaining operational performance of equipment is critical to customers who are dependent on its availability for production, information, manufacturing, and so on. While diagnostics are increasingly built into equipment which communicate conditions or repair requirements to users or field engineering staff, the ability to restore the equipment quickly and correctly is a performance must.

Increasingly, customers are creating their own hardware configurations by mixing and matching alternatives. This possibility of mass-produced, yet customized, equipment results in less and less predictable situations. Just think about how unique each personal computer is once users add their choice of boards, media possibilities, monitor and graphics capability, and software. This, of course, is affecting customer service and field engineering staff in that each situation they face is virtually unique. And often problems occur when things are combined for the first time—so the problems don't fall into predetermined categories with straightforward procedural solutions for diagnostics and repair. Add to this the rapid introduction of new capabilities, various versions of support software, and so on; you have a situation where it becomes almost impossible to keep people informed, never mind trained.

Information about products, problems, and processes is contained in voluminous paper manuals. Information search and retrieval is time-consuming and difficult. When information isn't immediately available, the service rep must either return to the office for the information and make a second client site visit or request telephone support or a joint repair call with a more experienced representative.

Assigning staff to field calls becomes a problem with less experienced staff. If problems come up that a given field engineer has no experience with or has not yet been trained on, the assigning manager must either delay the service call or reschedule the work of other engineers to assure proper assignment. Neither of these is an attractive solution. Customer Service managers want and must have:

- knowledgeable and skilled employees that can perform work as it appears

- employees who can function independently

- immediate solution to customer problems or fulfillment of their needs

- high staff productivity

- high work quality.

To the extent that there are performance gaps, there are serious business consequences:

- customer service delays

- customers whose business results and operations are negatively affected by faulty or inoperable computers

- expensive service due to multiple calls to resolve a problem or high overhead support costs (such as technical hotlines, joint calls by field engineers, and so on)

- associated business loss.

Amdahl conducts one of the most successful classroom and computer-based training programs for field engineers in the world. Even though they currently use the most advanced training techniques known, the Amdahl training staff and management knew that the rate of change, range of conditions, and equipment a field engineer would be presented with (including business volume growth) would require additional support.

Approaches to the Business Problem

Rich Schmieder and his Field Engineering and training staff have been developing effective simulation-based interactive training programs since 1988. Flexible, individualized programs was their goal. Employing various techniques, they managed to shift the Field Engineering training mix at Amdahl from one hundred percent lecture and lab programs to fifty percent self-paced interactive instruction and simulations. In the process of working with interactive CBT, they explored various hypertext alternatives and began to integrate hypermedia structures within the interactive training programs. They had also worked in developing concurrent interactive training programs in which learners could access support, help, and structured learning sequences while working actively within a simulator. Incrementally, they had moved away from tutorial structures into more flexible, task-oriented programs with learners doing—and accessing information to learn while doing.

But something was missing. Field engineers are taught to work with their documentation. And the documentation was not integrated with the training. Documentation and other support mechanisms, such as hot lines, were in other functional departments. Training staff couldn't directly make changes to the process, the structure, the content, and the distribution of such information and services. Of course, each of these other functions was also working to apply technology to their tools, so evaluation of on-line reference and other alternatives was occurring independently of the work done by Training. Schmieder and his staff knew that this would all come together some day, but grew increasingly concerned that each staff department would be selecting and implementing its own approach to supporting field engineering support. And each would be doing it in a unique technical environment employing different tools, establishing different standards. The fear was that when the time to bring things together was at hand, nothing would be designed or technically available in a form that would permit integration. Work would have to be redone, and precious time would be lost. It was also clear that the longer a given department went on with a set of tools, the more committed they would get to them. And it would become increasingly difficult to convince people to change.

So the Training group took a proactive approach.

The Performance Support Solution

The Training group stepped back and examined the field engineering performance needs without limiting their vision to previous solutions. They established a clear vision of what an ideal environment would be. They defined it as an integrated, electronic performance support system that would make information, process support, advice, and learning opportunities available on demand in the workplace at the moment of need. And they decided to prototype what such a system would look like to help crystalize their vision, assess development and technological requirements, and provide a basis for communicating alternatives to other functional support groups and Amdahl management. The prototype is detailed below in the Design section.

In the process of establishing the performance support system vision, the Training group defined the organizational and political realities facing such an effort. And they developed a specific strategy to address them and build commitment on the part of all required functions and management.

The importance of this case study lies as much in the process of orchestrating the political variables as it does in the very elegant design solution that was prototyped. Unless a given functional area or individual directly controls the political, logistical, and economic resources necessary to pull such a concept off, developing adequate commitment and sponsorship is the number one critical success factor (see the chapter on sponsorship and critical success factors).

The Process

The Training group's strategy was classic (for comparison, see the chapter on strategy):

- create a powerful, compelling example of an EPSS that would obviously address the business problems, including information search and integration of information with a given problem situation

- using the prototype, connect both system features and functionality directly to business benefits

- demonstrate the technological feasibility in the anticipated operating and technical environment for the next five years

- be certain not to raise expectations and hopes that could not be realized either technologically or with available human resources

- develop a basis for development costing and time requirements

- identify available, usable technological development tools to use in constructing and integrating the various EPSS components

- create understanding of and commitment to EPSS concepts and solutions in sister departments such as Support and Technical Publications

- limit perceptions and realities that would threaten sister departments or create a belief that Training was trying to "take everything over"

- identify key individuals that must be sold on the EPSS concept, its benefits, and its practicality

- along with sister departments, develop a specific proposal to proceed with EPSS development to Amdahl senior management, including development of a compelling business case and specific funding and resource requirements.

This was a very tall order—and one that was accomplished over a period of eighteen months. First, let's look at the prototype design.

Performance Support System Design (overview)

Goal Statement: *The purpose of the system is to provide an electronic environment through which Amdahl employees and customers can self-sufficiently and independently access authorized resources to achieve their business objectives in a timely manner.*

Mark Walus, with input from Schmieder and each of the affected groups, designed the system, which is based on user requirements within Amdahl. These include: 1) transparent demand access to information and applications, 2) a common user interface that's easy to use, and 3) hardware platform independence.

Additionally, the system is designed to accommodate the needs of the entire corporation. At Amdahl this means dealing with an extremely sophisticated computing environment made up of multiple desktop platforms (PCs and laptops, workstations, Macs), multiple mainframe and desktop operating systems (MVS, VM, UTS, *Unix*, DOS and so on), and multiple mainframe and desktop databases (DB2, IMS, IDMS, *Oracle*, and *Ingres*, among others).

To meet these demands, the mainframe and desktop must work together. The performance support system joins these two environments by using three key elements: a graphical user interface, expert system technology, and hypermedia. In this configuration, the mainframe and the desktop provide a complete solution by doing what each does best. That is, the mainframe handles centralized dynamic information while the desktop handles static information via CD-ROM.

To implement such a solution, the three essential system elements require extensive re-engineering to accomplish "seamless" integration. The GUI, the expert system, and hypermedia elements must communicate easily with one another and be portable to all platforms. Moreover, the expert system must be capable of accessing data from all databases.

Once these elements have been integrated, the system provides on-demand access to a full range of resources. These include the most accurate up-to-date information available, tools that make it possible to work with the information, and learning experiences, graphics, and expert advice in order to clarify or support the information. Furthermore, it allows users to manipulate existing information to develop new information to meet individual needs.

A Day in the Life ...

After double-clicking the system icon, the employee goes through the traditional corporate security checks by typing an ID and password. In addition to the security checks, the system profiles the user by job title and creates a customized working environment known as the "Information Bank." This environment is equipped with all of the datasets, tools, and applications the employee will need to perform on the job.

While profiling the user, the system uses expert system technology to check the user's environment for areas of exposure (things the person absolutely needs to know about). If exposures exist, the system notifies the user. If they don't, the system automatically takes the user to the Information Bank. In this example, the user has logged on and the system has identified the user as a Field Engineer (FE). Checking for exposures, the system finds five open service orders and proceeds to notify the FE (see Exhibit 1). The FE then exercises the option of either reviewing the service orders or continuing on to Information Bank.

Opting to see the service orders, the FE is presented with a point-and-click list of accounts to explore (see Exhibit 2). The FE then selects an account and obtains the necessary information to size the problem. If the account has a problem, and the expert system can identify it and match it to an existing solution, the system displays a "solution" button (see Exhibit 3: "HWS 33987"). If no known solution exists, the FE can investigate the problem using the resources provided in the Information Bank.

Until this time, all activity has taken place on the mainframe because of the dynamic nature of the information. Once the FE selects the "solution" button, however, the system downloads the solution to the desktop. At the same time, the system asks the user to insert a CD-ROM disk (see Exhibit 4). The solution, in this case HWS 33987, serves as the central hub to which all supporting CD-ROM information is linked. This support includes documentation, training, advice, graphics, and video. These resources reside in hypermedia environments and continue to provide links to additional information.

In many situations, the information in the HWS will be sufficient for the FE to complete the work. In others, more information may be needed in order for the FE to clearly understand what the problem is and what must be done. A visual learner may want to see graphics or perhaps even a short video showing the actual task being done. Maybe advice is needed on how to proceed. Perhaps review of a specific training module or completing a simulation of the tasks needed to solve the problem are required. All are possible in the EPSS. The FE can get whatever support he or she needs to ensure complete understanding of the problem and the proper resolution before actually performing the work.

In addition to a "known problem with a known solution" scenario, the system may be used to browse or perhaps prepare for

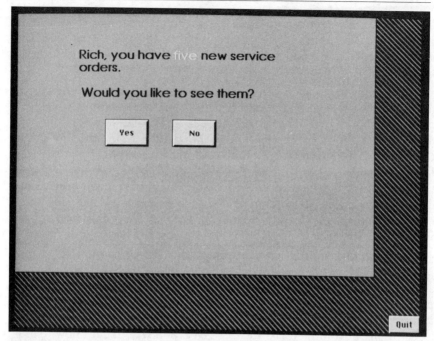

Exhibit 1. The system notifies the field engineer of five open service orders.

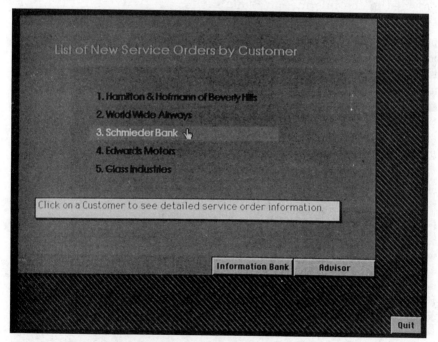

Exhibit 2. The field engineer can access one of the open service orders by pointing and clicking.
Courtesy Amdahl Corporation

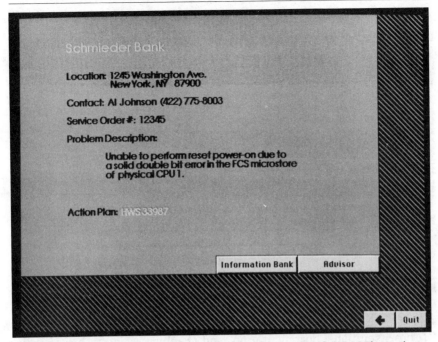

Exhibit 3. The system shows a solution button (HWS 33987) to show the expert system has matched an action plan to the problem.

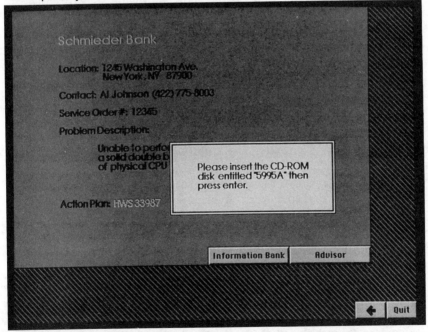

Exhibit 4. The system prompts the user to insert a CD-ROM disk containing up-to-date information relating to the solution.
Courtesy Amdahl Corporation

future tasks. For example, next month the FE is required to install a new product at a customer's site. Although he or she has been already trained to do this, the training occurred a year ago and review and refresh are in order. To do this, the FE uses the Information Bank to get the information and learning experiences needed.

In the customized working environment of the Information Bank, the system provides on-demand access to a full range of resources. The system's graphical user interface allows the FE to select a series of conceptually organized topics to form a request. For example, in Exhibit 5, the user forms a request by first selecting a product followed by a topic, a function, and finally an action. This graphical selection mechanism provides structured access to the information. It also lets the user know what information the system can provide.

Once the user forms a request and clicks the "resources" button, the request is processed. The system then asks the user to insert the appropriate CD-ROM disk. Once the disk is inserted, the system displays an array of available resources (see Exhibit 6).

This "resource array" is made up of six types of informational support: solutions, documentation, training, advice, graphics, and video. Of these, solutions, documentation, and graphics reside in hypermedia environments. When accessed, they provide links to cross-referenced information. The training and video resources provide structured learning experiences while the advice resource provides expert guidance.

The expert guidance is broken into two levels. The first level provides the FE with helpful information when working with a known solution. Such advice includes: tips, cautions, and technical details. The other level of advice allows the user to consult an expert system about specific topics via a natural language interface.

When an FE selects a resource type, the system returns a list of all occurrences of that particular resource type that satisfies the FE's request. For example, in Exhibit 7, the "Documentation" resource is selected. The FE then decides which occurrence to investigate by clicking on it. Once the FE does so, the system takes the FE directly to the occurrence via a hyperlink (see Exhibit 8).

The Information Bank also provides transparent access to tools and applications. The tools and applications an FE has access to are determined at the moment of user profiling. In this example, the FE is accessing the corporate electronic mail system known as "AMAIL" (see Exhibit 9).

In addition, the Information Bank allows users to tailor existing information to meet individual needs. Users can cut and paste information to a temporary work space. From the work space, the information can be pasted into other applications to create new information.

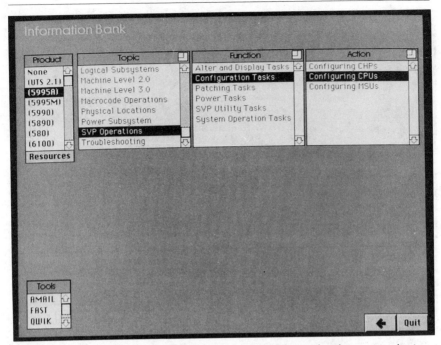

Exhibit 5. The user is able to form a request by selecting a product, followed by a topic, then a function, and finally an action.

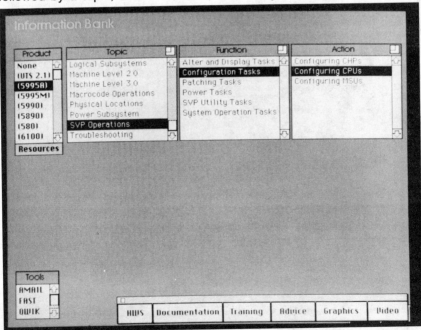

Exhibit 6. The system presents an array of choices across the bottom of the screen.
Courtesy Amdahl Corporation

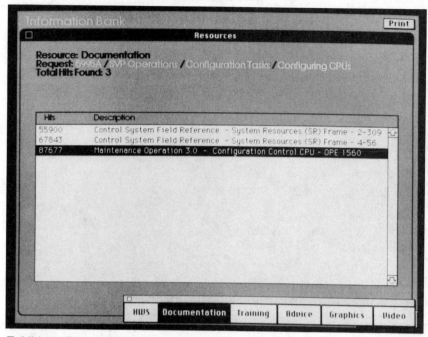

Exhibit 7. The user selects "Documentation" and gets further choices.

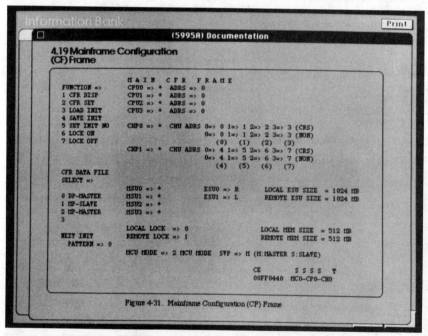

Exhibit 8. The system goes directly to the appropriate piece of documentation via a hyperlink.

Courtesy Amdahl Corporation

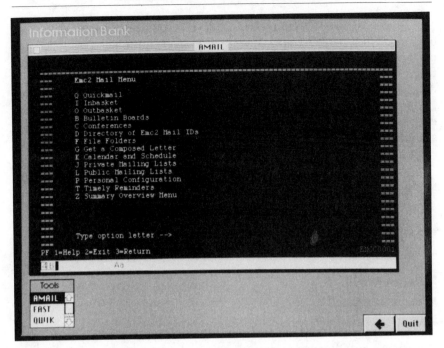

Exhibit 9. The system also has various tools, such as corporate electronic mail.
Courtesy Amdahl Corporation

A course designer will be able to get needed information from engineering to complete a training module while a person in Technical Publications will use the same information to prepare a hypertext module for the system. Because the system provides structured access to this information, single sourcing can become a reality, saving valuable time and resources and making it possible to end duplication of efforts and shorten development cycle times dramatically.

The system can also provide access to other valuable corporate information such as class schedules, major announcements, marketing information, policies and procedures, benefits, and organizational charts.

The Commitment-Building Process

In order to build commitment for such a large enterprise, it is necessary to get everyone in the corporation affected by or interested in (known or unknown) an EPSS together. This was started as a "common interest" group on a voluntary basis. Each group was invited to a "show and tell" meeting.

It was extremely valuable to use this approach because it not only identified similar requirements and needs but also introduced all participants to everyone else's technology. This was the start of identifying audiences for EPSS and establishing requirements for a standard system that would meet their needs. For example, who needs to get at what information and data, where are that information and data now, and how are they organized? The next step was to agree on standards and introduce the group to new technologies and processes: expert systems, hypermedia, and so on.

The education and commitment building process included interaction with individuals and managers in the following departments:

- Field Education (Training)
- Technical Publications
- Expert Systems
- Hot line support
- Engineering
- Marketing
- Business Intelligence Group
- Open Systems Marketing Group
- Manufacturing
- Technical Support
- Product Groups.

Participants from other interested groups are continuously being added as the work of the team becomes more widely known. Some have volunteered while others have been recruited. In order to keep the team at a workable size, membership has been limited to two per representative group.

Several show and tell meetings were followed by many education meetings in order to bring the group to a level of common understanding. At this point, it was possible to introduce the prototype and demonstrate its capabilities. Buy-in, in most cases, was immediate. In others, it took further work. A core of people representing organizations throughout the corporation, however, bonded and the swell began.

Educational activities included classes, readings, conferences, consultation, staff discussions, demonstrations, meetings with vendors, and benchmarking.

It is very important to include vendors in this process as they add immensely to the "education" process. They also help solve the "technical hurdles" and become advocates of the EPSS, once exposed.

Once these steps were completed, presentations were made throughout the corporation using the prototype to help the attendees to "see the future." Many of these audiences were organized by team members. One presentation begat another, so that soon much of the corporation was "educated" about EPSS.

The continuing process includes ongoing education activity on technical topics, such as creating hypertext, in order to prepare for actual implementation. It is important to note that outside presentations to other corporations are also important because the resulting benchmarking adds substance and political credibility to the project.

Key Learnings and Issues

The key learnings from this project, and the issues that it raises include:

- Never underestimate the amount of time and effort required to orchestrate a company-wide change.

- Expect to involve and have to communicate with more people than you would have believed could or would care about what you are doing.

- An elegant prototype quickly results in understanding. Make it so compelling that resistance melts in its presence.

- The user interface is everything! Simplicity, intuitiveness, and relevance must be the guiding principles.

- The business case is the best case to make. Selling technological wizardry is the worst case to make.

- Keep your eye on the goals and the outcome: accelerating and enabling employee performance. Always communicate how what you are doing will accomplish that objective.

- Cast your nets wide for expertise within and outside of your organization.

- Educate, communicate, and pontificate.

- Surface political, design, economic, and technological realities and problems.

- Manage expectations to be sure that neither too much nor too little is expected.

Anticipated Benefits

Since this project was limited to the commitment building, sponsorship development, and prototype development phases, no actual benefits were demonstrated or tested. The business case, however, articulated the following benefits projections:

- Cost reduction in creation, maintenance, production, and physical distribution of information

- Experienced staff can be leveraged resulting in more efficient use of expensive expertise, more complex work assigned to less experienced staff (novices perform expertly), and an explosion in productivity and performance

- Information can be "single sourced" making it possible to eliminate wasteful duplication of effort, improve access to latest information, improve information quality

- Traditional training is reduced or eliminated through a shift from the traditional training paradigm of "I know, thus I do" to the on-demand training paradigm of "I do, thus I know"

- Consistent and high quality Field Engineer work performance

- More rapid support and training development cycles

- Improved efficiency of training by elimination of training on unnecessary information and tasks or wasted training that teaches people too far in advance or covers what they already know

- More maintainable information environments

- Flexibility in Field Engineering assignments

- Increases in customer service and satisfaction

- Business benefits include potential revenue stream produced by selling shell as a product and customizing it for customers and selling datasets to be used in system

- Ability to distribute increasing equipment service capabilities to customers

- The company's expectations for a successful EPSS: world leadership, profitable products, improved quality, and satisfied customers.

Required Technology

The required technology for the prototype included:

- Macintosh II computer with two megabytes or RAM and forty megabytes of storage

- Silicon Beach *SuperCard*

- MacroMind *Director*.

The development platform and technology for the actual operational system includes:

- Any desktop computer with 386-like performance configured with four megabytes of RAM and eighty megabytes of storage (for optimum performance), a CD-ROM drive, video board, networking software and hardware, a 9600 baud modem (needed if user works from remote location), and a pointing device

- Amdahl Mainframe running the UTS operating system

- An expert system

- A graphical user interface

- A hypermedia environment (hypertext, video, and CBT).

Product Information

Steelcase Inc.

The Business Problem

What do you do when you are about to launch a major new line of some 350 products? How do you keep sales staff, customer service reps, dealers, and customers informed? Is it realistic to assume the market will readily appreciate the unique features, benefits, and use of these products as compared to others?

Steelcase Inc., the Michigan-based office furniture manufacturer, had this problem. The multiple-audience communication condition complicates the situation, but the product proliferation and complexity problems are not unusual. The renal products division of a pharmaceutical company, for example, has 2500 products and services in its line. A computer manufacturer makes 75 product announcements per month. An insurer has such product flexibility in its employee benefits product line that each customer essentially configures its own combination of product features, benefits levels, and variables such as second-opinion coverage and availability of HMO membership; and those benefits vary by geographic location and state law. As the concept of mass customization takes hold, customer-configured products will become more the norm than the exception. Just look at the personal computer. While they may look alike from the outside, the combination of memory, speed, storage, special purpose boards, operating system, system software, and other components make each one virtually unique.

In reality, irrespective of industry or product type, a very small percentage of the available product line is sold. The 80-20 law prevails: twenty percent of the available products constitute eighty percent of the sales. Sadly, the same ratio often holds for total sales volume: twenty percent of the sales representatives contribute eighty percent of the sales. With heavy emphasis on new product development, a shorter time period within which to establish a marketing beachhead and market share, and increasing desire to satisfy customers with the most appropriate product, companies need to significantly improve the overall potential for employees, distributors, and customers alike to find exactly what they need. And they must assure that they find that out in advance of a product order—not via the expensive, time-consuming, and dissatisfying processes of either order-return-reorder (i.e., trial and error) or ex post facto discovery (i.e., when the customer learns of something better, more appropriate, or less expensive after making an irrevocable purchase).

Information Dissemination and Control

Information about products, how to use them, and how to design with them is typically spread throughout the organization. Product facts are readily available, but the knowledge of how to use products well is often in the heads of experienced staff and is difficult to access.

Conventional approaches to the problems of product volume, product complexity, product communication, and unique configurations are:

- voluminous paper-based catalogs that present information in a specific structure and sequence (e.g., by type of product) when users need multiple views of the information, including relationships among and between the parts, qualities, costs, etc.

- memo-like new product announcements, change bulletins, or problem and troubleshooting announcements on paper or via electronic mail

- product announcement or communication meetings

- time spent on product information at sales meetings or meetings for other purposes

- establishment of product sales specialists who make joint calls or take over sales prospects

- hotline staffing with telephone information and configuration support.

Consequences

In addition to the information organization and distribution problems, associated costs include:

- reduced sales, market share, and profitability expectations

- high overhead costs

- development and implementation of paper-based materials that can't match user needs.

Steelcase Inc.

Steelcase is a major manufacturer of both traditional office furniture and contemporary modular office systems. The company sells its products through architects, interior designers, a direct sales force, and office furniture companies. While common needs exist, there are special needs for each group: architects and space planners need to select appropriate office systems and develop visualizations of office layouts for customer review; office furniture company distributors need to position the product in the showroom and allow customers to compare the Steelcase products—and often to compare them with products from other manufacturers.

Context, a contemporary freestanding product line, is a new concept in office landscaping. It consists of core units, boundary walls, screens, storage units, and utilities support. Literally hundreds and hundreds of components can be configured and reconfigured to create an infinite variety of space and equipment for general and special purpose work environments, such as work teams. With multiple audiences in mind, the business challenges include:

- developing an understanding of the product concept and its creative use in functional and aesthetically pleasing design

- creating functional, technical, and visual understanding of the product line

- representing colors, surfaces, and fabrics (traditionally carried around as samples)

- assuring that designers select appropriate components and relate and connect them appropriately

- maintaining current resource information

- accelerating design processes and the integration of specific product information into designs and orders

- reducing overhead support requirements associated with providing information (i.e., hotlines, technical support, requests to sales representatives)

- creating the perception of Steelcase as an industry leader and Context as a premier product line.

Steelcase Training and Product Marketing staff quickly recognized that conventional approaches to training, documentation, and support would not accomplish their objectives. They reexamined their problem in light of new technological alternatives and developed a different solution.

The Performance Support Solution

Steelcase decided to design and develop a multimedia infobase system for use in showrooms, exhibits, architect and customer offices, and wherever else it was needed. They developed the Macintosh-based *Context Information System*. The system includes a 160-megabyte multimedia product information database structured with the following major segments.

- *Portfolio.* Example applications (layouts) shown in plan, isometric, and island views

- *Details.* Features and benefits of Context furniture components, including product details and dimensions; graphical and text descriptions of all products, organized around types of product components (i.e., core units, storage units, screens, boundary walls, utilities, and accessories)

- *Surfaces.* Context's materials program, including the full line of fabric, wood, and paint samples; digitally-scanned images provide accurate visual representation of the materials; the surfaces are cross-referenced to the product components so users are clear on what surfaces, fabrics, and finishes relate to specific component parts

- *Tips.* Application tips discovered by designers using Context: what works and what doesn't, do's and don'ts, suggestions

- *Planning.* Differences in the planning process from other systems; development of a structured planning process

- *Resources.* Other available supplemental materials to help in understanding and designing with Context: related print materials, electronic, and human support.

The System Interface and User Orientation

The system's elegance is in its straightforward user interface, user orientation, and control techniques, the help system, and the sophisticated, interrelated infobase.

Users enter the system through a main screen, which provides access to all of the above information categories via buttons across the top of the screen. Mobility into each category is available from every point in the system via these buttons (see Exhibit 1).

The structure and content of each section can be viewed from a hierarchical map of that section (see Exhibit 2), and the map for the section they are in is always available via a button on the bottom of a screen. Users can go directly to a given section by clicking on the desired destination button and then pressing "Go Selection." Exhibit 3 illustrates the Details Overview and options available from that screen, and Exhibit 4 shows the Boundary wall details with hyperlinks to more detailed information. Hyperlinks appear as gray (rather than black) text on the actual computer screen.

Information can be accessed:

- from maps (see Exhibit 2)

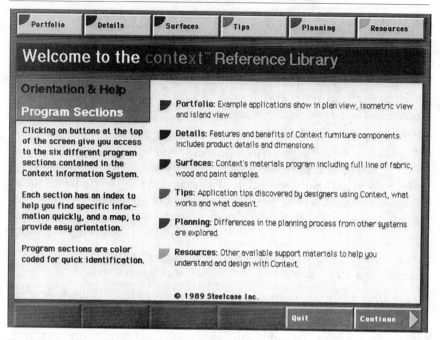

Exhibit 1a. The system provides access to its information categories through buttons across the top of the screen.

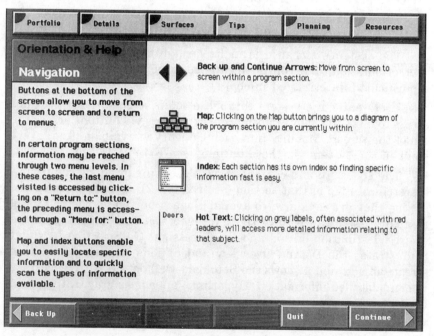

Exhibit 1b. Navigation is straightforward, and help is plentiful.
Courtesy Steelcase Inc.

- from hierarchical or logical menus, such as the boundary walls menu in Exhibit 3

- via relational or hypermedia links (see Exhibit 4)

- from alphabetical index listings of the main categories (e.g., Details, Planning, Tips—see Exhibit 5).

While there is no free-form keyword search option, users can easily go from anywhere to anywhere within the system effortlessly—and they can maintain orientation via map access, screen numbers (e.g., 1 of 4), and window labels. The information structure, combined with the interface, permits users to get any view or level of information detail they need or want. It can be used in a kiosk at a trade show, in a furniture sales showroom, or on a user's desktop.

Impact

The following impact and benefits have been achieved as a result of the Context performance support system and infobase:

- reduced costs (in creating and disseminating information)

- consistent information of high quality for users

- maintainable information

- reusability of a single knowledge base across several groups: Steelcase, distributors, and various customer groups

- established industry benchmark, in terms of information support required, for new product introductions

- increased company credibility and positive perceptions of the Context product line as innovative and contemporary

- broader product sales

- improved quality of office planning and representation of those plans to customers

- commensurate business impact.

Development Technology

Macintosh II, *SuperCard* (Silicon Beach Software), MacroMind *Director*.

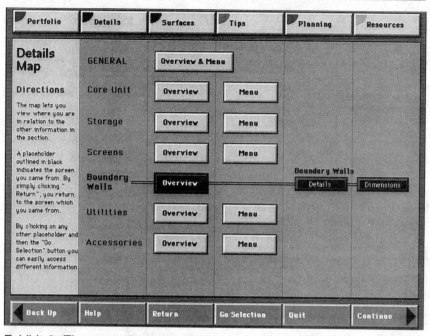

Exhibit 2. There are "maps" to show the structure and content of each section.

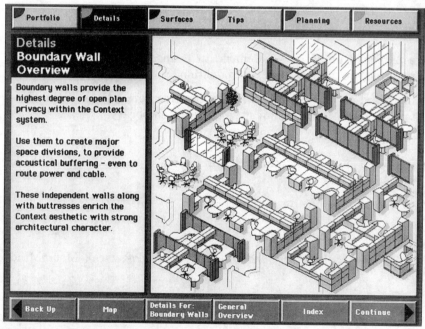

Exhibit 3. The system can provide an overview of a section.

Courtesy Steelcase Inc.

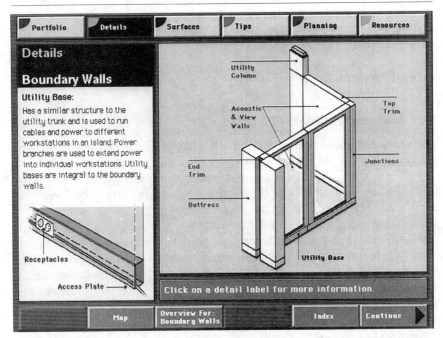

Exhibit 4. The system can provide detailed information at considerable depth.

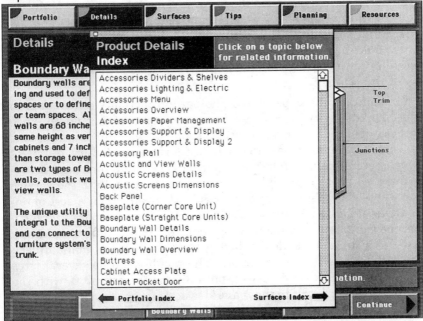

Exhibit 5. An alphabetical index allows instant access to the main categories.
Courtesy Steelcase Inc.

Manufacturing

Intel Corporation

The Business Problem

Intel, the country's leading manufacturer of computer chips, had a deceptively simple problem: how to consistently manufacture defect-free chips. The chips are inspected under microscopes, where operators examine the integrity of layer upon layer of tiny circuitry. Problem conditions *are* identifiable, but the amount of training required to learn to correctly identify and disposition the defects can be substantial—and the problem conditions change with each new generation of chip, which occurs more or less annually. Just as each new generation of chip changes in structure and shrinks in size, the defect conditions associated with each new chip can also change. Therefore, providing operators access to reference images becomes critical to identifying and eliminating defects.

The traditional way of training and updating the operators on the defects they were expected to recognize was to make photographs of the defects and distribute them via a reference manual. Unfortunately, instant prints shot through a microscope often are not sharply focused and suffer from shifts in color. Non-instant, high resolution, prints could be obtained, but they had to be sent out-of-house for processing thus jeopardizing the highly proprietary, intellectual property of the company.

In addition, the paper-based photographs actually contributed to reduced productivity in this case, because the workers could not keep the documentation near their workstations. Operator workstations are located in isolated cleanrooms because the manufacture of microscopic circuitry cannot tolerate paper-particle contamination. So every question about a possible defect necessitated a trip to the service aisle where the reference manual was kept, resulting in a sort of on-site travel time. In addition to the downtime, the trips back and forth from the workstation to the manual required an operator to maintain a mental picture of the defect during the trip from the manual back to the microscope in the cleanroom. The result could be several trips to the manual for a single defect, but only for the operators with the fortitude to do it. A trip to the manual is something of an event in this situation, possibly calling the attention of the rest of the staff and the supervisor to the operator's competence.

The operators could ask each other to look in their microscopes when they had questions, but that only provided a temporary solution.

A trip to the manual was required not only to confirm the second opinion but also to ensure that standards and uniformity were maintained.

The operators were charged with maintaining high product quality but felt their professional image was called into question when they sought help. Most workers, in a situation like this, will adopt a conservative and cautious approach in which they are reluctant to make decisions unless first consulting an engineer or other expert. From the worker's standpoint, it is better to be safe than sorry, but from the company's standpoint, there is a need to increase productivity via quick and accurate decision making.

Clearly, the company needed to provide operators with easy access to clear, visual models. The models had to be high-resolution, color-accurate, easily updatable, images of defects the operators could compare to what they were seeing in the microscopes.

The Performance Support Solution

Intel's solution to the paper-based reference manual problem was an on-line electronic performance support system available at the moment of need at the workstations of those who needed the information (see Exhibit 1). The system combines a readily-accessible visual database of known defects linked to a separate visual database of defect-free chips and chip conditions (see Exhibits 3 and 4). This enables the operators to immediately make comparisons against standards.

Through icon manipulation, the user is able to change views of the image in order to gain perspective and improve judgment. Operators can view highly magnified images of defect free chips at each of the twelve photomasking layers used to build the Intel 80386™ microprocessor (see Exhibits 7 through 9). They also have complete control to fade one image (layer) on to any other to aid them in their comparison. Currently, the operator navigates through the database with a trackball, but the system can be transferred to touch screen when required.

An operator can select expert coaching via audio icons linked to particular chip conditions. While listening to the voice-over audio expert, the operator can put full visual and manual attention to the job.

All of this information is based on views keyed to individual operator experience, knowledge, skill, and confidence. The operator always has complete control over how much and what types of information to display.

The system's display screen is flush-mounted in the wall of the production bay and is clearly visible to an operator from the workstation. The rest of the system is located in the service aisle in order to eliminate any possibility of contamination in the production bay. The controls—an on-off switch and a trackball—are easily accessible at the workstation so that an operator can activate the system at any time without having to leave the workstation.

Results

Increased time on task and increased operator productivity. Because the operators are provided with the information they need at the time and place they need it, they are able to devote more time and effort to their main task of identifying and eliminating defects.

Removal of paper-based reference manuals from the cleanroom and a corresponding reduction in cleanroom particle contamination. Implementation of the EPSS has taken Intel one step closer to accomplishing its mission of building their chips in completely paperless, particle-free factories.

Improved identification and dispositioning of defects on the factory floor with limited involvement of staff engineers or technical support. Consistent information on defect identification and dispositioning is available to operators on all shifts, twenty-four hours a day, seven days a week.

Decreased training requirements for new employees. The availability of information, precise visual standards, and situation-specific coaching at the moment of need has decreased, by forty-eight percent, the amount of time spent in training.

Increased skill and knowledge levels among experienced operators by thirteen percent. Availability of the EPSS to experienced operators has increased their on-the-job knowledge and skill levels. This gain was measured with tests administered both before and after installation of the system.

Empowered employees. Ability of operators to work independently without consulting external expert resources. Significantly increased feelings of control, competence, and self-esteem are expressed by employees: "The system has helped us to better identify defects and decide what to do to eliminate them without having to first consult with a training tech or an engineer. This has helped us improve productivity because we can keep product moving without having to wait for someone else to make a decision."

Reduced time to determine the cause of a defect and to provide feedback to key factory personnel to eliminate the defect and its cause. Reference screens linked to the defect images present detailed information on defect causes and expert advice on how to eliminate the conditions that cause defects (see Exhibits 5 and 6). With this information readily available to operators, the need for them to place product on hold—sometimes for hours—to secure engineering input has been eliminated.

Reduced involvement of experts in problem solving situations and the ability to leverage expert staff and engineering resources on other activities. Training technicians (who conduct the initial one-on-one training and who also serve as a post-training resource) and engineers (who serve as problem solving experts) have noted a decline in requests from operators for advice on solving problems on the factory floor. The training techs have therefore been redeployed to conduct other training or assist with critical manufacturing priorities, and the engineers have been able to concentrate their efforts on solving higher-level problems associated with sustaining the manufacturing process.

Information on new defects and inspection procedures can be quickly added to the system and is immediately available to all employees. Discovery of new defects can be added to the existing database and be available to all shift workers within a twenty-four to forty-eight hour time frame.

Demand-pull by operators, supervisors, engineers, and others. After implementation of the EPSS, both operators and management requested development of similar programs to meet other training and performance support requirements. The engineer who served as the SME on the pilot project has started development of a separate engineering-specific EPSS. Copies of the program were requested by and have been installed in other Intel manufacturing sites domestically and internationally. Sales staff use the system to demonstrate the capability of DVI, and executive management demonstrated the system at the annual shareholders' meeting.

Development Requirements

Development Team. One full-time and one half-time staff to conduct detailed task analysis, and to design, develop, and implement the DVI-based EPSS. Full-time staff person also served as project manager.

Subject matter and technical content experts. One engineer and two training technicians part-time for content development and review of program for technical accuracy.

Vendor for fifty percent of audio/video production. Half of all motion video and voice over audio segments, and all computer graphics, produced in-house.

Part-time contractor to write computer program.

Technical support staff. Access to internal hardware and software support organization to structure advanced technological environment.

Estimated total development requirements. Three person-months for project justification and preproduction planning; nine person-months for design, development, revision, and implementation.

Technology Required

Hardware. Intel Pro750 DVI Application Development Platform (ADP™)—an Intel 302 PC with a 25 MHz, i386™ microprocessor—later upgraded to a Pro750 Action Media (AM750™) system. 702 Mb hard drive, tape drive, SCSI controller, color and monochrome monitors. (See Figure 1)

Software. Microsoft DOS™; DVI Production Tools and Software Libraries for capture and display of still frame and full motion digital video; CEIT Authology: Multimedia™ for interactive programming; and Time Arts Lumena™ for graphics.

Additional technology. Three-quarter inch industrial video recording and editing equipment; vendor services to transfer three-quarter inch edited master to one-inch Type C videotape master; analog to digital conversion and compression services provided by Intel DVI Operation.

Key Learnings and Issues

Task analysis at the lowest level of detail is critical to design success and performance support usefulness. Development must never be jumped into without first conducting critical analysis and design steps, even if the technology is seductive and the pressure for results is substantial.

Detailed design, program flow, user navigation, and scripting are time-consuming and tedious but critical to successful programming and implementation. The more media, modes, and navigation alternatives, the more critical the detailed design.

Design criteria must include ease of maintenance and the ability to rapidly incorporate new information. The microprocessor industry, like all high-tech industries, experiences rapid change in its manufacturing processes. These changes must be immediately incorporated into all training and performance support systems to keep them current with the new processes.

Development is a multidisciplinary team effort requiring expertise in at least five separate domains. The team, at minimum, should consist of 1) Project Manager or Administrator, 2) Instructional Designer/ Educational Systems Technologist, 3) Subject Matter Expert, 4) Computer Programmer/Hardware Engineer, and 5) Audio/Video/Graphic Production Personnel. One person is not likely to possess all the knowledge, skills, and expertise necessary for successful program design, development, and implementation. (See Figure 2)

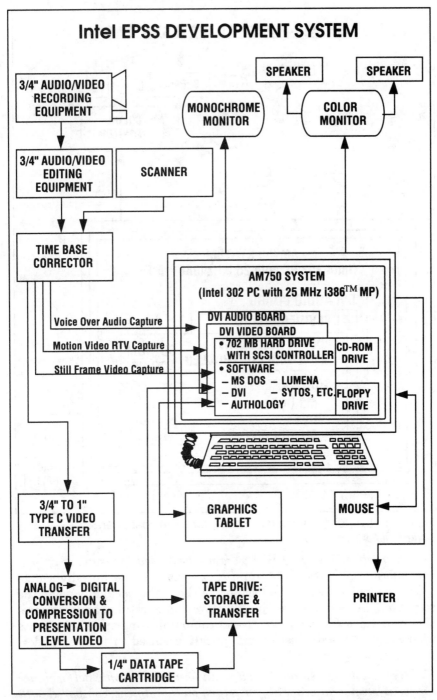

Figure 1. At the center of the development system is the Intel AM750™ system.
Courtesy Intel Corporation

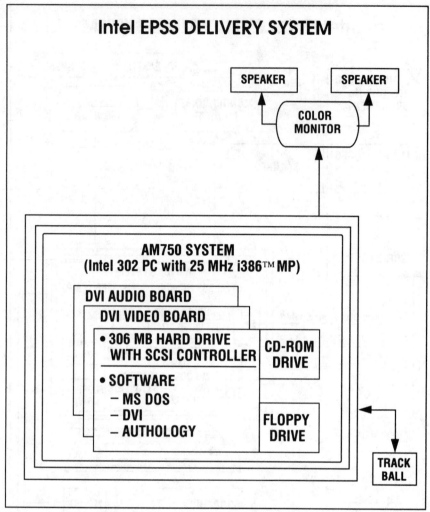

Figure 1a. The delivery system needs far fewer peripherals.
Courtesy Intel Corporation

Interactive video and DVI were not best used for transfer of general information within the training program. While initially seductive, advanced motion video technology should be used only when the return on investment can justify development time and expense. However, video was very effective in communicating specific concepts where sophisticated illustrations quickly resulted in learner understanding.

DVI, implemented on the job as an on-line electronic performance support system, realized a higher return on investment, compared with the system's use in a conventional training program framework. Although the time to train new employees was nearly cut in half, the

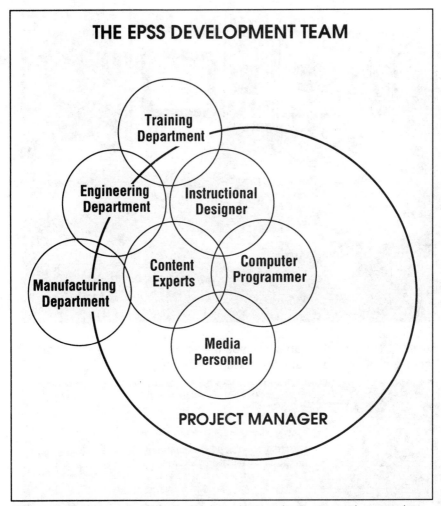

Figure 2. Development required close interaction among the members of the EPSS core production team. The content experts represented training, engineering, and manufacturing. The project manager was responsible for interfacing with all levels of management.

real value of the system was realized when it was used as an on-the-job aid. Experienced employees increased their on-the-job knowledge and skill level by thirteen percent and reported feeling more empowered to make critical decisions without expert input or review.

The greatest technical challenge with DVI was to correctly configure all the system hardware and software interfaces. Sophisticated technical support is critical to inexperienced developers, regardless of their level of motivation and design skills.

Exhibit 1. The operator can easily see the screen from the workstation. Note the cleanroom suit and the absence of papers.

Exhibit 2. The opening screen of the EPSS.
Courtesy Intel Corporation

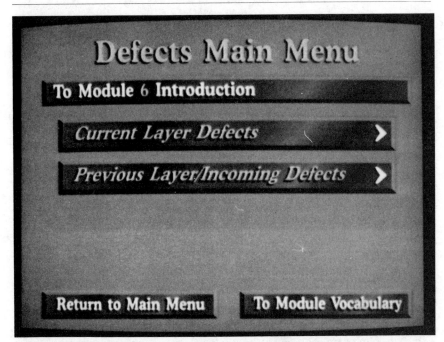

Exhibit 3. The defects main menu screen gives the operator access to visual information on defects and associated rules for eliminating defects.

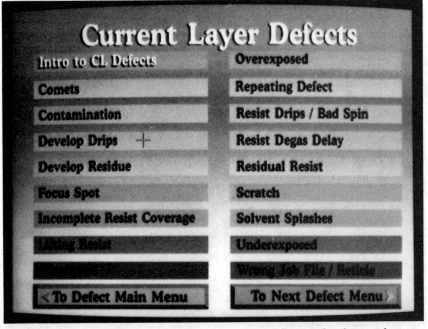

Exhibit 4. The current layer defects menu screen lists a database of known defects and provides links to expert advice on eliminating them.
Courtesy Intel Corporation

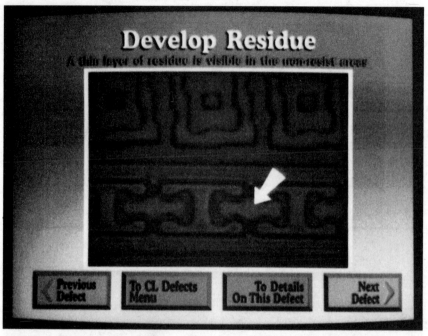

Exhibit 5. A reference image of a known detect helps the operator correctly identify a defect found during the inspection procedure.

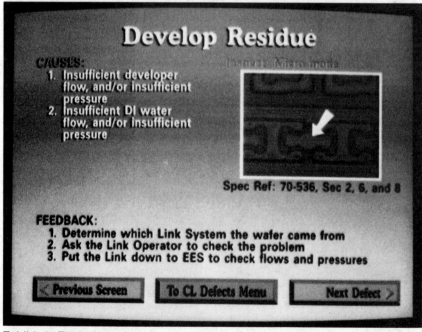

Exhibit 6. From the reference image screen, the operator can link to expert advice on eliminating the defect.
Courtesy Intel Corporation

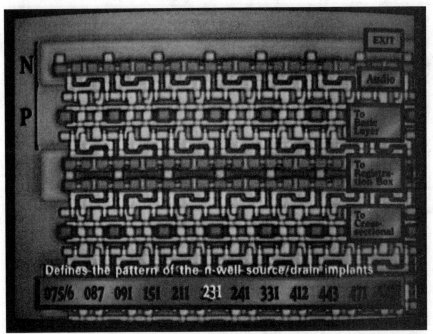

Exhibit 7. The system displays an image the operator might actually see through the microscope.

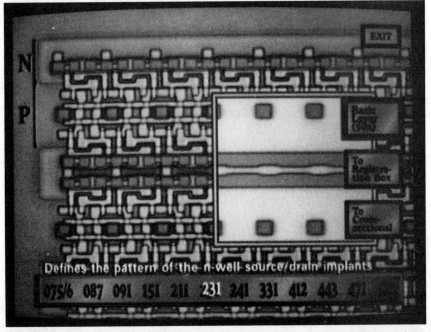

Exhibit 8. After clicking on the "To Basic Layer" icon, the operator is taken to one of the 12 layers used to build the Intel 80386™ microprocessor.
Courtesy Intel Corporation

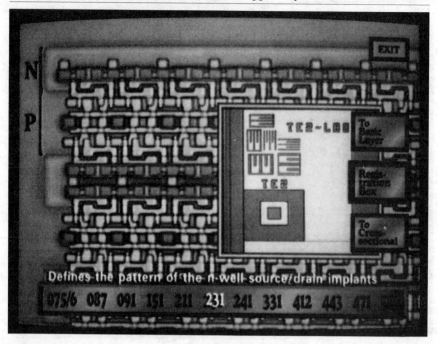

Exhibit 9. By clicking on the "To Registration Box" icon, the operator is shown another part of the chip essential to making critical inspection decisions.
Courtesy Intel Corporation

Total Quality Management

Dow Chemical

The Business Problem

Many corporations are actively addressing the need to increase and sustain quality in their products and services, processes, and systems. The quality movement has become formalized into processes and methodologies that support the use of workgroups to identify opportunities for improvement and to systematically develop solutions. This movement is called Total Quality Management, or TQM, and its proponents consider it nothing less than the salvation of the modern workplace.

It's not difficult to gain employee enthusiasm for the goals or the process associated with TQM. It is *very* difficult to get the process actually implemented and institutionalized as a way of life, however, without extraordinary staff support.

The Opportunity Identification and Problem Solving process is carried out in groups formed of work teams familiar with the task and operations at hand. The team must apply the methodology and process to the situation under consideration and construct a trail of the various analyses and proposed solutions. Ultimately, they must construct a presentation to management.

There are two fundamental issues at hand in supporting quality teams: first, they must understand effective team behavior and possess the knowledge and skills to perform in a team environment; second, they must understand and be able to execute the methodology associated with the task at hand.

The process is quite complex and requires sophisticated views of the situation, use of numerous tools to gather and organize information, and skilled group problem-solving. The typical approach to introducing the methodologies into organizations includes evangelical and educational sessions about the business problems and required solutions and then workgroup training in the specific processes, tools, and techniques required for success. In many companies, entire quality departments have emerged to train all company employees and then to provide direct consultation or facilitation support during actual project activities. When a company is in active pursuit of the Malcolm Baldrige Award, the quality department staff are akin to religious orders attempting to convert all they contact.

The fundamental reasons for this substantial effort lie in the complexity of the TQM process: the number and interrelationship of the required activities and processes is large.

Successful work groups must know about and be skilled in:

- Total Quality Management methodology
- Group process techniques, including brainstorming, communicating, and consensus building
- Feedback processes and appropriate use of qualitative and quantitative research techniques
- Flow charting
- Statistics
- Problem analysis
- Software tools
- Reporting the team's research and marketing and selling ideas.

The TQM methodology itself is stable, but how it is implemented varies widely, based on the tasks and the project group's perspective. Finally, individuals or workgroups might be simultaneously working on multiple opportunity-identification or problem-solving projects while also performing their normal job tasks at the same time.

The implementation problems of Total Quality Management are endemic and not exclusive to any individual organization. "Total Quality Management (TQM) and continuous improvement opportunities are cited regularly, but rarely implemented successfully," according to Claudia Twardy, communications consultant with Hartford Insurance Group in Hartford, Connecticut. "The complexity and high cost of the resources and techniques used to increase workgroup performance cause the majority of these quality improvement ideas to never realize fruition."

"It would be typical," says Randall Jensen of the Training Technologies Group of Dow Chemical, "for a person to go to a training session on something like Opportunity Identification and Problem-Solving and then not have a chance to use it for four months, six months, or even a year. The question is, how much of what was learned from the formal presentation will be retained after all that time has passed? Probably not much. And the printed information in the binder will probably not help much, either."

Work on a given project is intermittent and characterized by fits and starts. A work group might meet for several hours to focus on a sub-task within the process, make some progress in brainstorming, develop information needs for which surveys must be conducted, document their progress on paper flip-charts, and then return to work. People don't bring the flip charts to the next meeting or the flip charts are numerous and not consistently organized. So momentum and information are often lost. In short order, files are thick with random pieces of paper. People lose track of where they are in the process.

The skills involved are numerous and interrelated. Team members need to attend training programs in more detailed aspects of the TQM methodology and related activities, such as survey construction. More delays ensue. The process becomes fragmented and frustrating. Facilitators can, of course, help, but scheduling yet another resource introduces more delays—and external facilitation talent is expensive. Facilitators often don't know the work tasks, so their value-added is largely in managing group process. Educating the facilitator about the work tasks and flows takes even more time.

As momentum fades and the energy required to maintain the process increases, what seemed like a great idea often sours. The inability of workgroup participants to support their own group performance without facilitation and the continual breaking up of the process for additional training or organizing materials results in dissipation of effort and energy. Cynicism about the TQM goals and processes can follow. Without large organizational commitments, progress deteriorates, management pressure increases, and an idea with enormous potential gets shelved or ritually performed as yet *another* company program.

The Need

"We need a performance support tool that can alleviate the resource burden and help sustain the level of enthusiasm necessary in developing, implementing, and nurturing successful quality improvement programs," says Claudia Twardy.

Even organizations with substantial management commitment to and employee enthusiasm for the process can find it draining. Says Bill Shaffer of BellSouth Services: "Employee training associated with just the initial orientation of the quality concept is consuming, and then subsequent implementation training to equip our associates with the needed tools is enormous."

At Dow Chemical, they sensed that technology could reduce the problem to something more manageable. According to Randall Jensen, "We are trying to implement new and innovative processes that require sophisticated, long-term group involvement. We have been wedded to the use of flip-charts for too long. We now have technology that allows us to quickly capture the information through group work."

The Performance Support Solution

It is a situation tailor-made for electronic performance support. Dow Chemical and Santa Fe Interactive came up with a tightly integrated electronic performance support tool (the company calls it a PST) to support work teams in opportunity identification and problem solving. This groupware PST is designed to structure individual project activity and deliverables and to maintain all project documents in a single repository. Figure 1 illustrates the PST structure.

The prescribed methodology or Total Quality Management (TQM) process is represented in a flow chart. Major steps and their sequence and relationship to each other are presented. Sub-tasks related to each major step are presented when the user clicks on the primary step. Exhibits 2a and 2b are PST screens illustrating that structure.

Users have access via the Tools button to context-sensitive ongoing recommendations for tools and techniques appropriate for the task or sub-task they are working on at the time. Included are descriptions, explanations of use, and examples. (Sample screens appear in Exhibits 3a and 3b).

The Reference button provides context- or step-sensitive explanations and examples of the process, outcomes, pitfalls, and deliverables. Sample screens appear in Exhibits 4a and 4b. Similar to the information available from the Tools button, the coaching and instruction are granular and specific. Explanations, models, advice, and considerations are an implicit form of instruction and coaching. There are no formal structured training sequences, nor is there a rule-based expert system involved. Nor does there need to be. The nature of the task, combined with the structure of the program, provides sufficient guidance and support.

From the continuously available pull down menu, users can invoke interactive software support such as flow-charting, brainstorming, diagramming, graphing, and surveying tools. These are encapsulated versions of stand-alone products that permit on-demand construction of documents, lists, charts, and so on. Exhibits 5a, 5b, and 5c illustrate menu choices and selected tools. In addition, users can customize the tool set and add software tools they know and need via an automated process. On demand, they can access embedded and external tools by a simple menu choice.

Project teams must employ statistical analysis and graphing to represent their research and voting results. Enabling tools are available within the PST.

As users construct documents with the various tools, they are stored in the project folio and are available via the documents window. This dynamic encyclopedia structures the project file and permits

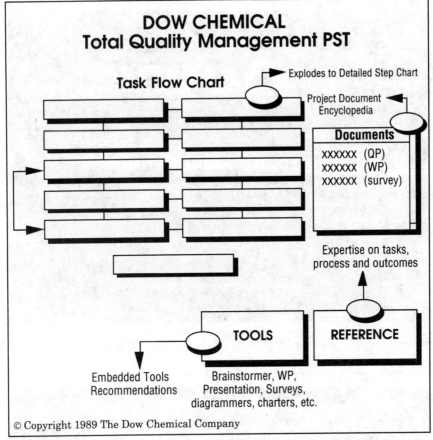

DOW CHEMICAL
Total Quality Management PST

Task Flow Chart

Explodes to Detailed Step Chart

Project Document Encyclopedia

Documents

XXXXXX (QP)
XXXXXX (WP)
XXXXXX (survey)

Expertise on tasks, process and outcomes

TOOLS

REFERENCE

Embedded Tools Recommendations

Brainstormer, WP, Presentation, Surveys, diagrammers, charters, etc.

© Copyright 1989 The Dow Chemical Company

Figure 1. The structure of the Total Quality Management performance support tool.
Courtesy Dow Chemical

immediate document availability at the moment of need. In addition, content can be lifted from the documents and inserted in various reports, including the prepared slide presentation called the *QP Story*, which is illustrated in Exhibit 6. The presentation is designed to assure that all relevant steps and information are represented in the marketing presentation during which the project team communicates its findings and generates commitment to its solutions. The team doesn't need to worry about the structure and display of their presentation. They can focus exclusively on the content, which is their area of expertise.

A Day in the Life...

Work groups convene in team rooms in which the computer is centrally located and projected through a large screen. They set up an

Exhibit 1. The opening screen of the Dow Chemical PST.

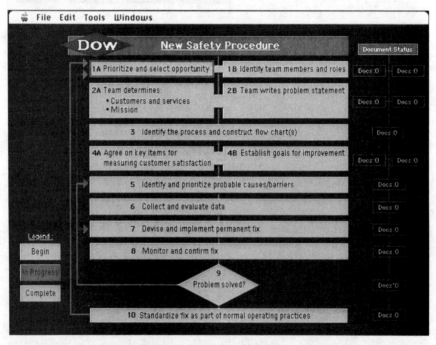

Exhibit 2a. The Total Quality Process appears as a flowchart.
Courtesy Dow Chemical

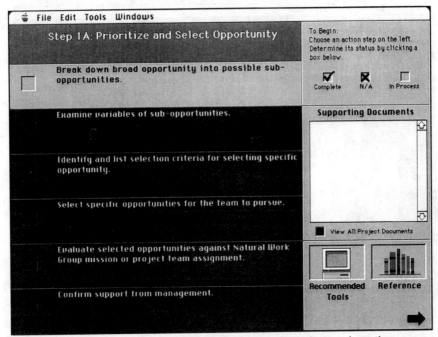

Exhibit 2b. Selecting one of the steps in the flowchart takes the user to a deeper level of detail for that step.

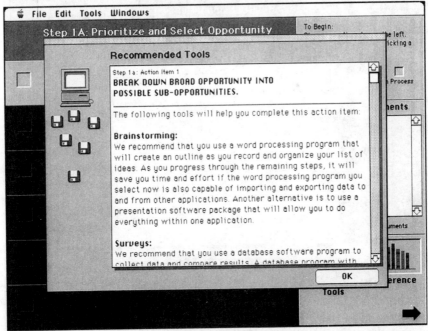

Exhibit 3a. The system provides background information for the first action item in Step 1A.
Courtesy Dow Chemical

131

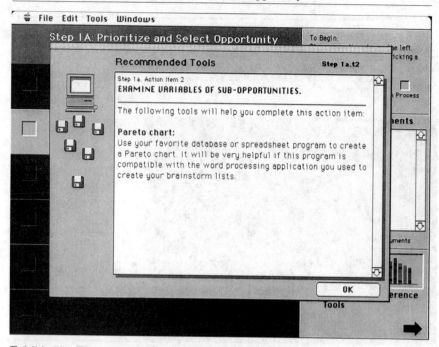

Exhibit 3b. The second action item in Step 1A.

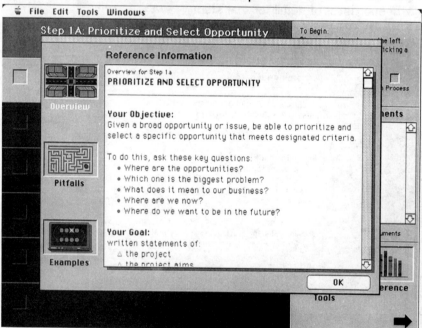

Exhibit 4a. The user has asked for reference information (via the reference button) on Step 1A. This is the Overview.
Courtesy Dow Chemical

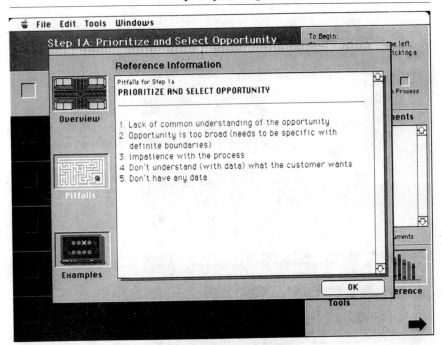

Exhibit 4b. The user has selected "Pitfalls" from the reference facility.

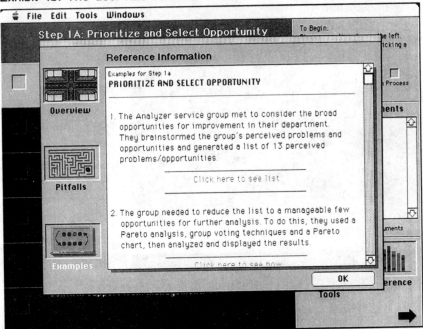

Exhibit 4c. The user has selected "Examples" from the reference facility.
Courtesy Dow Chemical

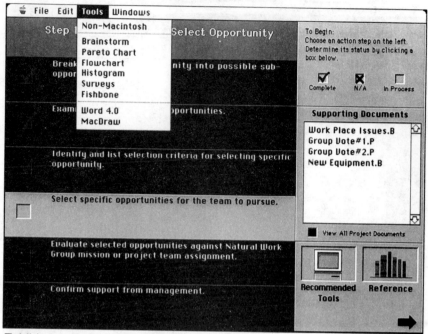

Exhibit 5a. From the pull-down menu, users can invoke interactive software support.

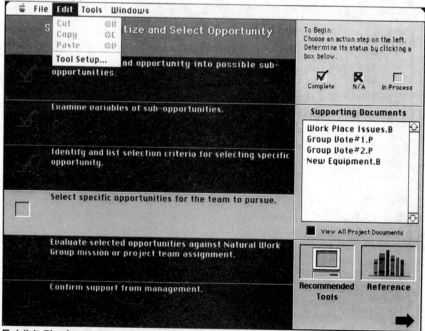

Exhibit 5b. As users construct documents with the various tools, they are stored in the project folio and are available via the documents window.
Courtesy Dow Chemical

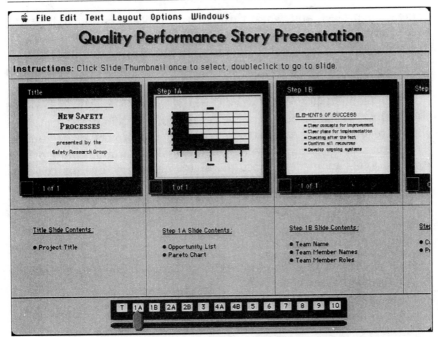

Exhibit 5c. The project team will have to make a marketing presentation on its findings, and the software assists in its development, including the creation of thumbnails for slides.

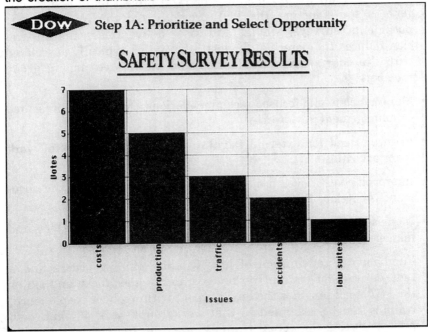

Exhibit 6. A slide from the marketing presentation.
Courtesy Dow Chemical

individual project and work through the process supported by the step chart. During initial group activity, a quality facilitator or TQM-trained staff member assists the group in learning and using the tool. Gradually, the team comes to work in and reference information from the PST.

The team structures its work through the PST, creates its project files online, prints documents for review and distribution, and then inputs results into the reporting tools and the project presentation. The team can check any given project's status, as monitored by the system, and can elicit project detail as necessary during reviews. During presentations of results, analysis, and recommendations, all relevant documents and illustrations are available on-demand to answer questions, reinforce points, and so on.

Anticipated Results

As of this writing, the system is not fully implemented, but the following results seem assured:

- Improved and consistent implementation of the TQM process across work groups and quality teams

- Improved project analysis with reduced probability of missing or superficially treating individual process steps and tasks

- Improved quality and timeliness of TQM project team results due to both the structure the PST provides *and* the integration of documents, surveys, graphs, and other deliverables; this integration reduces the potential for lost information typically associated with flip charts being dismantled and distributed among group members

- More complete and focused recommendations, consistently presented to management reviewers

- Reduced need for external facilitators and staff support of work team activities

- Improved control over project team work-in-progress via the documents encyclopedia

- Increased information availability to Project Team, facilitators, and managers

- Fundamental redefinition of how Quality training occurs and a reduced need for training on process, techniques, tools, and skills; the PST itself provides the environment within which people learn; training can be redefined so that workgroups work on their own projects during the actual training program, thereby learning the process and making progress on their activity at the same time;

within the training event, the teams also have increased time to focus on team behavior; there is increased time available for training and education on group process skills, such as negotiation and communications

- Sustained momentum and commitment to ongoing quality management
- Institutionalization of the TQM process into daily work life
- Improved business results accruing from project team recommendations.

Development Requirements

Project Team. The Training Technologies Group at Dow developed the PST with Santa Fe Interactive of Santa Fe, New Mexico, an outside consulting group. They visioned the product and provided client management, subject matter or process expertise, and review and approval of project deliverables. Santa Fe Interactive provided additional design expertise and programmed and technically tested the result.

Required Development Environment

Technology. Macintosh computers with eight megabytes of memory. *SuperCard* (Silicon Beach Software) development platform.

Key Learnings and Issues

The degree of explicitness required about the process, deliverables, and techniques is much greater when institutionalizing them in a software tool than is required in classroom instruction development or when facilitators work independently with groups. Developers must be very clear on what they intend to build into such a software product and must be prepared to manage the political process of gaining agreement.

Decisions about the power-simplicity tradeoff were difficult. A PST for a complex analytical process must contain features and tools that are adequate to the required task. The support tool must not, however, be so complex that it requires an extended learning curve. A decision was made to optimize power and to implement the tool so that supervisors, team leaders, and facilitators would be skilled in its use. Individual work team members would not be required to learn the tool itself.

Examples are a powerful way to communicate expectations, and deliverables should be incorporated into PST's whenever possible.

Articulating pitfalls associated with a given approach or step in the process is valuable to users.

Getting individuals responsible for implementing a methodology such as Total Quality Management to reexamine how training should occur once a PST is available is difficult. Traditional methodologies and activities, such as task analysis, are performed with a conventional frame of reference. It is difficult to get professionals to *let go* of their valued approaches and requires a sustained effort. Generating creative alternatives to conventional "teacher tell" training is a deliberate and time-consuming task. Gaining adequate sponsorship for such changes must be a priority.

Issues in implementing computer-mediated group process activities are untested and unknown. It is clear from initial activities that:

• An electronic PST is best implemented in a work team with a large screen projector available so all team members can collectively work with the tool's structure and view and process the information together. Small screens are inadequate in a workgroup environment.

• Questions about whether it facilitates or impedes group process must be studied. There is definitely an initial reorientation required to working with a tool. Team members must be committed to both redefining their process and working with the tool for it to be successful.

The requirement to use a computer to support group process requires a sufficient installed base of equipment in locations where teams are likely to meet.

Developers will always be fighting the tradeoffs of implementing their vision in an environment where inadequate technology is already installed. There is good news and bad news here: designing to limited technology increases potential for use, but it also reduces the power, relevance, and impact of the PST, which can affect people's motivation to use it.

The structure and resources of a PST for a complex process are reusable across other processes. The Quality PST flowchart could be populated with other methodologies and the examples, reference, and so on could be populated with other information. If a "front end" were available to tailor a flowchart to the number and sequence of steps *and* there were a word-processing type interface to permit content experts to load the information, this PST structure could be used as a shell or development environment for other similar processes. Designers should think about this when developing tools.

Direct Sales

Prime Computer

The Business Problem

Every dynamic and growing organization depends on a knowledgeable, confident, and productive sales force to develop customers, represent products, and generate revenue. Successful sales representatives know their products, understand individual customer needs, and are able to effectively and efficiently sell products to a wide variety of businesses, industries, and organizations. Successful sales reps also need to spend time wisely and maximize time with high probability sales—not with prospects who will consume time and be unlikely to buy.

Many organizations are experiencing increasing difficulty in creating these conditions due to several universal trends.

Increasing product volume. The sheer number of products is overwhelming. A medical products company has 2700 products, including drugs, electronic instruments, and services. A leading financial services organization has over seventy-five financial and insurance products its representatives can sell. Each product is represented and described in paper manuals organized to provide everything a sales person needs to know about specifications, markets, appropriate use, sales, business policy, related legal requirements, and so on. Often there are multiple manuals covering similar information produced by multiple departments (e.g., marketing, product development, sales, operations). The reference material often contains redundant, inconsistent, and overlapping information. There's either too much of something—or the desired information is not covered at all!

Dynamic and frequently changing product lines. Updates occur almost daily and are communicated through an array of channels, including paper bulletins, electronic mail notes, meetings and seminars, training programs, and satellite announcements.

Increasing product complexity and sophistication. This is particularly true when any electronic components are involved. This complexity requires greater understanding by sales reps, since customers are often intimidated by new functionality and increasing integration of features that were previously offered in independent products.

Product customization by individual purchasers. Customization permits substantial tailoring of product components, features, service, pricing, product power, and so on. The computer, financial services, and instrumentation and equipment industries represent this trend. For example, group insurance health care products permit customers—and even employees—to configure their own combination of what's covered by the policy, employee contributions, who can provide medical services, and so on. Computer sales reps know that almost nothing is standard. They can configure memory, speed, storage capacity, storage media, media, operating system, multimedia capabilities, user interface, communications capabilities, and, of course, software. Computers can emulate other machines and systems or be something they are not. Good grief! A computer is not a computer anymore.

The merging of different disciplines in products and services. The medical sales reps referred to above must know pharmacology, biology, physiology, physics, electronics, computers, sales, the medical marketplace, the retail marketplace, and so on. Gone are the days an insurance salesperson could succeed knowing only the products. Now insurance salespeople must master tax law, finance, security law, accounting, numerous insurance and financial products, computer software, and sales—while they are selling to an increasingly diverse marketplace in terms of life situations and needs.

Increasing competition and decreasing product differentiation among competitors. Subtleties prevail! It often seems that every company has (or soon will have) everything. This limits the window of product advantage a given company has in the marketplace. It increases the requirement for sales representatives to know and sell against competitor products and services. And sometimes the differentiation is only on pricing, financing, or service.

Increasing customer sophistication and expectations for quality, service and support. Consumers are less and less willing to resign themselves to unacceptable product, quality, or support. And there are willing vendors to step in when a vacuum emerges. One sales rep I know walked into a customer presentation to find that the customer had researched all competitive products on a CD-ROM library and had constructed an expert system using a $250 expert system shell to help him compare available products against his specific needs. It turned out the customer was far more informed that the sales rep and had more and better tools available to help him buy. The sales rep was helpless to compete against the customer's knowledge—never mind the competition. Not a high potential situation, to be sure.

Need for rapid sales force growth, including redeployment of non-sales staff into sales. Many companies need to get more people selling quickly. Sometimes it's new product or marketplace demands. In other cases, there might be need to increase revenue or reduce overhead. IBM and AT&T essentially reassigned tens of thousands of technical and support employees to sales jobs to increase revenue. These widely documented efforts were not as successful as anticipated—largely because the redeployed employees could not control all of the variables quickly enough to be successful. Whether or not they possessed the personal characteristics and motivation necessary for success in sales could be strongly debated. But the point is that organizations may need temporary or permanent boosts to their sales force—and they must be able to quickly gear those assigned up to speed.

Prime Computer

Prime Computer, a Fortune 500 company in Natick, Massachusetts faced these trends. Its 3,000-strong field sales force were also experiencing information overload: the paper-based information distributed to the field was said to be so enormous it would fill a twelve-foot wide bookshelf over a two-year period. Materials described products, marketing, and selling strategies and competitive information. These manuals and sales bulletins included the core materials needed by the sales and support personnel to perform their jobs.

The company had to make sure that salespeople would:

- access only that portion of the information that is relevant without being overloaded by a large volume of non-relevant information

- quickly find answers to specific task-related questions

- access the most up-to-date-information

- get information appropriate to different levels of knowledge, interest, and need within the target audience

- acquire knowledge when it was needed (just in time) rather than in prescheduled training events.

In addition to the information search and retrieval problems, the following business needs existed:

- assure that sales representatives spent time on qualified prospects and did not waste time with prospects who were not likely to buy Prime products

- assure that sales reps understood and could credibly communicate in the various industries and marketplaces they were faced with and could adequately understand the nature of the business, types of computer solutions available, and the language and business environment of each organization

- assure that a comprehensive customer needs analysis was conducted and that the broad range of Prime products were analyzed and compared with customer needs—and that the proper products were recommended

- assure that sales reps understood competitor products in relation to Prime products and could effectively sell against them

- create a productive environment for sales reps, including one in which the production of proposals, correspondence, analysis, and reports could be performed efficiently.

Traditional Approaches

In addition to providing paper-based information, traditional approaches to meeting the above needs included various formal training programs, peer and local management coaching and support, telephone hotlines, and various job aids. Of course, as business pressures increased, the desirability of taking sales reps from the field to sit in classrooms for each new product announcement or change declined accordingly. And adding more and more overhead to informally inform, coach, and support novice reps added expense and kept experienced staff from working on more difficult sales or other assignments.

Businesses throughout the world are experiencing increasing pain around assuring competency at reduced cost and in record time. And Prime was no exception. So the company turned to another approach, electronic performance support.

The Performance Support Solution

An Electronic Performance Support System (EPSS), code-named the "Prime Source," was designed by Barry Raybould for Prime Computer to address these needs and provide a competitive advantage for Prime. Prime's definition of an EPSS is "a computer-based system that improves work productivity by providing on-the-job access to integrated information, advice, and learning experiences." In addition to productivity, the goal of the Prime Source was to further improve the performance level and results of sales representative activity.

The Prime Source included three primary components: Information, Expert Advice, and Learning Experiences. Each component stood alone as a powerful environment within which to address a particular type of support or information need. The tight integration among and between components provided even more power to the users. Let's look at each component structure, design, and capability in turn.

The Information Base

The Information base provides users access to all of the information required to do their jobs. This was designed for users who did not want or need to be led step-by-step through a process, as in the

Advisor (described below), but wanted to work through the task themselves and be given easy access to all required information. The Information base contains text databases including product information, policies, procedures, specifications, facts, concepts, and explanations. In the Prime Source, information is organized as a hypertext data base and various views are available, including by industry, marketplace, product, competitors, and so on. Users can browse the database employing a range of search mechanisms. Note that the text database does not equate to putting the manuals on line. Rather, it represents how data can and should be reorganized for on-line use. (For a discussion of this, see Gloria J. Gery, "Issues in Computer-Based Reference," *CBT Directions,* March, 1991.) Exhibits 1A and 1B illustrate the display and options from competitor information on product benchmarks. User options are displayed. Exhibits 2A and 2B illustrate a single frame screen with embedded menu buttons permitting users to review Competitive Product Specifications. Exhibit 2B illustrates how a user would navigate via a pull-down menu to other competitive products.

The access methods in the Prime Source Information Base are varied and are designed to accommodate substantial diversity in user knowledge, experience, motivation, need, and style. Users can employ query-based retrieval techniques permitting key-word text search, browsing techniques using association-based retrieval (as in hypertext), hierarchical outlines, menus, indexes, or tables of contents.

Exhibit 2B shows the embedded menu buttons across the top of the screen illustrated by the pull-down menu for the Encore 320 product). Exhibit 3 shows the structure of the table of contents for each module in the Prime Source. Exhibit 4 illustrates the manually-created electronic index in which users can click on any line of the index and be taken to the appropriate part of the system. The index is context-sensitive and differs for each module. Not all modes of search are available from all Prime Source modules, but the available options are always clear to the user.

Exhibit 5 illustrates the main access screen of the Prime Source. Exhibits 6A through 6D illustrate the structure of the Prime Source and illustrate the module opening screens (accessible from the main access screen) by which users navigate through the structured hypertext information to meet their needs.

The *HyperCard*-based Information base is incredibly rich and provides excellent design models for developers. For more detailed information on the hypertext design and the various modes of user access and navigation, refer to the original articles on which this case study was based, plus others by Barry Raybould in the Bibliography.

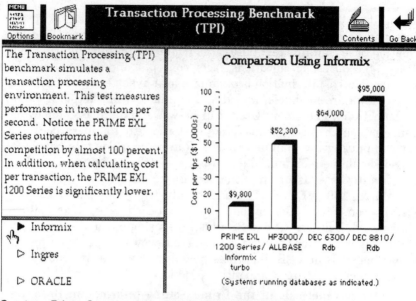

The Transaction Processing (TPI) benchmark simulates a transaction processing environment. This test measures performance in transactions per second. Notice the PRIME EXL Series outperforms the competition by almost 100 percent. In addition, when calculating cost per transaction, the PRIME EXL 1200 Series is significantly lower.

▶ Informix

▷ Ingres

▷ ORACLE

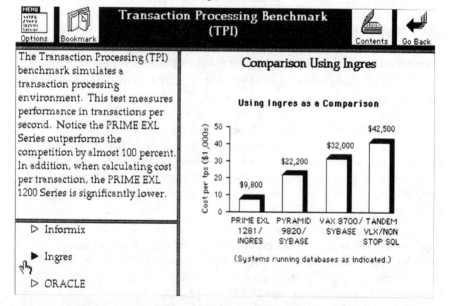

Exhibit 1. The Prime Source allows the user to access benchmark information and make comparisons with competing products.

Competitive Product Specifications

Options   Bookmark   Contents   Go Back

Features 1 of 2	PRIME EXL 1227	PRIME EXL 1281	Encore 320
Processor	80386	80386	NS32332
No. of Processors	2 - 10	2 - 30	20
Operating System	Dynix	Dynix	Umax
Std compliance	System V	System V	System V
Max Main Memory	8 - 80 MB	8 - 240 MB	16-128MB
Memory Increments	8, 16, 24 MB	8, 16, 24 MB	16MB
Disk Capacity	4.3 GB	17.3 GB	67.2GB
Disks Supported	150, 540 MB	540 MB	415,655MB
Cartridge Tape Capacity	60 MB	60 MB	
Reel to Reel Drive	45 MB	45 MB	180MB
Tape Controller	SCSI, Pertec	SCSI, Pertec	SCSI
DBMS Supported	Oracle, Ingres, Informix, Unify	Oracle, Ingres, Informix, Unify	Oracle, Informix, Universe
Max Terminals Connected	256	1000	1,000

Competitive Product Specifications

Options   Bookmark   Contents   Go Back

Features 1 of 2	PRIME EXL 1227	PRIME EXL 1281	Encore 320
Processor	80386	80386	**Encore 320**
No. of Processors	2 - 10	2 - 30	**Encore 510**
Operating System	Dynix	Dynix	**Encore 520**
Std compliance	System V	System V	**NCR 825**
Max Main Memory	8 - 80 MB	8 - 240 MB	**NCR 850**
Memory Increments	8, 16, 24 MB	8, 16, 24 MB	**Pyramid**
Disk Capacity	4.3 GB	17.3 GB	**Unisys 6000-70**
Disks Supported	150, 540 MB	540 MB	**Unisys 6000-80**
Cartridge Tape Capacity	60 MB	60 MB	
Reel to Reel Drive	45 MB	45 MB	180MB
Tape Controller	SCSI, Pertec	SCSI, Pertec	SCSI
DBMS Supported	Oracle, Ingres, Informix, Unify	Oracle, Ingres, Informix, Unify	Oracle, Informix, Universe
Max Terminals Connected	256	1000	1,000

Exhibit 2. A pull-down menu (from the button labeled "Encore 320") enables the user to call up specifications from any of a number of competing products.

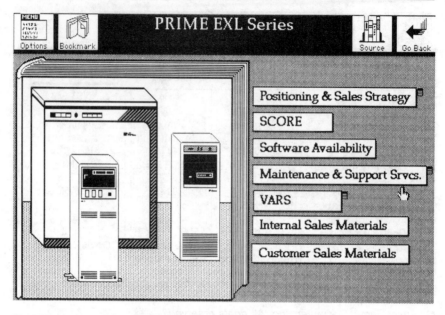

Exhibit 3. A table of contents from one of the modules.

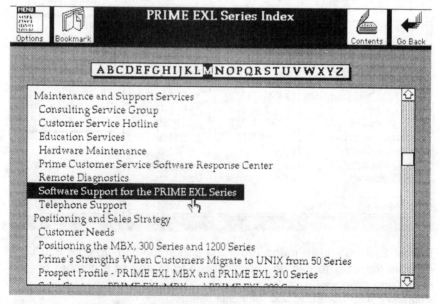

Exhibit 4. Clicking on a line in the electronic index takes the user to the appropriate part of the system.

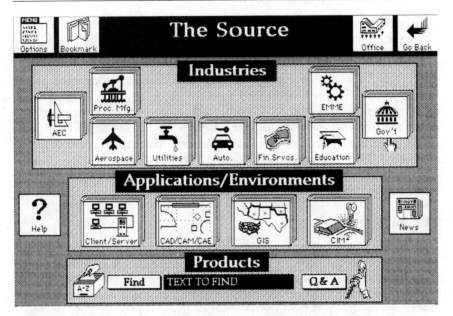

Exhibit 5. The opening screen gives the user direct access to many information areas, and it includes buttons to summon a search facility and an advisor.

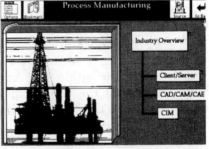
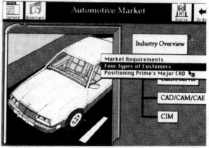

Exhibit 6. Individual module opening screens accessed from the main screen in Exhibit 5.

Integration of Information base with Advisory System and Learning Experiences

The Information base is hyper-linked to the Advisory System and the structured learning experiences. This integration permits users to move from freeform browsing to structured advice, to structured learning experiences (e.g., CBT) and back again in a fluid manner. As users require varying amounts and type of structure or as they feel needs to access and review associated information, they are able to do so easily. This accommodates user diversity in knowledge, need, situation, learning style, and motivation. It also accommodates differences in learning and analytical styles among users.

The Advisory System

The Prime Source Advisory System provides interactive advice on how to perform a task or to make a decision. This is the component that provides the maximum amount of assistance. The EPSS takes the place of a coach or an expert at the end of a telephone and leads the user step-by-step through the job or task. Working with the Advisory System does not require an in-depth understanding of the task involved, just the ability to follow a series of steps and to provide proper input when asked for it by the system. The goal is to permit novices to work through complex, branched analytical, and decision-making processes as if they had been performing the tasks for extended periods of time. These expert systems essentially provide intelligent job aids to users.

Exhibit 7 demonstrates a series of screen interactions a sales rep would experience within the Advisory System. The example illustrates support of the task of qualifying leads. This single-question dialog represents the simplest level of analysis since recommendations could be developed following the user's response to a single question. Far more complicated situations are supported within the Prime Source. Analytical processes involving numerous questions, user input of information or data, and comparisons with alternatives are performed. An example is the process that requires sales reps to structure customer needs and compare them to the Prime product alternatives and recommend an appropriate product solution.

In the Prime Source, there is a small, embedded rule base that works users through an interactive problem-solving session that results in a solution in two or three minutes. If the paths and decision points were mapped in a decision tree format on paper, over sixty nodes, or decision points, are involved. Obviously, tracking responses on paper would be impossible. And summarizing the information in a static, linear sequential text document would not have provided

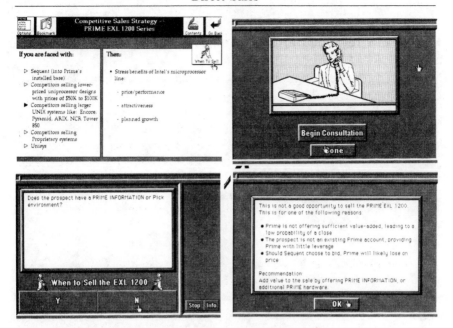

Exhibit 7. The Prime Source offers intelligent job aids.
Courtesy Prime Computer, Inc. All rights reserved

sales reps with the support they required in the processing of identifying information and comparing alternatives in relation to a situation. A novice performer would have taken more than the two to
three minutes it takes to work through the Advisor to find the phone
number of someone to call for help!

These task-specific advisors are linked via a hypertext button to
the text data bases and menus, thereby permitting context-sensitive
support.

Results

The Prime Source has been implemented in two field offices for
beta testing. Beta testers reported that the Prime Source provided
faster access to information, presented complex information in a more
readily understood form, and reduced the problem of information
overload in an information-rich environment.

Note: This case study is based on two articles by Barry Raybould:
"Solving Human Performance Problems with Computers. A Case Study:
Building an Electronic Performance Support System." *Performance and
Instruction,* November-December 1990 (published by the National
Society for Performance and Instruction); and "A Case Study in Per-
formance Support," *CBT Directions,* October 1990.

Barry Raybould is principal of Ariel Performance Systems, Inc., 100 View Street, Suite 114, Mountain View, California 94041 (415) 694-7880.

Specialized Analysis

AT&T

The Business Problem

Training department staffs typically include people with various backgrounds. At AT&T, as in most organizations, there are professional instructional designers on staff to provide training expertise. The bulk of the organizational staff consists, however, of individuals on assignment from line departments. These professionals bring business, functional, and technical knowledge and skill. They serve as both course developers and instructors. Their value to the training function lies in their business expertise. To remain too long in training diminishes their value to the students—and it limits their ability to be productive on returning to the business unit. So the rotation to the training department can last from 18 months to two or more years.

Within training, there are critical activities other than teaching tasks that are performed only intermittently by some staff. Those tasks include test construction and validation and media selection for course development. Both of these tasks are complex and require considerable technical knowledge about the discipline, as well as knowledge of the content or skill area. These tasks are important— and professional performance is required to assure that programs are effective, monies are wisely spent, and individual employees are evaluated and, in more and more circumstances, *certified* as capable of performing various tasks or knowledgeable in a subject, product, or business area. In the case of test construction, there are further implications: tests must be reliable and valid—and they must not discriminate based on irrelevant variables. Both the moral and legal requirements are clear.

As with many complex analytical and decision-making tasks that are only occasionally performed, the chance for error based on incorrect assumptions, faulty process or logic, or improper assumptions or mathematical calculations is high. The need to assure knowledgeable and skilled performance is commensurately critical.

The traditional approach to developing these skills is classroom instruction. AT&T tried that, offering a three-day instructor-led training program on test development. Skill development in this program was limited for the following reasons:

- the course was only taught intermittently—and it sometimes preceded need or wasn't available near the point in time when an individual needed to attend

- many attendees lacked prerequisite knowledge and skill—particularly in statistics and mathematics

- the content is not intrinsically interesting to most people—and it didn't offer much in terms of career development in non-instructional fields

- the content was too large and complex to do more than treat it superficially in a three-day program; some of the components alone are fields in and of themselves; many of the calculations required use of computer programs—and participants were not always familiar with the software to construct the calculations

- only limited labs and practice activities could be conducted within the program since the ability to actually conduct evaluations with sample learners and perform the calculations to determine reliability and validity was not possible during a three-day event.

All in all, the outcomes for learners were familiarization with terms, awareness of the processes, and generally less confidence than desired in their ability to successfully construct valid and reliable tests. Even though students could check "complete" on their course curriculum and employee development plan, they were effectively unprepared to construct and validate tests.

The other reality is that many supervisors within training lacked the technical knowledge to support or evaluate the tasks. The on-the-job developmental coaching potential was low as a result—unless there *happened* to be a resident expert in the unit who had time available.

Traditional training and unsystematic performance support on the job had some unsatisfactory results:

- trial and error was the basis for too much test development

- tests were sometimes mismatched with desired instructional outcomes

- substantial overhead support was required to guarantee proper results (i.e., consultant resource, use of internal experts, specialization for mathematical tasks, and so on)

- test development was expensive

- delays were the norm

- file documentation was often inconsistent, incomplete, and inadequate to stand potential investigation or complaint.

The Corporate Training Support Group in Morristown, New Jersey reexamined the problem and came up with an alternative solution: a Performance Support Tool (PST) to support the test development and validation process. The Training Test Consultant was developed for AT&T by Comware, Inc. of Cincinnati, Ohio. University professors, expert in test construction and validation, were used as subject matter experts, as were experts from the AT&T training community.

The Performance Support Solution

The AT&T Training Test Consultant (TTC) is a stand-alone resource available to internal AT&T training developers for installation on AT&T's installed PC hardware. As far as possible, it is available at the developer's workstation. Since the PC installed base at AT&T at this time of the development of this PST included CGA graphics and exclusively keyboard input, windows and scrolling had to be simulated, graphics were limited to character graphics, only keyboard navigation options were available, and only a single text style could be used. The developer challenge was to structure a complete and flexible information base, powerful and rich support mechanisms, and a flexible interface and navigation system without advanced hardware and software features such as buttons, multitasking, and so on. The system had to accommodate enormous user diversity in background, knowledge, skill, and motivation to learn a body of knowledge about test construction—although presumably, all users were motivated to produce good results. Glitz and software wizardry were not available to cover up inadequate design. The resulting system reflects clear and precise understanding of user needs. The development team accomplished its objectives.

The product is distributed to trainers throughout AT&T in a plastic case with brief documentation, including information on the PST organization, directions for use, and information on content. The package includes a tutorial diskette that provides structured computer-based training to users not familiar with the PST structure and navigation. No other training on the TTC is required. The TTC *is*, however, used in any classroom training on test construction at AT&T.

The Training Test Consultant PST is an integrated environment consisting of three components (see Figure 1). The components are the Advisor, the Infobase and the Tutor. Navigation is via function keys available across the bottom of the screen (see Exhibit 1). The QR, or Quick Reference, screen available via Function Key, summarizes user navigation options (see Exhibit 2). The Inquiry line permits free-form search of the infobase (explained later).

The Advisor is a consultant resource that structures the process of test development and validation for users. It employs a dialog-based question-and-answer sequence that requests relevant information from the developer about the task, situation, test goals,

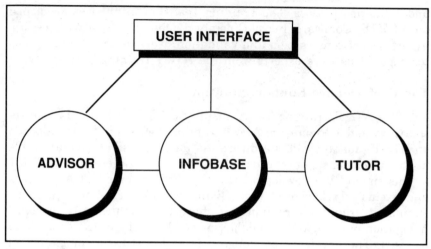

Figure 1. Diagram of the AT&T Training Test Consultant (TTC).

data, and so on. The Advisor provides support for the six major tasks associated with development (see Exhibit 2).

The Advisor is based on a decision tree structure, rather than an expert system, since it was determined that simply getting into and staying on the same logical path was sufficient to result in performance. So, as the user responds to a given question or request for input from the Advisor (see Exhibit 4), he or she is next presented with the question or input request appropriate to the previous response. Figure 2 illustrates the tree-structure within the Advisor.

At certain points in the test validation process, developers must perform complex calculations. Within the Advisor, users are requested to input specific information. Behind the scenes, the TTC is constructing a spreadsheet that reflects the responses (see Exhibit 5). Users then input the data and the TTC makes the appropriate calculations. In other words, *software* is constructed that is task-specific to limit user requirements to learn other software in order to perform the task. In a conventional performance situation, test developers would have to learn a spreadsheet or database package, learn how to construct the appropriate templates, develop the formulas (which is problematic for many), and then input the data. Within this PST design, the developer simply focuses on the task and is less aware of what is going on behind the scenes. Of course, in more advanced technical environments, design could incorporate entire software packages. But frankly, it's not needed in this case. And the availability of *specific and appropriate* pre-organized software environments

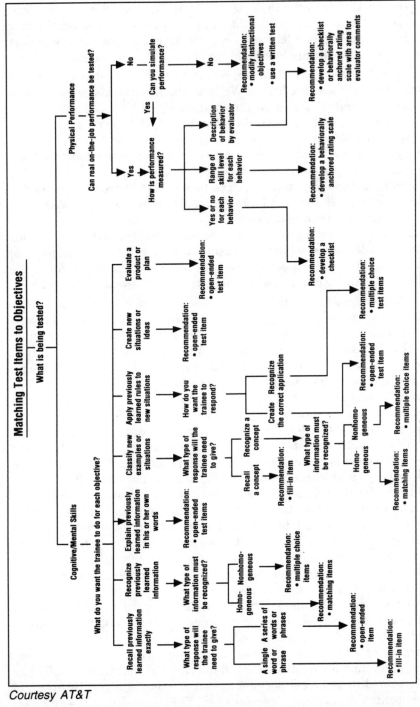

Figure 2. The Advisor component of the TTC is based on a tree structure.

Courtesy AT&T

guarantees that the results are complete and correct. What more could be asked? Oh, of course. Printing output is possible so that the test documentation is complete and accurate for either manager or expert review or for use during later analysis of the test construction activities.

The Advisor is available on a stand-alone basis and it is linked to the Infobase and the Tutor. While in the Advisor, users can access on-demand context sensitive information about the concepts, formulas, guidelines, and so forth. In other words, the user has a further expert available during use of the "expert" Advisor. This second expert provides information and explanations that either put the Advisor questions or activities into a broader context—or provide information that the user requires to respond appropriately to the dialog or request for input. For example, if a user is asked "Has content validity been established?" and is not sure what content validity means, pressing the F1 key accesses the related explanations and examples. Once in the Infobase, the user can take advantage of all its flexibility and alternative access methods (described under the Infobase below) without losing the active place in the Advisor.

Remember, the goal here was to enable people without knowledge or skill to successfully perform the various tasks required in test construction or validation and to provide them only what is needed to do that. At some points during the Advisor, developers determined that user discretion in seeking related information was not enough, so explanations and descriptions were included *within* the Advisor. For example, preceding the Advisor question on test item *criticality*, an important and relatively sophisticated concept, a four-screen narrative explanation of *criticality* is presented. The decision of whether to include *content* presentations within an Advisor or whether to link it to an Infobase is critical and takes understanding of the users from a knowledge and learning perspective. In my experience, this analysis and consideration does not always occur during design of expert systems. When expert system design is exclusively from a task performance perspective and does not consider enabling the users' access to relevant information, the expert system is less than helpful in that users lack prerequisite knowledge to employ the Advisor. In such cases, users will either abandon the task or simply enter any information into the Advisor to move on to the next point. In the latter case, the Advisor becomes virtually useless, regardless of how well it is constructed technically. This example argues strongly for ongoing and active involvement of people who understand the user from a learning or educational perspective during advisory system design. And when the task requires related information that traditionally has been stored in technical documentation or other sources, inclusion of documentation specialists becomes key. This brings us to the Infobase part of the Training Test Consultant, which illustrates the point.

The Infobase is a hypertext reference environment within which a sufficiently complete and relevant body of knowledge associated with test design and validation is included. This knowledge was analyzed and broken down into standalone *chunks* of information, each of which contains a complete piece of information. The Infobase is organized according to a type of hypertext called Hierarchy Replacement hypertext. The Infobase is designed to provide both relational and hierarchical organizing schemes and to permit multiple ways for users to search and retrieve information based on their frame of reference at the time of look-up.

Users can call up the Infobase and view a menu that looks like the table of contents of a reference book. In fact, the menu *is* a table of contents. There are both *contracted* (i.e., headings only) and *expanded* (i.e., headings and subheadings) views available (See Exhibits 6 and 7). By moving the cursor and using the enter key, the user can select a topic. The appropriate chunk of information appears in a window; behind the window are up to four other windows which keep the information hierarchy in view at all times. This maintains user orientation to the knowledge as it relates to a topical hierarchy (see Exhibit 8).

Users can also locate information via a free-form search capability. The system then searches the headings and sub-headings for a match and presents the exact or near matches to the user. Users can select among near matches. When the appropriate heading or node is selected, the information appears, in its proper hierarchy, on the screen. Users can scroll through the window to view information that extends beyond a given window. While most nodes require no more than two or three screens, some include considerably more. When the user reaches the end of the textual information within a topic, related and subordinate subjects are listed and are available for selection.

Users can also perform a search by highlighting up to ten words within the text display using the F7 key. The enter key results in an information search of the entire text file and, again, exact and near matches are presented to the user for selection. This file scan is effectively the hypertext capability of the system. The information within the text file is not hard-linked in hypertext mode. A glossary is also available via a function key.

The Infobase is cross-referenced to the Advisor and the Tutor, as well as being directly accessible as a stand-alone component. This integration with the Advisor and the Tutor have a significant impact on user performance—and PST design.

The Tutor. The Tutor component is essentially a designed collection of activities and questions that permit users to assess their knowledge, practice application of knowledge on case studies and examples, or increase their knowledge while interacting with the PST in various ways. While the name, Tutor, might create an initial expectation that this resource is a CBT tutorial, it is not. The Tutor is better described as all of the practice exercises of application problem interactions you might find in a tutorial, with none of the content presentation. As Exhibit 9 illustrates, the Tutor components relate to the Advisor tasks (see Exhibit 3), but when a given task is selected, the user gets practice problems as illustrated in Exhibit 10. Most of these interactions occur in a series that works users/learners through a carefully designed sequence of complex activities to achieve integration of knowledge and skill. For example, the interaction shown in Exhibit 10 that requires users to determine whether an item represents a good matching test item is followed by a question that asks "why or why not" by asking the user to judge the item against all of the guidelines for constructing good matching questions, depending on the user's initial response. Following that, the user is presented with an improved item if the initial item was not a good one.

You will note that these interactions are not trivial cognitive questions that simply assess memory and recall about facts, definitions, and so on. They require analysis and thought—and can only be successfully completed when the users *know and understand* the content. Of course, users can always employ the trial and error mode to work through the problems and exercises. And employing that strategy, learners learn through experiencing the series of interactions and receiving feedback to their responses. For those users who want *information or content* related to the questions, they can select F1 from the menu on the lower screen to receive specifically related content. The relevant content is extracted from the Infobase by a simple key press. The prior integration of content was accomplished when developers cross-referenced the content to the activities or tasks. Users can select the content before, during, or after working on a given question or problem exercise. Once in the Infobase, they can cruise through it relentlessly via its rich and alternative access methods while the system holds their place in the Tutor (or Advisor). Users also have access to a glossary component via a function key.

In designing this performance support tool, the goal was to support and guarantee performance, not to produce cognitive knowledge. While knowledge is definitely acquired by users in the process of using the PST, the developers did not have knowledge transfer and retention as a goal. Therefore, no assessment tests per se were included. Of course, this PST structure could be used in business applications where internalization of knowledge was the goal. In that case, more exercises or application questions could be constructed and identified as a "test" for certification. User activity would be tracked and stored, and results would be reported. It's critical to understand the *objectives* for the tool or system to be sure the design reflects it appropriately.

The Training Delivery Consultant. AT&T also developed the Training Delivery Consultant (TDC) which is designed to assist the same user audience in the task of evaluating and comparing alternative delivery systems for a given training application. The structure of the Training Delivery Consultant is similar to the Training Test Consultant in that it includes a hypertext information base, tutors, and advisors. But the TDC is different in that it also serves as repository of organizational information on costs, assumptions, and so on that relate to conducting cost analysis for individual applications. The cost comparison of various delivery alternatives for a given training application is conducted following the construction of an organization-specific database of current costs associated with media development and training delivery. That database consists of loading information into about fifty questions and requesting data on classroom costs, average student day costs, video production costs, CBT development ratios, and so on. If the information is not available, it must be researched. Once it is available, data entry into the Training Delivery Consultant takes about an hour. Once that database is loaded, it can be used and reused by all course developers comparing delivery system alternatives. It can also be updated as costs change.

Responsibility for the database construction and maintenance varies. In some units, a single individual is responsible for loading and maintaining the database periodically. In others, maintenance of information is a function of utilization. As with setting up a spreadsheet program, there is an initial investment of time and information gathering associated with the Training Delivery Consultant set up. But this activity can be leveraged quickly in that all subsequent users can perform analyses virtually instantly with their specific project information.

It's important to note that the Training Delivery Consultant goes beyond cost comparisons in assisting users about media appropriateness decisions. The TDC advisors request user input on issues relating to logistics, culture and media acceptability within the organization, and effectiveness, as well as costs. This provides a more robust and practical evaluation. User input, of course, then is subject to review by subsequent decision makers which will be discussed under implications.

Another important TDC feature relates to the ability of users to modify the rules and weights associated with various factors in the decision making process. For example, users can weight cost as more important than logistics, cost as the most important element, or reflect a "money is no object" condition. About seventy-five percent of the rules are modifiable, which permits considerable flexibility.

Results and Implications

The Training Test Consultant (TTC) was implemented in 1989 as part of a formal training program on test construction. Within that program, learners were informed about the TTC's availability and capabilities and used it as part of lab exercises within the course. The TTC includes a tutorial that focuses on understanding the available resources and their structure and navigating successfully within the TTC (i.e., function key mobility, relationships among and between the resources, and so on). During the initial class, many participants basically suggested that the course might be reduced, restructured, or eliminated since this tool could support them in their work on test construction and validation. Those experienced in the ways of organizations know, however, that whether or not the TTC would permit such a decision has limited impact on whether such a decision is made. The availability of formal programs is linked to many things besides need (for example, training certification processes, contracts with vendors, organizational philosophy, and so on). The TTC continues to be used within formal training on tests and measurements with ongoing initial user acceptance. An interesting implication for training should be noted. Classroom instruction on test design, development, and validation still occurs at AT&T. But the class content and student activities have changed as a result of TTC availability. Now, students are able to perform significantly more lab activities—and the assigned lab activities are more complex. Students perform the activities within the TTC. The potential for additional and more sophisticated exercises that will increase skill level and depth, to make the impact of the conventional training programs greater, is being explored.

Naturally, ongoing utilization of a tool such as the TTC or TDC is a function of perceived benefit by individual users, local management sponsorship, or corporate requirements for its use. (See the chapter on sponsorship and success factors). In a relatively decentralized organization such as AT&T, it is unlikely that anything other than legal requirements is used as a basis for corporate-wide required utilization. In addition, these tools were initial products in a new category whose benefits were anticipated, but not proven, so the likelihood of gaining sponsorship for required utilization was low.

Prior to widespread release of the TTC, two university-based research studies were conducted. The research results indicated that the TTC performance support tool had the potential to result in equal or better tests at lower cost—and the effectiveness of the tests was likely to increase following TTC implementation due to the structure and resources provided by the TTC.

In addition to the formal university-based research, the following represents AT&T's belief about the utilization and impact of the tools within the Education and Training community at AT&T.

- Ongoing classroom utilization provides learners with additional resources for learning and lab exercise performance within a training event

- Increased confidence of learners in their abilities to perform test construction and validation while on the job

- Utilization on the job when developing tests as a resource tool and support system by individuals developing and validating tests

- Time log information on developer time expenditures indicates a potential reduction in time for developer construction of individual test items.

- Improved test and test item quality, including reliability and validity, as perceived by users and training management

- Improved documentation of test development process, including statistical calculations

- Reduced elapsed time in test construction due to increased structure (and therefore both confidence and quality of results) to less experienced test developers

- Successful use as a "proof of concept" of performance support systems, creating an alternative or complement to traditional training programs

- Increased ability of prospective EPSS sponsors to conceive of how they can support other types of performance improvement, such as equipment configuration and sales support, using this concept

- Increased explicitness about underlying assumptions developers make during test construction and validation and media evaluation, costing, selection, and development (assumptions are surfaced earlier and can be discussed between developer, supervisor, staff technical resources, and clients; whether or not actual recommendations have been improved may be less important than the surfacing of assumptions to all involved)

- Increased consistency of delivery system evaluation process, cost basis development, and calculations in training delivery evaluation; overall improved implementation of the required process that had not been implemented successfully in a less structured and demanding environment than the PST required

161

- Expected decrease in developer bias about delivery system selection due to the increased explicitness about assumptions and costs and the associated documentation of those assumptions and costs

- Anticipated improvement in overall recommendation and product quality.

Required Technology

The performance support tools were developed for use on the AT&T PC machine with 640K of memory and a hard disk. It employs CGA graphics.

The PST's were developed by Comware, Inc. of Cincinnati, Ohio employing their proprietary development tools and KSS Author and KSS-HELP, Comware authoring and development tools.

Note: AT&T performance support tools, as described in this case study, are available only to internal AT&T employees.

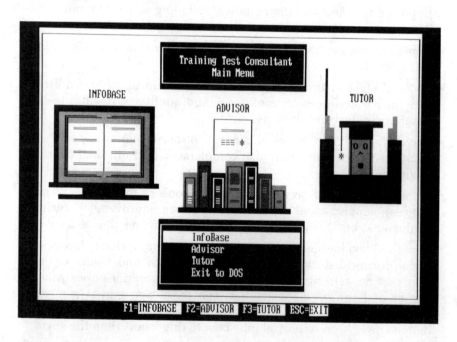

Exhibit 1. Navigation in the TTC is through function keys.
Courtesy AT&T

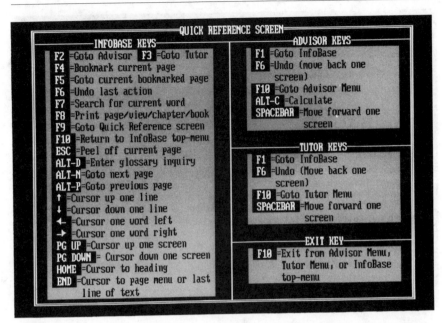

Exhibit 2. The QR, or Quick Reference, screen available via Function Key, summarizes user navigation options.

Exhibit 3. The Advisor menu.
Courtesy AT&T

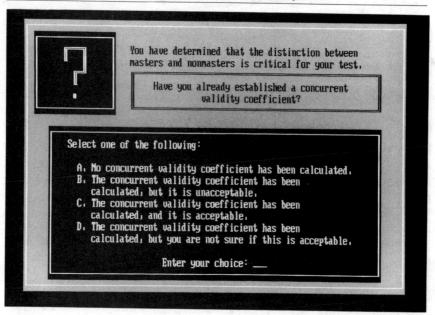

You have determined that the distinction between masters and nonmasters is critical for your test.

Have you already established a concurrent validity coefficient?

Select one of the following:

A. No concurrent validity coefficient has been calculated.
B. The concurrent validity coefficient has been calculated, but it is unacceptable.
C. The concurrent validity coefficient has been calculated, and it is acceptable.
D. The concurrent validity coefficient has been calculated, but you are not sure if this is acceptable.

Enter your choice: ___

Exhibit 4. The Advisor questions the user.

◆◆◆◆ DIRECTIONS ◆◆◆◆

At the cursor location, type the values of each of the masters' scores. Use the arrow keys to move the cursor cell. Press return to enter the default value of 0. After entering the masters' scores, press ALT-C. Enter each of the nonmasters' scores in the same manner. When all cells are complete, press ALT-C to calculate the master, nonmaster, and raw cutoff scores.

To exit the matrix without saving data, press SPACEBAR and type "y" at the prompt.

MASTER	Scores	NONMASTER	Scores
11	92	1	86
12	84	2	73
13	74	3	79
14	82	4	81
15	91	5	92
16	78	6	94
17	84	7	71
18	82	8	94
19	86	9	95
20	92	10	0--

Exhibit 5. Behind the scenes, the PST is constructing a spreadsheet that reflects the responses.
Courtesy AT&T

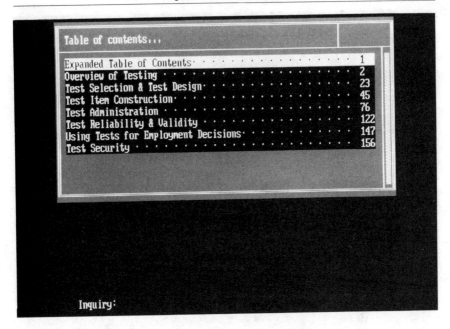

Exhibit 6. The table of contents in contracted form.

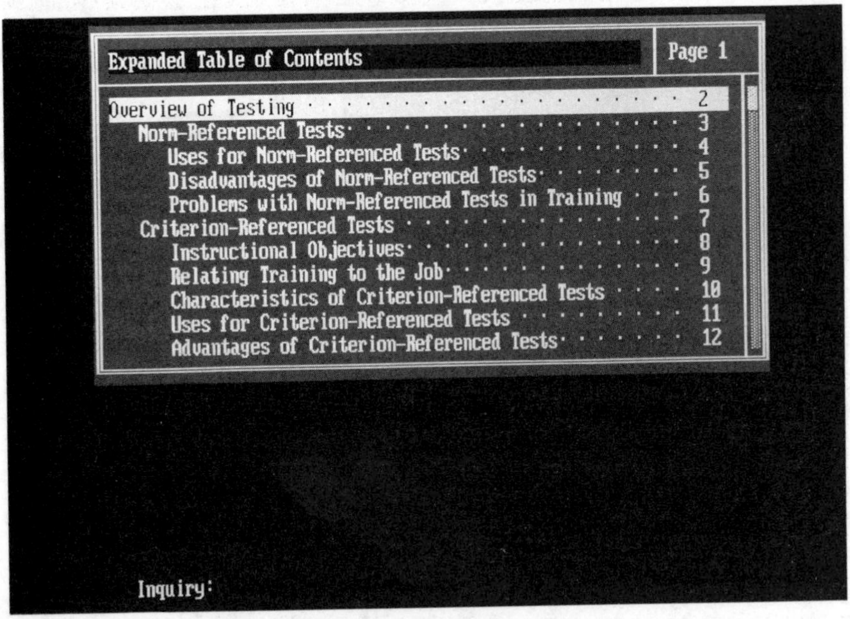

Exhibit 7. The expanded table of contents.
Courtesy AT&T

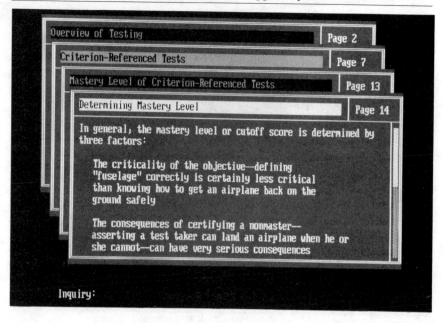

Exhibit 8. Behind the current window are up to four other windows that keep the information hierarchy in view at all times.

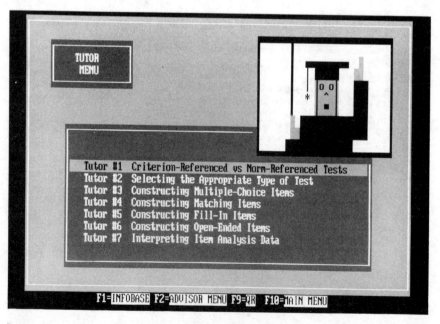

Exhibit 9. The Tutor components relate to the Advisor tasks.
Courtesy AT&T

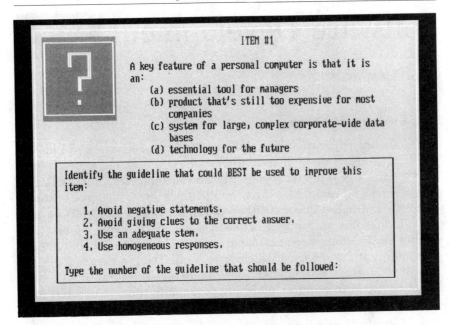

Exhibit 10. After the user determines whether Item #1 is a good
matching test item, the system asks the user to judge the item
against all of the guidelines for constructing good matching questions.
Courtesy AT&T

Software Development

IBM Corporation

The Business Problem

Software applications development takes too long. The bases on which software is developed—data, business processes, and user requirements—are often inconsistently and incompletely analyzed, developed, and represented. Often, applications are developed without complete and sound models of these data, processes, and entities and the relationships among and between them. As a result, application quality varies, change requirements increase, maintenance becomes a nightmare, and user dissatisfaction is high. Today's demand for accelerated systems development and more easily maintainable and adaptive software requires more improvements than structured programming and traditional techniques alone can generate.

Historically, applications software was developed for each particular business activity or function, depending on individual customer requirements. The broad and deep organization-wide view was rarely taken. Structured development methodologies and database technologies and concepts improved the situation, but the strictly data-driven view was still insufficient to speed application development. Among the reasons: the sheer number of variables, amount of data, and complex interrelationships are largely beyond people's capacity to understand them as a whole when using paper-based representation techniques such as data flow diagrams, bubble-diagrams, and so on. The static analog media was insufficient to represent either the data or the relationships.

CASE Tools as a Solution

Enter computer-assisted software engineering (CASE) tools. On to the scene strode computer-driven development environments, represented by such products as Knowledgeware's *Application Development Workbench* (ADW), Index Systems' *Excelerator,* and Texas Instruments' *Information Engineering Facility* (IEF). Information systems management recognized their potential for addressing the applications software development productivity bottleneck.

CASE tools are among the fastest-selling software products in the country. These tools permit automated, interactive design and representation of complex data, complex and interrelated processes, and the links to entities (functions, users, departments, and so on) via a set of structured design representation and sophisticated programs. Once information is entered into the system, developers can coordinate and structure alternative views of the information. Developers and customers can clearly view what information is used for various processes. They can determine whether data is used by one or more processes and how each process relates to various business entities.

The tools are powerful and flexible. As specific information is developed, it can be organized as super- or subsets of other information and expanded, or summary views can be generated, much like the expanded and concentrated views of documents available in word processors that will display or hide format commands, provide various levels of detail in outlines, and so forth.

Rarely do current or potential users fail to see CASE's potential to have an impact on design and development quality, productivity, maintainability, efficiency, and system performance. But in reality, CASE tools have had limited impact to date. There are many reasons for the limited impact thus far, but many are related to the considerable differences in process, technique, and developer mind-set that are required to perform many of the abstract tasks, such as data modeling, that are required. Even when there is limited resistance based on power and control issues, capability to generate required paradigm and skill shifts is limited. Table 1 summarizes the fundamental differences between conventional software design and CASE requirements.

Table 1
INFORMATION ENGINEERING

CHANGES: PARADIGM SHIFT

TRADITIONAL PROCESS	INFORMATION ENGINEERING
● EACH TASK, SEPARATE FUNCTION	● ALL TASKS, ALL RELATED FUNCTIONS
● USER ROLE LIMITED	● USER ON TEAM
● PROCESS BEFORE DATA	● PROCESS WITH DATA
● LIMITED TOOLS	● AUTOMATED TOOLS
● PAPER DOCUMENTATION	● ON-LINE DOCUMENTATION
● CODING BY PROGRAMMERS	● CODING AUTOMATIC

Courtesy IBM

IBM Corporation's Project

IBM's desire to accelerate quality software design is similar to that of all other organizations. The company's needs apply to software used within the corporation as well as software sold as product to customers or software that is part of hardware systems. Information systems management and education management recognized that conventional training in the new methodology was not generating adequate change within the desired time frames to achieve the desired productivity gains. As in many other organizations, the developers were having difficulty making the shift and were in some cases using the powerful automated tools to represent old ways of designing systems, rather than restructuring their views of the process. In addition, the scarce expertise of those developers who understood CASE methodology was required for critical software development. The experts could not be consumed with training and supporting those who had not yet mastered the use of the new tools. A different approach was willingly evaluated.

The Year 2000 Study

IBM Education had developed a vision for human resource performance in the year 2000. In analyzing future conditions and requirements, it developed a future vision and compared it with 1980 realities (see Chapter Three). Table 2 summarizes IBM Education's beliefs about the future. Education management realized there was opportunity for change. The year 2000 vision included integrating the concept of electronic performance support with other approaches to employee education. Figure 1 models the paradigm and summarizes the year 2000 education attributes.

In identifying potential pilot activities for a performance support system, education met information systems management, and the two units teamed up for the task. Senior management from each function were joint sponsors of this project and funded and supported the activity.

The Performance Support Solution

A working prototype Performance/Learning Support System (P/LSS) was developed for the data modeling task associated with information engineering. Data modeling was selected, based on an analysis conducted to answer three questions:

• What tasks will cause the most difficulty?

• Why?

• Of these tasks, which is the most critical to business success?

Table 2
DIRECTIONS FOR EDUCATION

TODAY	2000
• MANAGEMENT INITIATED	• EMPLOYEE INITIATED
• CENTRALIZED	• DISTRIBUTED
• LOCAL COURSE CATALOG	• INSTRUCTIONAL MODULES
• LIMITED MEDIA	• MULTI-SENSORY
• EXPERTS MUST STRUCTURE	• LEARNER CONTROLS STRUCTURE
• PLAN BY JOB	• PLAN BY SKILL
• KNOW = DO	• PRACTICE FOR PROFICIENCY
• HOMOGENEOUS GROUP	• HETEROGENEOUS GROUPS
• EDUCATION = EVENT	• LEARNING = PROCESS
• JOB IS STATIC	• JOB IS DYNAMIC

Courtesy IBM

The project goals included:

- A P/LSS that would work in parallel with the installed software, Knowledgeware's *Application Development Workbench* (ADW)

- Demonstration of the future attributes of education identified in the education 2000 study

- Validation of the paradigm through rigorous evaluation of the system's effectiveness with novice, intermediate, and expert data modelers and ADW users

- Development of understanding of P/LSS design and development requirements, including required skills, staffing levels, project management, and development methodology

- Documentation of a repeatable process.

If successful, the plan was to extend the performance support concept to other critical information engineering tasks and to use the data modeling prototype to introduce the P/LSS concept throughout IBM.

Project parameters included finishing on schedule, utilizing leading-edge technology (including OS/2, video, and audio), and supporting IBM's information engineering methodology utilizing existing

171

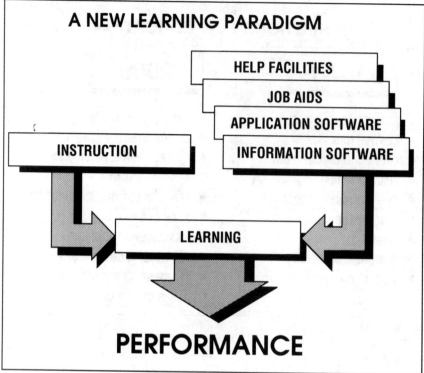

Figure 1. A New Learning Paradigm
Courtesy IBM

support materials. Phase One of the project included feasibility studies, task design, development, and evaluation. The project team was multidisciplinary and included a project leader with instructional design skills, instructional designers, programmers, and expert system developers. Consultant resource was used intermittently. Users were actively involved as both domain experts and designers and were part of the team as well.

Components and Features of the P/LSS

The data modeling P/LSS is represented in Figure 2. The P/LSS is an interrelated and integrated structure with a large number of features and components.

Software. Knowledgeware's ADW operating on a PS/2 under OS/2.

Monitor. A monitoring system that observes user activity and deduces actions within ADW. Based on defined conditions, it presents the user with context-sensitive support material. In addition, the Monitor works in conjunction with the Advisor and the Time/Path Log.

Advisor. This feature works in conjunction with the Monitor to provide system-initiated "Helps." If the system recognizes either a violation of a procedure or "rule," or perhaps recognizes an individual taking excessive time in a task, the Advisor will interrupt and recommend specific support material for the current task.

Time / Path Log. Tracking mechanism to summarize user activity within the P/LSS to be used in understanding P/LSS resource utilization, pathing, and time spent within various components. This mechanism may also be used to track task performance within the application software tool.

Library. The Library consists of two sections. The first is a "public" library containing articles and reference material just as one would find in a reference library. This may be represented by both actual reprints of articles and reference to other sources. The second section is the personal library that contains To-Do steps, examples of actual data models, other examples of outputs from the application software, and finally a quality assurance checklist to assist in the system assurance process.

Interactive Reference and Training. This component consists of several different support levels, in order to support all users regardless of expertise or learning style preference. The design is significantly different than traditional computer-based training lessons or stand-alone reference. Within the component:

- A *tutorial* guides new users through how to use the Performance/ Learning Support System so they can become familiar with all of the resources and components.

- *Interactive reference* information is organized in a question-answer structure. Users can *directly access a menu* of contents that is hierarchically organized. The interactive reference can also be accessed in context-sensitive ways from the ADW application and the structured training described below. Users who need quick answers can return to their tasks. Others can browse, if so inclined. Those who wish more depth or structure can proceed to the interactive learning components.

- *Training lessons* support all application tasks and levels of expertise, as well as alternative learning styles. There are suggested navigation paths so that users can take the hypermedia-like CBT if they wish. There are case studies for the novice or new user to test skills in new application areas.

- *Assessments* are available so learners can check their knowledge and skill if they desire.

The training lessons are organized in a question-answer structure in which each question and answer are self-contained. Actually, the question-answer text material is the same material that is available through reference, reorganized for the training. As a result, each is linked to a specific application task and can be independently accessed and organized in various hierarchies based on need. This design structure specifically addresses both flexibility and reusability. Each question and answer set covers a specific topic like "What is an entity?" as well as related questions such as "How are entities defined?" "What are the different types of entities?" and so on. The related questions are designed to accelerate integration of knowledge, task, and context. Conventional topical reference structures require user-learners to integrate the information themselves or to integrate the information with task, software, or context. Inexperienced learners are often not capable of sufficient integration, since they lack the universe of knowledge and experience from which to compare, contrast, combine, analyze, and synthesize.

The question-answer structure accomplishes many things, including reflection of user-learner thought processes, simulation of user-learner thought processes, and advanced and consistent integration of information.

The instructional design task was to provide users with granular structure in question-and-answer form that would guide learning on various cognitive and task aspects of the subject matter. When users access the Training component in a free-standing mode and work with the material in a linear, sequential process, they have access to fifteen plus hours of computer-based training, including some interactive video components. They still have complete control to construct their own learning paths. In their learning, they can skip topics, tasks, or activities, or they can take the entire section or the entire "program." From within ADW, the user is directed to context-sensitive training and receives only material relevant to the task at hand. Again, the goal was to integrate training with software and task performance, rather than require users to search, retrieve, and integrate the training outside of the task or software context. The goal was to provide specific and related on-demand learning at the moment of need.

Consultant. This component is a library of tips and techniques that are new information, material specific to a team's project, or new discoveries in the use of a tool. This section can also be used to communicate across a community of system users and reduce the number of calls to a central site for user support or enhancements of the support material. It is the first place to look when starting a new project or returning to a project after some time away from it.

Glossary. This is a set of terms specific to the application software and the use of the software in a project, and it helps users to distinguish between the system's definition of something and the more common definition in everyday usage.

All of the hypermedia support was authored with Asymetrix *Toolbook* software.

Evaluation and Results

IBM evaluated the Data Modeling P/LSS with six particular questions in mind:

- Does it enhance skills?

- Does it improve work quality?

- Is it motivating to use?

- Is it technically reliable?

- What improvements are needed?

- Does it present a feasible opportunity for further development and extension of the concept?

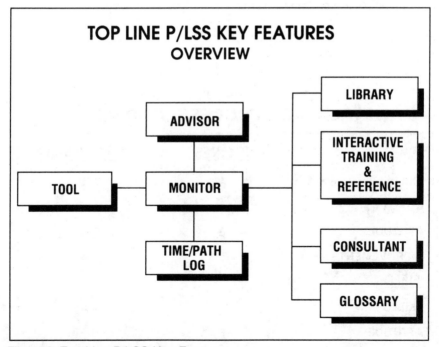

Figure 2. Top Line P/LSS Key Features
Courtesy IBM

The evaluation process was designed by two IBM research psychologists. An IBM human factors psychologist provided quality assurance services. Two external data modeling experts evaluated and scored the actual data models produced by the participants. Pretests and post-tests were used to measure skills.

The evaluation process included a usability lab, field tests, and focus groups. Participants in the evaluation process were IBM programmers, analysts, and requirements analysts. They represented a wide range of data modeling expertise, training in information engineering and the software tool, experience with OS/2 Windows environment, and time in their position. Ten people participated, and their results were analyzed. Five people participated in the field tests with results that were analyzed. Table 3 summarizes the findings.

The P/LSS results were statistically significant in both learning and skills that translated to data modeling performance. People liked having the environment available, and they liked the structure.

Some additional findings and observations of note:

- Performance/Learning Support Systems can be used effectively on a stand-alone basis as well as to accelerate learning within the formal training context, whether it is a self-paced CBT environment or a classroom program.

Table 3
EVALUATION PROCESS: FINDINGS

LAB	SCORES	SIGNIFICANT?
SKILLS	↑	YES
QUALITY	↑	YES
ATTITUDE	↑	YES
IMPROVEMENTS NEEDED	YES	N/A
FIELD		
SKILLS	↑	N/A
ATTITUDE	↑	N/A

Courtesy IBM

- Users expressed the belief that while concept learning and skill development can occur "off the job" in training programs, they are enhanced when done in the context of the job.

- Some users expressed interest in a more structured training experience, while others expressed delight with the freedom to build their own learning paths.

- Individual learning styles were evident in not only the use of the support material, but in which parts were perceived to be most helpful and in which medium was preferred. Audio and full-motion video are clearly not the best media for all information and all learning preferences.

Post-Evaluation Results

The P/LSS sponsors and information systems management strongly value and endorse the concept. There is enormous potential in the systems development sites to have the prototype system enhanced as a tool and made available to multiple users. Richard Scott, IBM Education, who was a part of the prototype team, says, "The success of the prototype and the reaction we have from the users, and more importantly the user management, has been fantastic. The concept should prove to be most effective and efficient as we address cycle-time reduction and increased levels of quality in all tasks. The ability to combine support and education with the actual task will allow new levels of productivity in employees of varying levels of skill."

Issues and Learning

Several key learning issues and barriers were surfaced during the development and prototyping:

- Traditional training department measurements, such as student day counts and student/instructor ratios, will probably not be satisfactory if applied as P/LSS measurement.

- Traditions and organization structures that were built around conventional solutions, such as training, must be reevaluated and changed to reflect new development requirements.

- A pervasive vision of P/LSS does not yet exist.

- There are few experienced practitioners in the field. Development resources will need to be grown and their thinking reframed.

- It will be easier to quantify the return on investments from P/LSS than it is from classroom training. This will eventually provide the cost justification that will help accelerate the P/LSS concept through organizations.

- Performance/Learning Support Systems require linkages among and between functional counterparts such as training, documentation, expert systems, system developers, and subject matter experts within an organization.

- Limited models, procedures, and tools are in place for rapid and full development. Their emergence will be critical to exploitation of the concept.

CHAPTER

Justification and Resistance

The first step in selling an organization on electronic performance support systems is to demonstrate business impact.

I recently checked into a hotel. The desk clerk wore a button that read "I'm new, and I'm trying." I'm typically so late and so tired that if *I* wore a button as a guest, it would read, "I'm tired, and I don't give a *#&$!" The immediate impact of his button was to gain my sympathy and, as it turned out, patience, while he fumbled through check-in, finally to be assisted by his coach. This is not the norm for this hotel, but if it were—or if I were waiting on a phone for someone to figure out a transaction, I would do my business elsewhere. I certainly wouldn't *ever* want to see my financial advisor, the underwriter on my property insurance, or the person piloting my flight to Dallas wearing the "I'm new, and I'm trying" button! Believe me, I am not unique in this attitude. To justify an electronic performance support system, the first place to look is at business impact.

Whenever change is proposed, there are always driving and restraining forces. And nothing changes unless there is clear relative advantage associated with the change. In this chapter, we will look at the primary basis for justifying electronic performance support systems (EPSS) over conventional alternatives—and we will examine the major sources of resistance that have surfaced to date. Responses to objections or resistance will be proposed as well.

There are various approaches that could be taken to adopting the EPSS frame of reference. Some net out to we-should-do-it-because-we-can type of argument. Other arguments favor EPSS because of its newness or its trendiness. Some decisions makers will, in fact, make a leap of faith. But in the end, the primary justification must be based on the impact of EPSS on human performance. While there is limited systematic research to date on which to base such decisions, there are straightforward ways to compare the probable effects of EPSS on employee competence.

As will become clear, benefits—and therefore justification—are largely a function of program design, rather than technology. So the understanding of EPSS justification dovetails with the information in the chapter on design. Comparisons must be made with both computerized and non-computerized alternatives because benefits, of course, are relative.

COMPETENCY CURVES, COSTS, AND CONSEQUENCES

In purchasing diamonds, buyers focus on the three C's: clarity, carats, and color. "Buyers" of electronic performance support systems should also adopt three C's: competence, costs, and consequences. One of the necessary conditions for success is to present a clear picture of both the actual current situation and the anticipated outcomes of the EPSS solution. Information must be assembled for

• the current competence curves for the job or task

- the direct and indirect costs associated with formal and on-the-job competence development, and

- the consequences of the various inadequate, adequate, and excellent levels of performance that result.

Competence Curves. Competence develops over time and is a function of both formal *events*, such as training programs, and the informal *experiences and processes* that occur while on the job. The comparison of the activities and outcomes associated with training events, in contrast to the requirements for *learning* that occur over time on the job were developed in Chapter 3. In the process of justifying EPSS, it is crucial to make these general observations *specific* to the job or task at hand that EPSS is being proposed to address.

A picture is, of course, worth a thousand words. And a picture that translates into dollars is worth its weight in gold (as is the developer of such an outcome!). The best way I know to identify both the potential for an EPSS and to sell it is to graphically represent both the current and proposed situations and to plot the dollar costs and consequences associated with each.

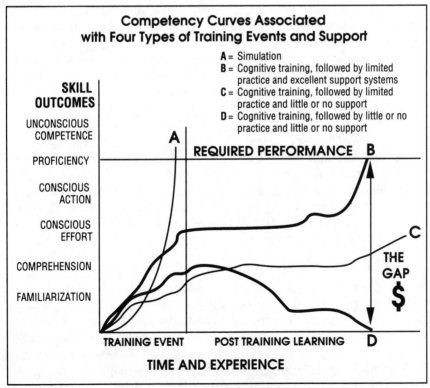

Figure 5.1

Training events are the most commonly implemented tactic for developing knowledge and skill. In Chapter 2, the virtual impossibility of achieving competence within training programs was discussed. Of course, if the training program is a *simulator,* competence can occur. Curve A in Figure 5.1 represents training to proficiency. Typically, this occurs only at enormous expense and is justified for jobs or tasks with enormous human and social consequence such as flying a commercial airplane or operating a nuclear power plant. The more typical outcomes are represented by Curves B, C, and D. These curves are not based on actual measurement, but their shapes do describe what I have seen throughout the history of my consulting experience.

Curve B represents outcomes associated with training that is largely information-transfer oriented with limited and simple task practice, followed by excellent post-training support systems (coaching, information access, positive behavior modeling, and reinforcement).

Curve C represents similar training and limited or inaccessible on-the-job support systems. Typically, learners plateau on a task or job at the level of learning that was achieved during training. For example, computer systems are used at only a very limited level of functionality and implementation. Usually, it takes another training event to change the slope of the curve to head it toward required performance proficiency. When additional learning *does* occur, it occurs in increments and is usually associated with either great learner frustration (following which he or she makes an effort to learn more) or it's the result of intervention by others who observe that things could or should be done better or differently.

Curve D represents the unfortunate situation in which there is limited learning within a training program and the post-training situation results in deterioration of knowledge or skill. This happens when the skill is inadequately developed to begin with (there is limited need to use it, the application of the knowledge or skill is complicated, or the application is not exactly like what was learned in class) and there is inadequate on-the-job support to sustain previous learning levels. This curve commonly occurs when training occurs in advance of need (or adequate learner motivation). For example, when people learn about products or systems long before the need to use the information, they simply forget about it. When the need finally arises, the learners dismiss it and simply go about doing their business the familiar way—selling products they know or performing tasks manually. Sometimes learners have *guilt* about not doing new things, but guilt doesn't typically translate into movement up the learning curve.

Plotting Actual Competency Curves. You should, of course, develop the specific curves associated with task or job competence for your organization. At first, this might seem simple, but it's often difficult because actual competence development can't be summarized with outcomes of a single training event followed by a single period of on-the-job learning. Reality is likely to include combinations of training and experience in sequence. I recommend making the attempt to represent your specific situation, but because that often gets very complicated, I suggest additional alternatives. For example, I find that often simply presenting the generic curves in Figure 5.1 *or* plotting the overall job or skill competence curve as described by credible line managers or new employees is sufficient.

When describing competence with personal computers, for example, it's easy to gain agreement that it takes up to two years to become reasonably proficient at working with the operating system and various types of productivity software. Heads simply nod in affirmation. Or sales managers will readily agree that it takes several years to get a good sales rep who knows products, territory, systems, policy, and good sales process and technique. Be sure to physically plot the acknowledged curves to assure agreement. The physical representation will come into play later in the justification process.

Be sure to:

- use research-based representation when you can—but don't make a career out of ferreting out impossible-to-find information

- establish face validity of your competence curves with credible supervisors, managers, and new employees

- be specific about time-frames to competence (which, in stable situations, typically range from six to twenty-four months, depending on job complexity)

- reinforce the competence curve descriptions with specific anecdotes or quotes from those involved, including customers

- narratively describe performance levels to assure agreement.

A chart can help summarizing knowledge and skill typically represented at certain levels of experience. Table 5.1 illustrates such a description.

Establishing Acceptable Competency Curves. The next step is to establish and plot an acceptable competence curve for the job or skill you have in mind to support with an EPSS. Recognize that managerial fantasy will enter into play here: everyone wants instant outstanding performance. You can manage such expectations, however, so they don't bind you to some unfulfillable fantasy. This curve should be expressed in specifics as it relates to both time and skills. For example, the goal can be defined in terms such as "enabling six-

Table 5.1
LEVELS OF COMPETENCE IN FIELD ENGINEERING

Three Months

Has conceptual understanding of products, repair process, and business practice. Can repair X types of problems in X products without additional support in a single call when problems have been previously diagnosed. Requires additional telephone or peer support on problem diagnosis or repair. Cannot be assigned a, b, or c product or problem situations. Assignments restricted to noncritical customers.

Six Months

Knows and can diagnose and repair Y products. Understands X types of repair processes. Operates with limited additional support on X product class. Requires periodic multiple calls to resolve problems. Assignments resistricted to noncritical customers.

Twelve Months

Knows and can diagnose 60% of product line and 100% of X types of problems. Requires external support or multiple calls on high-end products or X type of problems. Can be assigned critical customer situations when senior field engineers not available. Must verify diagnostics and repair activities with telephone support when working with critical customer situations.

24 Months

Can be assigned any work to be performed on any product. Assigned to critical and difficult customer situations. Assists less experienced staff. Performs telephone support to field on rotational basis.

36 Months

Assigned project development work with product development. Participates in task forces on problem resolution and maintenance procedures. Teaches in schools as required. Assigned supervisory responsibilities for work assignment and staff development.

month employees to perform at the current performance level of eighteen-month employees." This performance acceleration is the ultimate reason for developing EPSS. It will be the basis for economic justification, as you will soon see.

Table 5.1 is just one way of articulating current reality. In organizations where work has already been done in defining job competencies by position or organization level, this will be a simple task. In organizations that represent job performance with titles or responsibilities or by "time in grade" only, this task will be somewhat formidable. It is, however, an important part of lifting the drapery that covers up current unacceptable realities. You will quickly find that adequate and sufficiently placed sponsorship is important, even at this stage of advocacy. There is often strong vested interest in not surfacing the current situation.

COSTS

In the EPSS justification process, there will be a critical need to focus on development and implementation costs such as designing and programming the EPSS itself and assuring adequate hardware and software installations to support its use (if such technology is not already in place). Those costs are treated in the chapter on development. Often, those development costs are compared with the formal, visible, and accepted costs associated with competence development. These include:

Formal Training Costs, including development, delivery, facilities, and student time. Consider classroom training, computer-based training, announcement meetings for new products, system changes, and so forth that occur in either central or site locations, written and self-paced training materials, and so on. Include costs for developer and student salaries, facilities, equipment, materials, production costs, organizational overhead, and so on. The identification of direct training costs is a common practice in organizations, and there are often agreed-on formulas and costs associated with such activity (e.g., student-day costs for training delivery, average student costs for salary and overhead, and so on). Check with the training department for this information. Be sure what you use is consistent with accepted information to avoid death by gunfire from resisters.

Documentation Costs, including development of manuals, announcements, specifications, technical publications, job aids, on-line help systems, and whatever else is published as formal job support materials. Include those developed centrally by those with organizational responsibility for such activity, as well as those that are developed locally by supervisors, trainers, and job incumbents who find the centrally-developed materials unusable. You will likely find there are multiple organizations creating such materials, including product development, information systems, marketing, documentation or technical publications, and other functional groups.

Informal Training Costs are often defrayed by line organizations developing additional training programs to supplement centrally developed and sanctioned programs. You will often find substantial, but "hidden" training program development occurring as the recognition develops that single formal events are inadequate. These informal training events can be actual training programs, or they may be disguised as activities in staff or development meetings which include presentations, role plays, discussions of how to sell, service, repair, etc. The key thing to look for is *time spent in developing employee knowledge or skill that is not associated with specific tasks, sales, or projects* (e.g., developing a specific sales proposal, underwriting a specific risk, and so on).

Formal Support Costs are found in job support functions such as hot lines, help desks, positions or organizations providing technical support to novices or supporting new product introductions, complex problem solving, and so on. Sometimes these are formal organizational units with clear costs associated with staffing, facilities, and management. These formal organizational units also track their activity in units such as number of calls, number of field visits, and so on. Ironically, many help desks measure their success by *increases* in the number of calls, which, in my opinion, indicates *failure*. What success is there in a work force dependent on a support group? Or in inadequate documentation and help systems? Or in computer systems that are inherently unusable?

In identifying formal support costs, also look for *jobs or positions* that are formally structured to do nothing but support novice or inadequate employees. Sometimes those are supervisory jobs, sometimes lead or senior staff. The key thing to look for is whether the people are actually doing productive or value-added work themselves—or if they are exclusively supporting, working with, reworking or compensating (read doing *damage control*) for others' work.

Informal Support, Production and Overhead Costs are harder to find. They occur in the form of peer support, work being performed many times before it's right, inadequate work that must be compensated for informally, and so on. Sometimes these costs are hidden in production realities such as multiple calls per sale or equipment repair, etc. Again, these might be viewed as the "inevitable" costs of incompetence (see Chapter One). The costs, nevertheless, are real and substantial. Document them if you can.

Management Costs. Historically, management span of control has hovered around the one-to-five or one-to-seven ratio. In the pursuit of self-managed teams or independent work groups, senior management is often flattening the organization to limit non-value added activity. The underlying assumption of flat organizational structures, self-managed teams, or self-sufficient employees is either adequate employee competence or adequate performance support systems that don't require excess overhead. Sometimes, a small span of control really reflects compensation for inadequate employee performance. Talk with managers of the work you are considering EPSS for and determine how much time they spend on inadequate employee performance. It will be called coaching, employee development, evaluation, and so on. But it all adds up to hidden support costs. Recently, a manager told me that he spends the bulk of his time on one poor performer. He essentially leaves the excellent employees alone and occasionally monitors the "average" performer. He said "if I had two poor performers, I wouldn't be able to manage at all." This type of support cost is best documented by anecdotal evidence. It will be easier to describe it by comparing it with the benefits and outcomes associated with truly competent employees.

CONSEQUENCES

In building your business case, the final area to research and describe are the *consequences of both performance and non-performance*. In Figure 5.1, the various competence curves are in relation to the horizontal line at the top of the diagram referred to as *Required Performance*. Required performance levels are, of course, a function of organizational standards, competitive requirements, customer expectations, available labor pool alternatives, and so on. The bar may be raised or lowered based on situational circumstances. Whenever there is a *gap*, however, between actual and required performance of a task or job, the gap has associated consequences.

The exact consequences are organization- or job-specific, but they typically fall into the categories listed in Table 5.2, Consequences of Performance Gaps. Each of these gaps has directly related costs in earnings, other business results, customer satisfaction, employee morale, confidence and pride, and so on.

Table 5.2

CONSEQUENCES OF PERFORMANCE GAPS

- **Errors,** the costs of errors and the activity and costs associated with error recovery

- **Inadequate quality** and the associated consequences and costs of achieving adequate quality

- **Inadequate productivity**

- **Increased costs** of goods, services, and related reductions in profitability of sales

- **High overhead support costs** associated with compensatory staffing, small spans of supervisory control, peer support, hot-line support, and so on

- **Turnover, morale, and confidence problems** among inadequate performers and those who work with them

- **Failure to achieve anticipated benefits** from new systems, products, programs, procedures, organizations, methodologies, and so on

- **Other costs,** such as delayed results, lost sales, customer dissatisfaction, limited business growth, delayed product introductions, inability to implement desired business strategy, and so on.

In developing the business case for performance support, the costs associated with non-performance or inadequate performance must be calculated into the justification equation. This is typically a very different cost than is built into training or documentation business cases. These costs are often built into the business cases associated with justification of expert systems development. The reasons are largely related to the rewards and measurement systems and the ability (and sometimes willingness) of training and documentation personnel to connect their activities to results. Often, it is difficult to measure the results of training and documentation. Even more often, there is no direct benefit to training and documentation managers to even attempt such measurement since they are rewarded mostly for *activity*, rather than impact. Measures such as student days, student day costs, course completion rates, facilities utilization levels, numbers of pages of documentation, and so on, prevail. With help desk management, number of calls received and responded to are measured and rewarded, as is the rate at which calls are answered. Rarely, if ever, is any effort placed on determining whether callers can operate independently in the future—or whether they simply continue to call when they have a question. Since most people adjust their performance to focus on what is measured, the *impact* of these activities is never assessed. It is either assumed—or ignored as impossible to determine. In the meantime, the costs of non-performance increase and the benefits of proficient performance aren't achieved. Perfectly fine products are withdrawn from the market when they are not sold— and it is assumed they didn't meet market needs; it's equally possible that they weren't sold because sales reps and customers didn't understand them.

The *benefits* of proficient performance are often the opposite of the consequences of performance gaps, but there are others. A sampling is listed in Table 5.3. You will have to develop a cost-benefits list for the particular task or job you are advocating EPSS to support. Those costs and benefits are the primary part of the EPSS justification process.

CRITICALITY, RISK, AND DEPENDENCE

The *criticality* of proficient performance, the *risks* associated with inadequate performance, and the organization's *dependence* on the outcomes of specific performance multiply the costs and benefits. For example, if establishing early market share allows the company to *own* the market, such as happened with Lotus *1-2-3* in the spreadsheet software market, then successful performance at the early stages of product introduction are primary dependencies. Getting to market late—or not quickly penetrating the market—can be the kiss of death in some cases. The risks are simply too high, so EPSS development

Table 5.3
A BENEFITS LAUNDRY LIST FOR ELECTRONIC PERFORMANCE SUPPORT

- Consistent, high-level performance
- Ability to train previously "unreachable" or difficult-to-reach learners
- Accelerated performance and improved rate of learning
- Decreased costs associated with teaching people things they already know and teaching them things they don't need to know
- Increased control over information dissemination and maintenance and its application to performance situations
- Organizational flexibility; ability to assign work to a broader range of individual; ability to reorganize with less concern about existing employee knowledge and skills
- Decreased use of hot-line support by employees or customers
- Decreased product returns, service calls and "call backs" by customer service or field engineers due to improved user competence
- Broader span of management control
- Improved product quality with fewer product returns or less waste of materials
- Rapid integration of new products, systems, services, methodologies, processes, policies, and so on
- Larger volume sales
- Assignment of expert staff to more complex, innovative, or developmental work (vs. using them to support less-expert staff)
- Additional utilization and impact from technological investments
- Ability to truly implement Total Quality Management, self–managed teams, flatter organizational structures, employee empowerment, and other desirable, but difficult-to-implement approaches to organizational effectiveness.

costs pale in relation to the situation's criticality, risk, or organizational dependence. Sponsorship is often simpler to get in critical and high risk cases—but the requirements to actually have an impact on the results take a higher profile as well. Sponsorship is also easier to obtain when the organization is dependent on a particular individual, group, or situation for its success. Watch for these situations. But always be certain that your solution can deliver what is promised. And remember: *manage expectations carefully*—and be sure the EPSS solution is put into perspective with other activities that support the critical situation. While electronic performance support systems can be powerful, they are not a panacea for complex or high-risk circumstances.

Technical Wizardry and Results. It is easy to get attention—and sometimes sponsorship, when interesting and sexy technologies first appear. The wave of energy around multimedia technologies and workstation technologies are examples of such technical attention-getters. Very quickly, however, the power of the hardware or media must be put to relevant use. And the use that has the impact is software design. Pretty pictures will never compensate for inadequate design. And computer-generated sound quickly becomes annoying when it doesn't add value.

Figure 5.2 summarizes the various benefits associated with interactive program designs that range from standalone computer-based training and on-line manuals through sophisticated electronic performance support systems. Obviously, these comparisons can also be made against traditional analog training and support approaches. The benefits simply are greater when individualized interactive technologies are employed. More advanced workstations and technologies can permit, but never guarantee, sophisticated and relevant design that supports user performance. And high-impact solutions can be generated with simple computer terminals operating with mainframe computers. Remember, in EPSS, the power is in the design, not in technological wizardry.

THE SALES CAMPAIGN

Let's be honest. Managers and professionals seriously involved in the business couldn't care less about benefits to the training department. They care about what training does for them. They frankly would prefer never to spend a dime on training for its own sake. And for the most part, the corporate platitudes on desire for employee development are translated into serious commitment only when managers see that the development translates into some meaningful business results. When managers see *business value,* arguments about the relative costs per development and delivery hour completely disappear, and out come the checkbooks. They now see value for the money spent from a *business* rather than a training perspective.

Good sales people know that customers buy benefits and solutions, not features. Sponsors of EPSS buy business payoff, not training process. Just show them what it does for them that's advantageous from their perspective, and you've got the sale and lots of follow-on sales. If you can't show the benefit, be prepared to be making presentations about EPSS's wonderful features for years (if you last that long) and to watch your personal and professional credibility declining with each sexy pitch.

LEVELS OF BENEFIT FOR
FOUR TYPES OF SYSTEMS

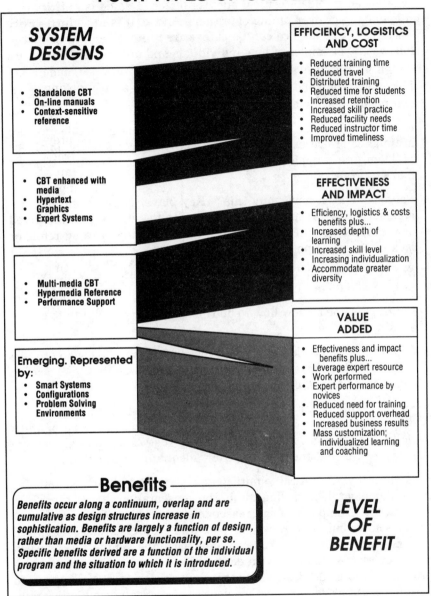

SYSTEM DESIGNS

- Standalone CBT
- On-line manuals
- Context-sensitive reference

EFFICIENCY, LOGISTICS AND COST

- Reduced training time
- Reduced travel
- Distributed training
- Reduced time for students
- Increased retention
- Increased skill practice
- Reduced facility needs
- Reduced instructor time
- Improved timeliness

- CBT enhanced with media
- Hypertext
- Graphics
- Expert Systems

EFFECTIVENESS AND IMPACT

- Efficiency, logistics & costs benefits plus...
- Increased depth of learning
- Increased skill level
- Increasing individualization
- Accommodate greater diversity

- Multi-media CBT
- Hypermedia Reference
- Performance Support

VALUE ADDED

- Effectiveness and impact benefits plus...
- Leverage expert resource
- Work performed
- Expert performance by novices
- Reduced need for training
- Reduced support overhead
- Increased business results
- Mass customization; individualized learning and coaching

Emerging. Represented by:

- Smart Systems
- Configurations
- Problem Solving Environments

Benefits

Benefits occur along a continuum, overlap and are cumulative as design structures increase in sophistication. Benefits are largely a function of design, rather than media or hardware functionality, per se. Specific benefits derived are a function of the individual program and the situation to which it is introduced.

LEVEL OF BENEFIT

Figure 5.2

Sources of Resistance. Of course, good sales people also know that any or all potential buyers are likely to harbor some resistance to what's being sold. A critical success factor in sales is anticipating and managing or overcoming objections. And so it is in selling EPSS. The sources of resistance can be categorized into seven groups. Each is followed by examples of how individuals and organizations who are resisting on this basis express that form of resistance.

- *Logistics.* "We can't get there from here." (Time resource, priority, equipment, technology, etc. are lacking.)

- *Economics.* "We can't afford it." (The money isn't available or there are higher priorities for expenditure. Or, the costs of the business problem aren't apparent—or aren't being measured. But expense budgets are.)

- *Politics.* "They'll never buy this." (Key player support isn't obtainable, largely because of vested interest in the status quo, perceived or real risks, organizational measurement and reward systems, or lack of access to potential sponsors.)

- *Knowledge or Understanding.* "I don't understand what you're talking about" or "I don't see how this will solve our problem."

- *Skills.* "We don't know how to do this. We lack the ability to create such a thing."

- *Feelings.* "I don't like this type of thing." "I wouldn't want to use such a system myself" or "Our customers wouldn't like seeing someone go to the computer for information."

- *Values.* "This is the *wrong* thing to do." "We shouldn't try to support people with machines. Only people can do this type of work well." "This doesn't fit in our culture." "It's wrong to give up hope that we can find the right staff or adequately train them."

Naturally, it's critical to anticipate objections and include material to help manage them during the initial presentations about the EPSS concept. For example, you can reasonably expect that if your organization has never built such a system, potential sponsors or developers will be concerned about skills. You can emphasize the similarities between what you already know how to do, such as design interactive training programs, and EPSS design. For the newer concepts or skills, you can describe specific available methodologies, resources, consultants, training programs, and so on. And you can explain the process that other organizations have followed in developing employee capability.

When budgets are tight, the relative impact of your proposed solutions against other existing or proposed approaches will be the key to managing economic objections.

There are strategies appropriate to the nature and depth of resistance in each of the above categories. If the expressed or anticipated resistance appears value-based, you must either prepare yourself for a long and difficult sale, reexamine whether your timing is right, or try to identify another sponsor whose values and beliefs are more compatible with your proposal. Knowing your buyer and framing your presentation in relation to the various buying audiences is key.

Naturally, the more incompatible your solution is to the current culture, expectations, measurement and reward systems, organization structure, and power bases, the more difficult the sale. You can tolerate, manage, or overpower resisters. The strategies and tactics available to you are a function of your organizational level, responsibilities, role, credibility, and relationships. If you are a potential senior management sponsor, you have options that are not available to advocates at lower organizational levels. Always, it's best to avoid steamrolling resistance. The most powerful tactics available to you are:

- education

- demonstration

- case study descriptions on similar industry or functional applications

- reframing resisters' thinking to expand their point of view and have them see how your proposal is *compatible* with their goals, objectives, measurement systems, skills, responsibilities, power bases, needs for visibility, etc. (in other words, *enable* them)

- involvement of key influence leaders.

Of course, the most powerful options are the existing organizational reward systems that are administered by sponsors. This loops us back to the requirement of focusing on sponsorship. It's critical to understand that with the right sponsor and the sponsor's commitment to the EPSS vision and implementation, much resistance disappears!

CHAPTER

Sponsorship and Critical Success Factors

Your electronic performance
support system is more likely
to be wrecked by politics and
inadequate project management
than technical difficulties.
Make sure your organization is
ready for it.

Many people want to concentrate exclusively on design, performance, or technological aspects of support systems. Each of these is important, but none should be considered at the expense of establishing proper sponsorship for the concept. There is a reason the chapter on sponsorship comes before the chapter on development in this book. If your organization does not "buy" an eletronic performance support systems (EPSS) project, it simply will not happen.

Gaining Sponsorship for Performance Support. Whenever there are new undertakings proposed in an organization, the first critical step is to obtain an adequate level of sponsorship for the activity or project. *Sponsorship* is defined as the political, logistical, and economic *funding* of an activity. Because of its newness, the investment it represents, and its political and business implications, electronic performance support requires such sponsorship.

Essentially, the advocate of the EPSS concept must identify the individual(s) or group(s) who are in a position to provide such funding. The sponsor(s) must be at a high enough organizational level and position to control the resources (and establish the priorities) so that the strategy or project may proceed.

To the extent that the advocate's goal is strategic and involves changing organization *direction*, rather than simply developing an individual EPSS project, the sponsorship must be at a higher organizational level and involve multiple units in the organization. Inexperienced advocates sometimes think that getting dollars in the budget is all they must do. That's an incomplete, and somewhat naive, view. Experienced advocates know that they must build other support as well. Developing adequate commitment levels and securing appropriate levels of public and private political support at the right organizational levels and in the proper organizational units is one of the most critical success factors associated with EPSS.

Key Roles in Introducing Change. Introducing the concept of electronic performance support is essentially introducing change to an organization. It requires new technology, new roles and responsibilities, new skills, and a different development process (i.e., software development is superimposed on the traditional development methodologies of documentation and training). Unless all of the traditional support functions (technical publications, training, help desks, and expert systems development) are located in a single organizational unit, development of EPSS will involve multiple departments and multiple professional fields. In some cases, significant amounts of power and control are at stake: at some point, it must be decided which group will have corporate responsibility for decision-making about EPSS direction, technology, standards, use, staff, and so on. Companies and departments differ. In some organizations, no one wants to touch EPSS because of the real or perceived risks involved. In yet others, no one cares enough to even become involved in a discussion about it. In still others, everyone wants to be in charge.

Let's look at the general roles involved in planning the EPSS change:

Sponsor. The individual or group in control of the logistical, political, and economic resources necessary to implement the change.

Change Agent. The individual or group charged with implementing the change.

Target. The individual or group that must change or adopt and utilize the change.

Advocate. An individual or group trying to get sponsorship.

These seem straightforward enough when looked at in the abstract. The reality in most business or government organizations, however, is that these roles are overlapping and not always clear (see Figure 6.1). And when roles are unclear, or people involved don't understand that their roles are shifting, the right behaviors aren't likely to occur systematically.

In large, complex organizations, the necessary players are frequently in different departments with different sponsors. And training, documentation, or data processing functions (typically the sources of EPSS advocacy!) are fragmented and decentralized (i.e., there's sales training, management training, product training, and procedures training—and often responsibility for documentation is diffused throughout the organization as well). Individuals involved in expert systems development can either be in a centralized artificial intelligence group or, increasingly, be domain experts in line departments who are working with expert systems shells. Typically, individuals, managers, or even directors within any of these functional groups lack the ability or credibility to sponsor EPSS other than in their own organizational units (or, possibly, working with an individual internal customer or department on a given project). For example, the data processing department might have economic resources like a budget for software development tools or staff, but it cannot initiate an EPSS project to support a specific business need without line management approval and involvement. Or the training department can initiate and sponsor an EPSS project for a given need, but it may not be permitted to acquire certain types of software without review and approval by information systems. In some cases, corporate licenses for tools used in EPSS development (hypertext tools, authoring systems, and so on) are controlled by the unit that originally purchased the software. When another unit wants to use the software or wants to purchase a *different* tool, the fray begins!

CRITICAL ROLES IN THE CHANGE PROCESS

Change Sponsor   Individual/group that *legitimizes* the change.

Change Agent   Individual/group that is responsible for *implementing* the change.

Change Target   Individual/group that must actually *change*.

Change Advocate   Individual/group who wants to achieve a change, but who *lacks sufficient sponsorship.*

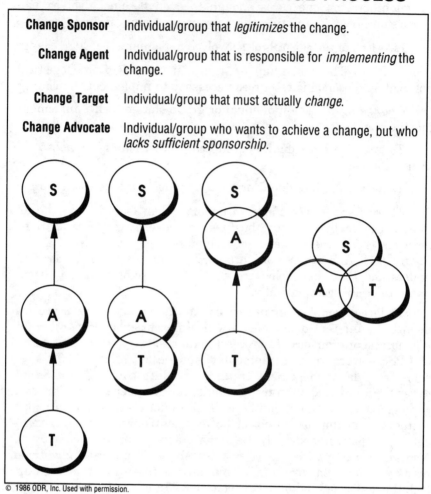

Figure 6.1

Understanding and Leveraging the Relationships. Figure 6.2 graphically depicts the three primary types of relationships in introducing and managing change: (1) the linear or "hierarchical" relationship, (2) the triangular or "staff" type of relationship, and (3) the square or "matrix" relationship.

If you advocate EPSS (or if you are a sponsor within one part of an organization, such as corporate training, trying to get sponsorship in another organizational unit, such as a line department or peer staff unit) you must understand your role. In any given situation, you might be a sponsor, a change agent, or an advocate. In addition to

THREE BASIC RELATIONSHIPS
IN THE CHANGE PROCESS

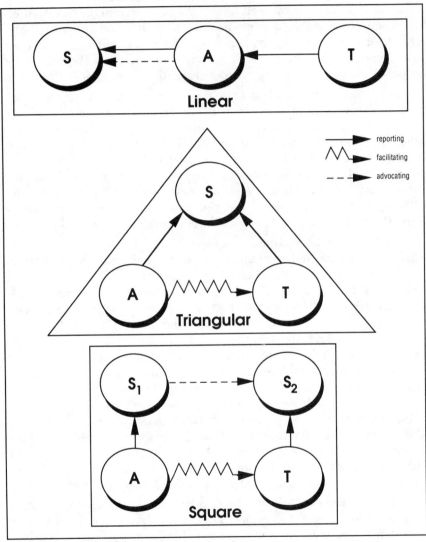

Figure 6.2

understanding the roles, however, you must understand the structure
of the organizational relationship you are involved in (i.e., linear,
triangular, or square) to leverage the time and resources you expend
in trying to build commitment. These organizational relationships are
described below.

To build commitments, you must become a *change facilitator.* What are the characteristics of the effective change facilitator? First of all, he or she is comfortable with the organization's overall business. If you simply consider yourself a training professional (or information systems professional or documentation specialist) and never give any real thought to banking, travel, government, or whatever business your organization is in, you will never be able to exert the necessary influence on upper levels of management to secure sponsorship.

Next, the change facilitator is a *manager;* that is, he or she must be comfortable in a realm where departmental objectives (and certainly individual objectives) are often in conflict. As a change facilitator, you must thoroughly understand the relationships between training, business decisions, and management principles. Finally, you must be multidisciplinary, operating equally well in the technical-procedural and human relations environments. You must know what the EPSS systems are capable of, but you must also know how to understand the personal interests of your targets and how to appeal to them.

The Linear Structure. The easiest organizational structure in which to advocate and implement electronic performance support is the linear organizational structure. In that structure, the sponsor can make all of the decisions and fund them—and has the resources (reporting directly to him or her) with which to implement them. The EPSS advocate needs only to convince the sponsor that EPSS is a good idea and worth the trip. Once that sponsor is committed, he or she can direct and institutionalize activities moving toward EPSS development and implementation (e.g., building it into objectives, funding it with budget dollars, establishing its priority in relation to other objectives, and publicly and privately wielding political might). Naturally, sponsors usually work to build commitment among those who report to them who must carry out the task of implementing EPSS so that full enthusiasm prevails. But when resistance is encountered within a sponsor's chain of command, there are always rewards, incentives, pressures, and sanctions available to increase momentum.

Consider the example of an EPSS integrated within applications software. When the EPSS project is advocated and sponsored within the information systems group responsible for the systems development project, it is not difficult to get the required resources involved at appropriate stages of development. When information systems must involve end users with content or expert system development—or when client organizations must *pay,* things get more complex.

Whenever possible, working within a linear structure is the way to go, because it's politically simplest, since ultimately all of us within organizations play to the priorities of the people we report to if we want to survive and prosper. But frequently the EPSS advocate, or the person who has been charged with implementing EPSS across organizational lines (such as the EPSS staff person or department), must work from outside the organizational structure he or she wishes to influence. That makes things much more interesting (read "difficult").

The Staff or Triangular Relationship. This relationship will be clear from an example. Suppose you are the EPSS change agent ("A" in the chart in Figure 6.2) and you report to a sponsor who says, "EPSS Change Agent, get Lee (the 'T,' or Target, in Figure 6.2) to develop an EPSS." Now Lee reports to your sponsor, but not to you. Unless your sponsor tells Lee that it's something that he (the sponsor) wants Lee to do, you are reduced to persuasion, political debt, or charisma to get Lee to develop or implement EPSS—unless Lee was already planning to do it. I wouldn't count on such a coincidence.

Let's revisit the integration of EPSS within applications software discussed earlier. A line department has commissioned applications software development and wishes to integrate EPSS within that software that includes *job task or business information* in the infobase and advisory systems—and not just systems-related information and support. The information systems department which does not report to the line department resists it. The line department (Advocate) will not be successful unless it convinces their shared management (the Sponsor) to allocate resources and require the information systems department to participate. In the opposite situation, where systems is advocating such integration of business information and the documentation group within the line department resists, the information systems group must get *either* line department management or their shared management to sponsor the effort.

Key rules in the Triangular structure type of situation:

1. Be certain the sponsor communicates expectations to the target and clearly legitimizes your change agent as a facilitator, educator, doer, or what ever else is involved.

2. Get the ground rules clear on which of you is responsible for what (e.g, technical development, subject matter expertise, project identification). Use your organization's standard procedures to ensure that responsibilities, expectations, time frames, and accountabilities are fulfilled. For example, if your organization operates with formal written performance plans or objectives, be sure EPSS is included. If a simple memo does it normally, use one. Include results in your business activity reporting.

3. If the target's priorities shift or interest wanes, but yours aren't changed by the sponsor accordingly, know when to go back to the sponsor for political, logistical, or economic support. Of course, it's

best to work one-to-one with the target. If you can't make progress, however, you have no way of reestablishing momentum: the target doesn't report to you.

4. If you don't have adequate sponsorship, you have four choices: educate your sponsor, get a new sponsor, try to get out of the assignment, or prepare for failure in the form of your expending a lot of effort with little or no meaningful result. Sorry, I wish there were another message. But there's not.

Frankly, savvy staff people try to assess the adequacy of sponsor commitment before they take on the task. They don't confuse positive comments from a prospective sponsor with the ability and willingness to fund the project logistically, politically, and economically. Less sophisticated, inexperienced, or overeager EPSS advocates take any interest—or even a request to "do something with EPSS around here" at its face value. Staff people, who typically lack traditional forms of organizational power, naively jump at anything that smacks of power. Be cautious and careful. And remember, the first thing to do is to accurately assess sponsor commitment levels (see Table 6.1).

The Matrix or Square Relationship. The matrixed sponsor, agent, target, and advocate relationship just complicates things further. Here's an example of this type of situation: The DP training manager has developed and implemented various performance support systems within her organization and has been successful in improving systems utilization and decreasing system support costs. She appoints someone (EPSS change agent) to get trainers in another area, like sales training, to use EPSS. The sales trainer doesn't report to, and may never have even heard of, the DP training manager. An EPSS change agent on a suicide mission runs over and tries to get the sales trainer to deal with the EPSS agenda (which, typically, is built into the EPSS change agent's objectives). It's a complete waste of time unless, as mentioned earlier, the sales trainer is predisposed and willing to accept the EPSS change agent's help, the sales trainer owes something politically to the EPSS change agent, or the EPSS change agent is so charismatic that anything he suggests to anyone is done right away. If so much charisma existed, my guess is that person would be in politics or in a very powerful management or sales job— not slaving away at the middle level of an organization like the rest of us only slightly charismatic folks.

For this scenario to work out well, the EPSS change agent must convince his manager (sponsor) to serve as an advocate to the sponsor in the *sales* department, thus building his or her commitment to EPSS and the things necessary to accomplish it. The situation is similar to the tale above. Without the ability and willingness to truly sponsor something within a chain of command where the sponsor can use

Table 6.1

SPONSOR COMMITMENT DIMENSIONS

The following dimensions must be assessed to determine EPSS sponsor commitment. The more the sponsor understands and feels about these issues, the greater the commitment.

Dimensions are not weighted equally. You must factor in relative importance in relation to both the situation and the sponsor's value system.

When commitment is not adequate, your strategy must include tactics to increase sponsor commitment on the more important (or the majority) of the dimensions. Only with adequate commitment will you succeed.

1. **Sponsor Dissatisfaction with the Status Quo.** The degree to which the sponsor is dissatisfied with current or anticipated performance.

2. **Vision of the Desired State Employing EPSS.** The clarity of the sponsor's vision of what EPSS will look like, cost, and how it will be administered. Your sales strategy will be even more effective if it addresses the reasons behind the prospective sponsor's dissatisfaction with the present situation.

3. **Need for the Change.** The degree to which the sponsor feels that EPSS is needed (versus simply useful, nice to have, or not necessary).

4. **Resources Necessary for EPSS.** The degree to which the sponsor understands the organizational resources (time, money, people, and so on) required for successful implementation of EPSS, and to which he or she is able and willing to commit what is necessary.

5. **Organizational Impact.** The degree to which the sponsor understands the true effects of EPSS on the organization and performance.

6. **Human Impact of EPSS.** The degree to which the sponsor can appreciate and empathize with what the people involved with developing and using EPSS are being asked to change about the way they operate.

7. **Scope of the Change Associated with EPSS.** The depth of the sponsor's understanding of the size of the group to be affected by EPSS.

8. **Sponsor's Public Role.** The degree to which the sponsor is able and willing to demonstrate the type of public support necessary to convey strong organizational commitment to EPSS.

9. **Sponsor's Private Role.** The degree to which the sponsor is able and willing to meet privately with key individuals or groups in order to convey strong personal support for EPSS.

10. **Consequence Management.** The degree to which the sponsor is able and willing to promptly reward those who facilitate the implementation of EPSS or to punish those who inhibit it.

11. **Monitoring Activities.** The degree to which the sponsor will assure the establishment of monitoring procedures that will track progress or problems occurring during EPSS's development and implementation.

12. **Importance of Sacrifice.** The degree to which the sponsor realizes that he or she may pay a personal, political, or organizational price for implementing EPSS; the degree to which he or she will support EPSS despite the costs.

13. **Sustained Support.** The degree to which the sponsor demonstrates consistent, sustained support for EPSS and rejects any course of action with short-term benefits if it is inconsistent with the EPSS implementation.

incentives, rewards, pressures, and sanctions toward a given objective, the EPSS change agent is better off going to the beach. Nothing is likely to happen in the organization without that sponsorship.

Evaluating Sponsor Commitment Levels. There are thirteen key dimensions of sponsor commitment to EPSS, or to anything else, for that matter. Think in terms of these dimensions when assessing sponsor effectiveness. The greater the number and intensity of these factors, the greater the commitment. Table 6.1 lists the dimensions. If commitment levels are low or inadequate to the EPSS development or implementation task at hand, you can use various strategies to build commitment by focusing on the most critical of the items listed in the chart. Not all are equally important, so you'll have to make some subjective assessments of the key factors with each individual in your organization. Understanding the specific areas that are lacking is an excellent first start at picking a commitment-building strategy that is likely to pay off.

Remember, no one sponsors a change—particularly an unfamiliar one—unless he or she sees sufficient benefit to make necessary risks worthwhile. Building commitment is an educational and sales activity (see the chapter on justification).

GAINING MOMENTUM: CRITICAL SUCCESS FACTORS

Each organization is different, of course. Gaining and maintaining momentum for any innovation is not easy. Some organizations never jump on the bandwagon; others fail to keep it rolling once they've begun. I've seen lots of activity but little movement in many places. For example, development tools are installed but not used. A pilot project is begun and is not finished, or it's completed, but it's laid to rest and not used to expand application of the concept. Or EPSS development is put in performance and business plans, but every year there's a reason for not doing it. Most frequently, performance support doesn't progress because sponsorship is inadequate, not coming from the right sources, or both (see the beginning of this chapter). This inertia can occur even when benefits are clear and definable. Often, the feelings of lack of control over *both* development *and* the political factors associated with multi-departmental development efforts are the things that hold sponsors back. Understand and carefully manage the critical success factors associated with EPSS.

Risks and Control Mechanisms. Every undertaking in life has risks. Risks are the most tangible in physical activities such as sports where injury (or even death) is possible, especially when those involved are inexperienced and the challenge is great, like in mountain climbing or skydiving. In organizational life also, risks are everywhere, although they are not as obvious as a cliff face.

When new activities such as EPSS development are undertaken, the risks are personal, political, and financial. Aside from the general risks detailed below, the fact that few people are *requesting* performance support systems adds risk to the situation. Since the concept is new, it must be sold. Often sponsors are requesting traditional solutions, even though they might not be adequate. In new situations reputations are at stake. Credibility can increase or decline based on the outcomes. Business results can suffer if adequate systems are not delivered for such critical efforts as new systems installations, improving business results, and so on. And all involved can be hurt. In addition, when we are at risk, anxiety increases dramatically. Not a pleasant working situation, to say the least: tensions and tempers rise, management controls tighten, and so on.

For those learning new and risky sports, instructors frequently teach basic competency and survival or risk-management techniques very early on. They also emphasize the control mechanisms so that the new learners don't give up because they feel overwhelmed or not in control. For example, in skiing you're taught the snowplow to slow yourself down. You're also taught how to fall. Usually these instructions occur on nearly-flat ground or on the "bunny" slope. In whitewater kayaking, you're taught how to right yourself while still in the kayak. You learn this in a swimming pool—not in a cold and raging river with rocks in every direction. In skydiving, there's a reserve chute that automatically opens.

Performance support system development is often a *team*, not an individual sport. In high-risk team activities, coaches initially focus on developing a team and a clear understanding of the members' interdependencies. When the EPSS development team is under a single sponsor and manager, that team focus can be easily accomplished. When the team members are in different organizational structures, it is much more difficult to accomplish.

Beyond the basic survival techniques, every sport also has control mechanisms and "tricks of the trade": in ice skating, edges give control; in bicycling, it's cadence; in running, it's pace. Control mechanisms exist in EPSS development also. One of the difficulties experienced by organizations getting started is identifying and developing proper sponsorship and in identifying and establishing control mechanisms. Often, they reject the task itself, or they spin their wheels in unproductive activity trying to avoid them.

In my experience, many EPSS activists have initial or ongoing feelings of lack of control. Those who stay with it learn that the way to decrease anxiety and increase control (and consequent quality, timeliness, and cost effectiveness) is to identify the controllable variables and reduce the uncertainty associated with them. Let's look at the critical control mechanisms now.

EPSS Management Control Mechanisms. There are several primary control mechanisms associated with the EPSS development process that, when consciously and carefully managed, increase the likelihood of quality and timely system development. Most of these control mechanisms are discussed in detail in the following chapters. I've combined them here to place a managerial perspective on them.

Assuring Adequate and Appropriate Sponsorship. The most critical and highest-leverage variable to attend to is developing adequate and appropriate sponsorship. Understanding exactly *who* must be committed and sponsor the project should consume your attention. Depending on your organizational structure, as discussed above, you may need an individual sponsor, multiple sponsors, or a *mega*sponsor over several others. Develop that commitment and be sure the commitment is institutionalized in goals and objectives and that activities and results will be monitored.

An additional note about sponsorship during implementation: It is crucial to understand that sponsorship activities must extend beyond system development. Often, advocates and change agents are concerned about getting the project sold *and they hand off the project* to someone else following completion. Electronic performance support systems have considerable impact on those who use them. Much of that impact is positive and enabling. There are those, however, for whom it means reduced autonomy or political significance (a single expert, for example, can be diminished in importance to others). Therefore, they are likely to both personally resist implementation and actively work to subvert confidence with the EPSS. In the chapter on justification and resistance, implementation issues will be treated. But the overriding success factor during both development and implementation is for the sponsor to appropriately administer rewards, incentives, pressures, and sanctions to those involved during both development *and* implementation

Knowledgeable Team Members and Limited Development Team Size. Clearly, having people involved who know what they are doing increases control. I include among these people a project manager and department management with knowledge about what should be done, in what sequence, and so forth. In the chapter on roles, the required knowledge, skills, and characteristics are covered in detail. There's also a discussion of ways to improve them all. In the absence of knowledge or experience within the team itself, it's frequently desirable to employ an expert external resource, such as a consultant, to work with the team at least through its initial EPSS development projects. The fewer people you have with the requisite skills, the more control you achieve, simply because communication is easier. Have enough people—and no more—with enough skill and time.

Clear Roles, Responsibilities, and Accountabilities. Put someone in charge. Define roles and expectations. Clearly articulate the decision-making process. Identify when you want to be involved and establish that you expect questions and discussions when there is conflict among team members, uncertainty as to how to proceed, or need for additional perspectives. "Legitimize" ignorance and establish a requirement that uncertainties be expressed. Make it unacceptable for people to proceed using their own assumptions or when uncertain.

Structured Development Process. Here, the establishment and use of the various structured development processes associated with the types of support components within an electronic performance support system can't be overemphasized (e.g., expert advisory systems, computer-based training sequences, interactive hypertext reference, and so on). This includes clear role definition, steps, quality control points, and evaluation criteria. Structured development is the highest-leverage item available to development managers. The process, including strict adherence to the walkthrough of prototypes and clearly defined deliverables at the end of each phase, is detailed in the chapter on development.

Standards. Establishing, communicating, building commitment to, and enforcing templates and design and interface standards provides up-front control. Such standards also tend to compensate for less experienced development team members and permit partitioning of development to multiple individuals, which can accelerate development times.

Third-party Perspectives: Insurance. Expertise external to the team can be an important quality-control mechanism. Either knowledgeable external EPSS consultants or more experienced EPSS developers or project managers from other groups within the organization can serve as a check on the team's or project manager's self assessments. Consultants can be used for education, advice, review and evaluation, supplementing the project manager, participation at stages where the team could use input (e.g., design phase, establishing standards), technological expertise, and validation of activities such as time and cost estimating, design, technological decisions, development methodology.

Using External Contractors. Sometimes it makes good sense to contract externally for initial or pilot EPSS development. This is particularly true when much up-front work on standards development, structuring a development process, or establishing design conventions needs to be done in addition to designing the system. For contracting to work well, the vendor you hire must have the relevant experience and knowledge. Sometimes vendors have developed excellent user interfaces, navigation techniques and design standards, and structures for other clients. Whenever possible, utilize those designs and conventions and adopt them as your own, unless copyright issues prevent you. At some point you will find that there are only so many approaches to the solution—and you can spend enormous amounts of time on incremental or trivial improvements. If you like what you see, adopt it! In contracting with a vendor to do the initial pilot or system development, you can institutionalize the vendor's design conventions in your application, with permission, of course. Be sure that your intention is clear during the proposal and negotiation phases.

When you contract with external developers, be sure to involve your anticipated internal EPSS developers as active team members to learn from and contribute to the activity. Working with a knowledgeable individual or group is a very good way to decrease risk and get results relatively quickly, even while you are gaining knowledge and getting productive work done.

Understanding and Consciously Making Tradeoffs. In EPSS development, understanding the specific tradeoffs in your situation and consciously analyzing and deciding about them is an important control mechanism. If you don't recognize the tradeoffs, you will make them anyway, but unconsciously.

Tradeoffs will fall into four general categories:

• time spent by the developer vs. time spent by the user

• power versus simplicity

• structure versus freedom

• productivity versus creativity.

There are likely to be others, but these apply specifically when you are selecting technological environments, establishing the content and support components within the EPSS, designing the user interface, determining specificity of standards or the development process, or deciding how rigidly you will enforce standards and process. Careful examination and conscious decision making and communication about desired tradeoffs give you up front control in EPSS development.

Project Scope and Complexity. Limiting the project's size and complexity from the perspective of structure, content, or outcomes can dramatically increase control. Some of the biggest failures I have seen result from the development team biting off more than it can chew while it is simultaneously learning how to develop EPSS and creating the initial EPSS infrastructure (e.g, standards, templates, and so forth). We have a long history of traditional data processing projects to learn from: both complete failures and those that are merely out of control. On the other hand, once you are beyond your initial development efforts, it is important to understand that significant business *impact* of the system might justify increased complexity and risk. Remember, you sold business impact in order to gain adequate project sponsorship. You must deliver it.

The minimum configuration of an electronic performance support system includes an infobase structured in hyper-form, interactive advisory systems, and structured learning sequences. Don't compromise on the choice of these minimal components. Make your tradeoffs within them and limit their complexity or range of alternatives—or limit nonessential interaction with other software.

Adequate sponsorship and close attention to the critical success factors will take you more than half way in your EPSS project.

Note: The material on sponsorship, key organizational roles in implementing a new activity, and commitment building is based on materials and instruments that are a part of the "Managing Organizational Change" training program owned by ODR, Inc., 2900 Chamblee-Tucker Road, Atlanta, Georgia 30341 (404) 455-7145. Models and content are incorporated and reproduced with the permission of ODR, Inc.

CHAPTER

Roles

Whether the development
group is three people or thirty,
there are sixteen distinct roles
to be played in the creation of
an EPSS.

Once the decision to develop and implement an electronic performance support system has been made, a development team must be created. In almost every circumstance, EPSS development is a team activity. While theoretically an individual could create an EPSS, it is unlikely to be the case when a robust system is to be designed, developed, tested, and implemented. This is certainly the case when the system addresses more than a single, simple task and integrates interactive reference, advisory systems, structured learning sequences and, probably, software applications.

It is important to note that differences among and between EPSS designs and the technology platforms they are implemented on makes a single characterization of roles, responsibilities, and methodology incomplete, inadequate, or possibly just wrong. This discussion treats roles, knowledge and skill requirements, individual personal attributes, and responsibilities that cross most integrated EPSS designs.

The number of people and the specific knowledge and skills required for EPSS design and development are determined by the task or job to be supported, the range of users to be accommodated, and the nature and scope of the EPSS design itself. The methodology and the jobs involved in creating an EPSS are similar to those for any development effort: systems design and development, training program development, documentation development, expert system development. The difference, of course, is that all these types of development come together in an EPSS project. The whole is definitely different from the sum of its parts.

FORGING A NEW DISCIPLINE

Some of the traditional roles, such as *domain expert* from the artificial intelligence field and *subject matter expert* from the training and documentation fields are both similar *and* different. For example, a subject matter expert (SME) working with a training unit focuses on *content representation, completeness, and accuracy*. The domain expert working on an expert system development team focuses on content and accuracy, but has the added responsibility of making explicit the *rules and relationships* employed in various analytical and decision making processes. During EPSS development, either or both of the role names can be used. But the activities might be either the same or different, depending on the size of the team and the language chosen by the team manager to express roles. Role labeling is far less important than assuring that the various activities and points of view are represented appropriately at specific stages of the development process.

And the methodologies themselves become somewhat different for a project that combines all those disciplines and that produces something as strange *and* familiar as an EPSS. These differences are explored in detail in in the chapters on EPSS definition and development.

There is a major development process pitfall relating to names. Individuals or managers associated with the original discipline or function from which they came may become preoccupied with terminology.The conflict over names of activities and functions is the visible battleground in the war for control. Don't let the war get started. This is where strong sponsorship will again come into play. The sponsor must require that the team leader forge a new methodology and set of descriptions by mixing and matching. It might even be appropriate to come up with entirely new descriptions or terms, although I don't believe that is usually necessary. Or a sponsor can autocratically decree terminology and minimize the issue by eliminating focus on such things, thus refocusing activities on outcomes and impact. In an extreme case, the sponsor might simply replace difficult people, clearly stating they are unacceptably committed to the past rather than forging future realities.

ROLE IMPLICATIONS

The number and nature of roles in EPSS development do not simply equate the number of people on the team. As a matter of fact, the fewer people, the better. In some situations, two or three individuals must perform all the roles or be certain that someone else does. In other cases, defined responsibilities are divided among several individuals in an EPSS development team. Situations vary enormously and each development team is unique. There are times when you will staff a team with fewer resources and then simply manage the expectations of the sponsor and the organization. The decision to bypass (or inability to include) critical knowledge and skills in the development effort will have consequences for the time, cost, quality, or impact of the system. To the extent a role is not adequately fulfilled, the EPSS product and its impact will suffer.

Using this Information. Managers and individual developers can use the detailed descriptions of activities and critical skills in this chapter to structure development team efforts or to compensate for the limited experience of an individual developer working alone.

The more of the requisite knowledge, skills, experience, and characteristics each of the players brings to his or her role, the more complete the team. Rarely, if ever, does a candidate bring everything to a position. Tradeoffs, as always, are necessary. A strong motivation to achieve in this field often makes up for a lack of experience!

At some point—and the earlier in the development process the better—it's important to assign these roles to people. Then the project manager must make very clear that team members are to respect one another's roles. Without a clear definition of responsibilities, team members will constantly try to redo each others' work, which can add enormously to development time and cost while decimating team morale and cohesion. For example, the programmer can spend considerable time challenging the infobase design, which is clearly not in the programmer role. Such challenges are expensive and not productive. Unless there is a software limitation preventing reasonable implementation of the design, the programmer should not be criticizing component design. Editing is another case. Everybody is an editor, but this is usually more a matter of opinion than qualification. The project manager's responsibility is to clearly state that writers write, designers design, and editors edit. And the editor's word is final unless the changes make the content inaccurate or affect the design structure. Naturally, this role assignment should not preclude reasonable discussion among team members, but the discussions should be focused at early stages of a project or phase, such as during template and standards development. At some point, each person must do his or her own job.

Integrating the Activities and Blending the Backgrounds. Orchestrating and integrating the activities is a critical project management activity. Each of these roles must be filled at one time or another in the EPSS development and delivery process. Typically, however, individuals in given positions play multiple and sometimes overlapping roles. To the extent possible, elements should be institutionalized in job descriptions and performance plans to assure results.

Careful creation of specific expectations, roles, and accountabilities is crucial to the EPSS effort. The EPSS development methodology is the structure through which the roles are integrated. Don't fall into the trap of thinking sound knowledge, skills, and experience are all you need to successfully develop an EPSS. These are necessary but not sufficient inputs. Good process and team management control the outcomes.

EPSS DEVELOPMENT ROLES

The sixteen roles in an EPSS development and implementation effort are project manager, EPSS sponsor or client, designer, subject matter or domain expert, knowledge engineer, writer, editor, programmer, media expert, graphic designer, technical systems expert, development software specialist, data input or entry specialist, user, production administrator, and EPSS implementation specialist. The responsibility for user interface and navigation design is a subtask that may require its own specialists, including human factors specialists or interface designers. That will depend in large part on whether you are working with established conventions (such as Microsoft Windows or the Macintosh) or you feel you need a custom interface.

Let's look at each of the sixteen roles in terms of skills, responsibilities, and activities. Remember, the larger the scope and complexity of the EPSS development and the larger the development group, the greater the probability of more specialization, both in functions and activities. And the larger the particular project, the more likely it is that you'll have several people performing the duties of the same role (i.e., designers specializing in individual components, multiple writers, and so on).

Project Manager. This person oversees and orchestrates the project from beginning to end. In my view, the project manager has the most critical role. The project manager role is most like that of a symphony conductor.

Activities

- Defines project: scope, time frames, responsibilities, schedules, development activities, evaluation criteria, approval process, reporting relationships, accountabilities, budgets

- Selects staff and develops full-time, part-time, or "borrowed" people for particular roles (e.g, content experts to review infobase content or domain experts to evaluate advisory systems), defines roles and has decision-making authority for each team member

- Obtains commitment from managers of team members to permit timely and attentive participation in the project. Logistical and political components must be considered, including building accountabilities into performance plans

- Creates and obtains agreement on the development process, including explicit definitions of deliverables and accountabilities at the end of each phase; communicates the process, procedures, and deliverables to everyone concerned

- Develops and monitors EPSS standards and conventions

- Creates and maintains an atmosphere conducive to creativity and productivity

- Manages communication among and between team members and with the EPSS program sponsor or client

- Manages activities during each development phase, including building consensus or making decisions as the project manager

- Establishes priorities; manages the review, evaluation, and approval of each deliverable; makes or recommends necessary tradeoffs; manages specification changes and modifies or gains agreement on resultant schedule and budget changes

- Negotiates support and enhancements with development software vendor(s)

- Evaluates, obtains, and implements tools and techniques to improve team productivity (anything from hardware and software to groupware, procedures, and work flow)

- Identifies evaluators, establishes evaluation process, and assures that proper evaluation and sign-off occur during each development phase

- With client, defines implementation requirements: hardware, software, communications, administrative process, implementation planning, and so on

- Manages team and client relationships; communicates, manages conflict, recognizes achievements, rewards team members, and so forth.

Knowledge, Skills, and Characteristics
- Team building skills

- Organizational skills

- Communication skills

- Negotiation skills

- Coaching (developmental, performance improvement) skills

- Conflict management skills

- Assertiveness

- Ability to learn quickly and to deal with complex abstractions

- Ability to propose and sell change

- Tolerance for ambiguity and ability to create structure

- Tolerance for pressure and working under deadlines

- Process orientation

- Work-flow management skills

- Ability to set goals and monitor performance

- Ability to handle multiple activities simultaneously

- Listening skills

- Ability to incorporate diverse views into the best solution; problem solving skills

- Task orientation

- Commitment to quality

- Ability to manage detail

- Whole-brained (both creative and analytical) approach

- Knowledge of structured systems design and development, instructional design, documentation development, expert system development, computers and programming management very desirable.

Note: It's *very* unlikely an individual will have all of these backgrounds, which brings us to the final skill requirement...

- Sense of humor.

Program Sponsor or Client. This person authorizes the EPSS's development and provides the logistical, economic, and political support necessary to orchestrate all the variables and the individual involvements necessary for success during *both* development and implementation. Sponsorship is so critical that it warrants a separate chapter in this book (see Chapter Six). In fact, *nothing* happens over time without adequate sponsor commitment and performance.

Activities

- Requests or approves the project

- Allocates necessary resources, including human, economic, technological, logistical

- Politically supports the effort and outcome both publicly (e.g., verbal support, expressed confidence in the project and its outcomes, expectations for its use) and privately (e.g., managing resisters, applying pressure, or administering incentives to key individuals)

- Assures that individuals meet their responsibilities if they are not within direct control of the project manager; requires that the project manager involve him or her as necessary when problems or needs arise

- Negotiates with and secures agreement of sponsors in other organizational units, as necessary

- Provides or delegates the responsibility and authority for input, review, and approval for program specifications and design and development deliverables; assures the program will meet intended objectives

- Monitors project activity from a customer perspective

- Signs off and accepts the program following completion

- Performs post-implementation evaluation in conjunction with project team

- Identifies whether future maintenance will be required; plans for when and how maintenance will be accomplished

- Assures development of adequate implementation plans, including communication, training, and administration

- Institutionalizes utilization of the EPSS in business and performance plans; develops appropriate rewards, incentives, pressures, and sanctions associated with EPSS utilization; monitors system utilization; generates required changes in design, implementation, and utilization

- Assures anticipated benefits are achieved; communicates results to management and serves as advocate for future EPSS development.

Knowledge, Skills, and Characteristics

- Understanding of relevant business needs

- Willingness and ability to use position power and credibility to manage resources and relationships during project activity and to authorize, review, approve, and accept deliverables

- Knowledge of users and criteria for product design and content

- Ability to learn quickly

- Commitment to the EPSS concept and to controlled development.

EPSS Designer(s). This person determines the EPSS organization, capability, structure, infobase content, components, functionality, user interface and navigation, and technological requirements to support identified needs and users.

Activities

- Participates in or conducts business, task, and user analyses to determine needs and requirements

- Develops EPSS objectives

- Evaluates related information, audiences, media requirements, and objectives to develop EPSS specifications

- Designs user interface, navigation mechanisms, infobase organization, required advisory and software support, learning and assessment mechanisms to achieve identified needs

- In conjunction with knowledge engineers, instructional designers, and writers, develops detailed EPSS structure and logic, including specifications for user options, navigation, media, support mechanisms (such as advisors), software functionality, and applications or productivity software elements to be included in the EPSS; articulates specifications to the required level of detail necessary for development and programming

- Works with all team members, including software experts and technical specialists to optimize both program creativity and development productivity

- Designs review and evaluation activities for each development and assessment phase

- Conducts a program qualification with target audience learners; identifies learning obstacles and recommends appropriate revisions.

Knowledge, Skills, and Characteristics

- Experience in developing one or more types of the interactive components within an EPSS (e.g., reference information, advisory systems, training); in the absence of such experience, ability and willingness to learn *very* quickly

- Experience with interactive media and systems development highly desirable

- Creativity; no deep ties to a past paradigm, tradition, process, or procedures; openness to ideas and willingness to expand point of view and incorporate the thinking of other disciplines

- Attention to detail

- Oral and written communication skills

- Strong team skills; commitment to synergy

- Listening skills

- High tolerance for ambiguity

- Ability to create structure

- Ability to work under pressure and deadlines

- Experience with and comfort with software, including various development tools such as hypertext tools, authoring systems, expert system shells, and so on; ability to quickly learn about and use various kinds of software

- Ability to "dig into" technical capabilities of software in order to maximize its capabilities and associated EPSS design

- Familiarity with, or ability to quickly grasp, business, task, or job content

- Ability to compromise

- Ability to accept and incorporate critical comment.

Subject-Matter, Content, or Domain Expert. This person develops or consults on content for the infobase and structure and rules for EPSS advisory systems, interactive training programs, assessments, examples, practice activities, and so on.

Activities

- Employs personal expertise on information content, task requirements, business process and conditions, and methodology required for proficient task or job performance supported by EPSS

- Educates team members as required for development of their part of the system

- Develops, validates, and reviews infobase content and rules/procedures in advisors or other EPSS components

- Reviews all deliverables for technical accuracy, completeness, clarity, and an assessment of whether the approach and content will achieve anticipated support, learning, and assessment objectives

- May be actively involved in the design activity, particularly if he or she has experience in teaching or coaching others in the task, system, or job or is personally an expert performer in the area

- Assists in program testing to respond to challenges related to technical detail.

Knowledge, Skills, and Characteristics

- Adequate knowledge of the domain or content area in relation to the EPSS objectives and the user populations

- Experience and skill in communicating the subject matter, process, and analytical or decision-making rules to others

- Knowledge of the user audiences

- Time and motivation to participate throughout the project

- Strong team skills; commitment to synergy.

Knowledge Engineer. This person constructs EPSS advisory systems to assist users in complex analysis, configuration, classification, decision making or other problems best supported by expert systems. Advisory systems can be rule-based, decision-tree, or other types.

Activities

- Extracts relevant knowledge about procedures, process, rules, and methodology from domain experts

- Designs and constructs advisory systems to perform such tasks

- Programs advisory systems using expert system shells, hypertext tools, or programming languages or communicates programming requirements to the programmer
- Evaluates results and integrates required changes into the system
- Maintains the advisory systems as new knowledge, process, rules, and so on are introduced.

Knowledge, Skills, and Characteristics

- Experience and skill in developing expert systems
- Ability to communicate effectively
- Ability to learn quickly
- Strong team skills; commitment to synergy
- Experience with development tools to be used on the project is very helpful
- Ability to work under pressure and deadlines
- Value for detail and high tolerance for working with it
- Ability to maintain a novice or user perspective about the task or job being supported.

Writer. This person writes infobase content and any other narrative material in the EPSS (e.g., advisory system interactions, practice exercises).

Activities

- Organizes and scripts infobase and EPSS components using established standards and information organization schemes, display templates, and interface conventions
- May participate in establishment of writing and information display standards
- Links, cross-references, or indexes information if design includes hypertext or hypermedia in conjunction with content or domain expert and representative users
- Revises scripts based on editorial, content expert, client, and user comments
- Coordinates with graphic and media specialists to assure alternative expression of information (e.g., a graphic representation of concept, equipment, process; sound representing conditions, etc.)

- Develops specific production notes describing linking, branching instructions, and screen dynamics (such as highlighting, motion, sound) to be executed by the data entry or programming staff

- Maintains content and instruction as changes require.

Knowledge, Skills, and Characteristics

- Ability to write concisely, clearly, and coherently for the visual medium of the screen display

- Ability and willingness to conform to established standards and templates

- Analytical and logical skills

- Attention to and tolerance for detail

- Ability to accept critical comment and incorporate ideas into his or her work

- Ability to assimilate large amounts of information quickly

- Knowledge of, or ability to learn about, the software tools, systems, or the computer programming required to execute designs, scripts, and displays

- Ability to work independently

- Ability to work under pressure and deadlines

- Strong team skills; commitment to synergy; motivation to communicate with other team members

- Flexibility

- Commitment to quality

- Ability to produce large volumes of work in short time periods

- Knowledge of content, job, or task, or experience writing about it very helpful.

Editor(s). This person reviews and edits text, graphics, sound, and images for communication effectiveness. Typically editors specialize in a particular medium, such as video.

Activities

- Reviews, alters, adapts, and refines scripts, images, graphics, and sounds to conform to EPSS standards and to assure clarity and conciseness from user's point of view

- Reviews production notes and programming instructions for completeness, clarity, and appropriateness (last cut before programmer involvement)

- Evaluates appropriateness and clarity of media combinations
- Evaluates user instructions and interfaces for clarity and conformance to standards and conventions.

Knowledge, Skills, and Characteristics
- Editorial experience; editing text, graphics, video, or sound for computer implementation helpful
- Ability to communicate
- Interpersonal and persuasion skills
- Assertiveness
- Ability to operate under pressure and deadlines
- Attention to and tolerance for detail
- Commitment to quality
- Knowledge of the subject area and learner population helpful
- Strong team skills; commitment to synergy.

Programmer. This person prepares executable code or works with development tools such as hypertext or authoring systems to create the actual programs. Consults on the capabilities and limitations of the tools or programming requirements with designers and developers.

Activities
- Educates and consults with project manager, designers, writers, and knowledge engineers on technical requirements for implementing design structures in relation to the development tool or programming language, available time, and ongoing maintenance implications
- Participates in defining and evaluating design alternatives in relation to available software tools; identifies needs and alternatives for tools based on design and user requirements
- Constructs design prototypes, as required
- Recommends alternative design approaches when initial approaches are not feasible or affordable
- Writes project requirements and schedules
- Reviews developer output for required programming and production notes (e.g., branching, screen displays, rules, and so on); assures clarity with writer, instructional designer, knowledge engineer, or other members of the development team

- Develops programming instructions or development tool commands to translate production notes or programming instructions on designs into executable code

- Conducts technical review of the program

- Tests and debugs the program

- Develops and maintains program documentation

- Develops and maintains communication with development tool vendors to resolve system bugs and to request problem resolution and enhancements

- Develops and maintains technical interfaces between software tools (e.g., word processing and authoring system software, graphics packages) to ensure development productivity.

Knowledge, Skills, and Characteristics
- Analytical skills

- Programming skills or knowledge and skills in using development tools, operating system, and specific hardware

- Understanding of programming logic

- Knowledge and skill in systematic software development testing

- Ability to project requirements and schedules

- Orientation to detail

- Communications skills

- Strong team skills; commitment to synergy.

Media or Graphics Expert. This person develops information to be represented in various media included in the EPSS. Media can include sound, graphics, full-motion video, and still images.

Activities
- Consults with designers, developers, and writers on capabilities, limitations, costs, and production requirements of various media

- Participates in the design process, including specification of media to be employed and information to be represented in multimedia form

- Produces or manages media production (e.g., develops video sequences).

Knowledge, Skills, and Characteristics
- Knowledgeable about and comfortable with computers

- Interactive media skills (e.g., graphics, video, audio, print)

- Creativity
- Communications skills
- Ability to operate in a team
- Ability to work under pressure and deadlines
- Ability to accept critical comment and incorporate it into his or her work
- Commitment to quality
- Tolerance for ambiguity and ability to create structure
- Strong team skills; commitment to synergy.

Graphic Designer. The graphic designer is responsible for the visual display of the EPSS and creates graphic views of the information and resources available to users. As graphical computers and multimedia machines become the installed norm, this role will increase in importance. Regardless of equipment used, the visual impact of screen displays, layout, and graphics is critical to effective communication. Involvement of the Graphic Designer should not be limited to the creation of *pictures*. Visual communication is critical; an experienced and skilled graphic sense should be applied throughout the design process.

Activities
- Participates in design of user interface, screen layout and display standards, text formats, and any other design considerations with visual impact
- Identifies EPSS content that would benefit from visual communication
- Designs graphic images and animation sequences to communicate EPSS content information; employs computer generated graphics, animation, still images, and full motion sequences, as appropriate
- Identifies available graphic images or creates and edits graphic images using selected graphics development tools
- Organizes visual database
- Participates in linking of visual images to corresponding text and other media representation.

Knowledge, Skills, and Characteristics
- Graphics and animation design and development knowledge and skill
- Creativity
- Ability to communicate

- Interpersonal and persuasion skills
- Assertiveness
- Ability to operate under pressure and deadlines
- Attention to and tolerance for detail
- Commitment to quality
- Knowledge of the subject area and learner population helpful
- Strong team skills; commitment to synergy.

Technical Specialist. This person assures internal and external technical integration of the EPSS within the organization's technical operating environment, databases, and information systems.

Activities

- Actively participates in establishment of technical specifications for the EPSS, including development software and integration of EPSS itself with existing and planned networks, communications systems, operating systems, hardware, and mainframe computers (if necessary).
- Evaluates development tools in relation to existing and planned technical environments; recommends acceptance, modification, or rejection as appropriate
- Provides technical support to assure access, links, and data exchange with required software and databases
- Identifies and resolves technical problems; develops alternatives if problems cannot be resolved without changes to EPSS or other technologies; recommends EPSS changes if design or implementation cannot be accommodated
- Serves as technical liaison with vendor(s) and internal development staff.

Knowledge, Skills, and Characteristics

- In-depth understanding of EPSS concepts, design, and technological requirements
- Strong commitment to EPSS
- In-depth knowledge of existing and planned technological environments and systems and communications architecture
- Established relationships and credibility with internal technical staff and technical management and software vendors
- Flexibility

- Creativity

- Strong team player; commitment to synergy.

Development Software Specialist. There will be numerous software development tools employed in constructing an EPSS. It's important that knowledge and skill in these tools is available and employed to be sure that design is neither limited nor expanded unrealistically in relation to tool capabilities, limitations, and programming or development requirements. The greater the tool expertise, the better the outcome—and the more quickly the EPSS will be produced. Many people on the team will be familiar with or know various software tools to varying degrees. Incomplete knowledge and skill will result in sub-optimal design and development. At a minimum, consultation with software tool experts is necessary. At best, experts should be assigned to the EPSS development team.

Activities

- Educates team members in software development tool capabilities, limitations, and programming requirements

- Participates in design activities with a responsibility for both expanding and limiting design alternatives in relationship to tool capabilities, limitations, and programming requirements

- Programs and implements design using available tools

- Structures macros, programs, templates, and other appropriate structures to be used by other team members in designing and constructing their output and deliverables; maximizes team productivity in design or software tools use

- May recommend tool evaluation and acquisition

- Develops and maintains relationships with software tool vendors, user groups, other users, technical specialists on other tools, networks, computer environments, and so on

- Identifies and resolves technical problems in development, implementation, and integration of tools.

Knowledge, Skills, and Characteristics

- Strong technical skills; knowledge and skill in installed software tools to be used on the project is very helpful

- Ability to learn quickly

- Strong team skills; commitment to synergy

- Articulate

- Ability to work under pressure and deadlines

- Understanding of the value of detail and high tolerance for working with it.

Data Entry Specialist. This person feeds the scripts, rules, graphics, sounds, and so on into the development tools.

Activities

- Enters program scripts into software tools, including programming instructions, if appropriate. Typically data entry specialists are familiar with a particular set of development tools or media.

Knowledge, Skills, and Characteristics

- Knows or can quickly learn development tools and how to execute program specifications or enter information into the tool(s)

- Operates independently

- Pays attention to and tolerates detail.

User. This person represents the intended audience and tests the effectiveness of the EPSS program. Several users are needed.

Activities

- Reviews and evaluates EPSS programs and provides feedback to developers

- Participates in the design, content, advisory system, or script reviews, as possible, to evaluate interface, approach, and specific content from a learner perspective

- Identifies confusing areas in interface and EPSS

- Identifies irrelevant or missing content or support mechanisms.

Knowledge, Skills, and Characteristics

- Representative of the user population

- Commitment to the project

- Communications skills

- Strong team player; commitment to synergy.

Production Administrator. Requirements for the Production Administrator will vary based on the technology used, geographic dispersion of users and delivery computers, data communications network availability, and the number and frequency of changes to the EPSS. Development of an effective EPSS is a necessary condition. Adding effective production and implementation activities is critical to EPSS distribution, use, and maintenance. Don't underestimate the importance of this position.

Activities

- Creates or manages the physical creation of required copies of the EPSS
- Assures appropriate and efficient use of computer storage, media, and data communications facilities
- Develops distribution and maintenance processes and procedures
- Develops packaging as required
- Develops instructions for implementation in geographically dispersed locations, including installation, configuration, technical support, maintenance, instructions for use, etc.
- May develop written or other announcement communications alone or with others on the development team
- Assures distribution and maintenance of EPSS in standalone or networked environments
- Provides troubleshooting and support to users or user management or technical personnel, as appropriate.

Knowledge, Skills, and Characteristics

- Well organized; ability to create structure
- Understanding of the value of detail and high tolerance for working with it
- Knowledge and skill in software reproduction, maintenance, distribution, networking, packaging, costs, storage media alternatives
- Understanding of the organization structure, locations, distribution systems, and technological environments helpful
- Strong team skills; commitment to synergy
- Ability to communicate effectively
- Ability to work under pressure and deadlines.

Implementation Specialist. This person oversees the actual production, distribution, and implementation of the EPSS.

Activities

- Produces or manages the production of program materials, including diskettes, tapes, print, and packaging
- Develops appropriate communication programs and implementation plans; assures that EPSS training, if appropriate, occurs
- Distributes program materials or oversees installation of EPSS systems and updates on individual computers or networks

- Maintains appropriate inventories or versions of product
- Manages production budgets and costs.

Knowledge, Skills, and Characteristics
- Organizational skills
- Communication skills
- Attention to detail
- Ability to work in a team
- Knowledge of production techniques
- Commitment to quality.

CHAPTER

Development and Implementation

No matter what technologies
you are using or what activity
you are trying to support, the
main issues in system
development are always more
organizational than technical.

I have tried to make the point in this book that EPSS is a concept, not a technology. It takes advantage of whatever technologies are appropriate to the delivery of support when and where it's needed and in the form it's needed. There are certain technologies—hypermedia, expert systems, text management, audio and video display, relational database management—that turn up frequently in EPSS implementations. But this concept is not limited to any machine, technique, or architecture.

It is therefore difficult to define a detailed development methodology for EPSS. Any one of the component technologies can boast one or more development methodologies, complete with action steps, deliverables, testing methods, and so on.

There is a standard development methodology, however, and it is usually described as having eight overlapping and iterative phases:

- Needs analysis

- High-level design, including prototyping

- Detailed design, including detailed prototyping

- Development

- Testing

- Revision

- Implementation

- Post-implementation evaluation.

These steps seem to be appropriate whether the ultimate product is a training program, an on-line transaction processing system, an orientation film, or a procedures manual. They are appropriate for EPSS, too. Beyond that, however, development methodologies vary, and it is enough for you to know at this point that you will need to make the acquaintance of a new methodology for each of the technological components in your EPSS.

What I intend to do here is give you guidelines and considerations for structuring your activities, commencing with needs analysis. As described in Chapter Four and in the introduction to the case studies, the focus of the needs analysis cannot be simply *tasks, content, or processes*. Those things are, of course, important, but the focus of the entire analysis and planning phase must be the *needs of the performer or learner in relation to the tasks, content, or processes.* In other words, the first questions to ask are how will the learners view the situation? What questions will they ask? What are their requirements? What must be available to them to respond to their needs, questions, and requirements? I refer you to Figure 4.1, The Face of a Complex Task (page 33) to review the situation.

Table 8.1 summarizes a general approach to developing EPSS that was created by Comware, Inc. of Cincinnati, Ohio, a leading developer of electronic performance support systems. Comware calls its products Knowledge Support Systems or *KSS*. Theirs is a useful general description of the process that helps first-time users know what to expect.

GUIDELINES AND CONSIDERATIONS

The following guidelines, considerations, and questions are offered:

Agree on process sequence. Recognize that the development process can be both linear and sequential *and* parallel. For example, once you've defined graphics requirements, development of the graphics database can occur even though all work on system functionality and content has not been defined in detail.

Agree on deliverables. The development process and deliverables will be structured differently for different projects based on what form information is currently in, developer skills and experience, tools, and so on. Issues that must be addressed and represented include:

- Who is the user audience and what are its characteristics?

- What source materials will be used and who is responsible for them?

- What hardware and software will the EPSS be presented on?

- What will the user interface be?

- What are the components of the EPSS?

- How will users navigate throughout the system and within a given component?

- What components and information can be linked or electronically cross-referenced within the EPSS?

- What are the media requirements for each of the components?

- How will design, functionality, media, and relationships be represented in the various deliverables?

- What software will be accessible from within the EPSS?

- What data will need to be accessed or exchanged when using the EPSS?

- Will users or administrators be able to customize the EPSS to address individual or group needs? If so, what and how will customization occur?

- What standards will be used in text layout, screens, and writing style?

233

Table 8.1

KSS DEVELOPMENT PROCESS OF COMWARE, INC

1. Identify the Need and Goals of the KSS

- What is the global goal or set of goals?
- What are the performance goals?

2. Identify the Audience

- Identify the audience job description(s)
- What are the goals of the audience in relation to the KSS?
- What range of skills does the audience already have?
- Is the audience diverse enough to warrant special design considerations?
- Is the audience too diverse for the creation of a single KSS?

3. Identify the Tasks that Meet the Needs and Goals

- What are the individual tasks required to meet the larger ones?
- What information needs to be available to complete the tasks?
- What information needs to be gathered to complete the tasks?
- How do the tasks interrelate?

4. Match Current Resources to the Tasks

- What information about the tasks is currently available?
- How complete, up-to-date, and accurate is the information?
- What format is the current information in?
- Identify what of the current information can be used in the KSS
- What rework is required of usable information?
- What conversion considerations are there?

5. Identify Additional Resource Needs

- What tasks are lacking resource information?
- How can this information be located/gathered?
- What effort (time, cost, resources) is required to gather this information?

6. Divide Tasks and Resources into Presentation/Learning Media

- Which tasks are best covered in hypertext?
- Which tasks are best covered in CBT?
- Which tasks are best covered in an advisor?

Reproduced with permission of Comware, Inc., Cincinnati, Ohio.

Table 8.1 (Continued)
KSS DEVELOPMENT PROCESS OF COMWARE, INC

7. Define the Relationships Between the Tasks and Media

- How is hypertext linked to the CBT, advisor, and application?
- How is the CBT linked to the advisor, hypertext, and application?
- How is the advisor linked to the hypertext, CBT, and application?

8. Create the Design Document

- Identify all of the previous steps in a formal, authoritative document

9. Convert or Create Resources into Selected Media

- Convert resources identified as usable in Step 4 into the appropriate media
- Create media (scripts) that do not exist in final or near-to-final format
- Multi-tasking environment (all this can be happening simultaneously)
- Involves many development/writing skill sets

10. Development of Media Components into a KSS

- Complete any custom programming
- Create on-line hypertext component
- Create on-line CBT component
- Create on-line advisor component
- Previous four are simultaneous
- Link components into KSS
- Testing

Reproduced with permission of Comware, Inc., Cincinnati, Ohio.

- Will templates be used to assure conformance to standards?

- What controls and access limitations are necessary to maintain security and proper utilization?

- What schedules and timetables exist for the project?

- What are the objectives for each deliverable?

- Who will review and approve deliverables?

Some deliverables can only be designed following completion of the tasks listed below. In fact, they may look like design questions. Deliverable definition is not an entirely clean and sequential process; often it's *very* messy. Those with a need for certainty and *neatness* may have a hard time about now.

There are as many deliverable designs and structures as there are developers. Figures 8.1 through 8.4 represent samples of various deliverables. These are simply snippets for your use and by no means an exhaustive sampling. Search out samples from vendors and other EPSS developers. And then create your own based on the nature of your application and the tools you will use.

Determine who should be involved at each of the development stages. Actively involve appropriate individuals and groups in providing input to the design and content of the EPSS. Depending on the EPSS nature, scope, and technological platforms for delivery, you may need to involve one or all of the following functions:

- Training

- Systems

- Systems training

- Information center

- Help desk

- Union representatives

- Documentation or technical publications

- Expert systems development

- Special interest groups (e.g., customer groups).

Of course, there may be others who should be included, even though not listed above.

Focus on the performer, learner, or user, not on the content, process, system, or anticipated product. I hope I've said enough on this topic in the early chapters of this book.

Describe the range of performers or learners who will be using the EPSS. Describe knowledge, skills, capabilities, computer experience, operating context, and whatever else is relevant. Resist homogenizing the user population into a single irrelevant description. Do not succumb to the pressure or pull to fantasize the mythical user for whom the EPSS will be designed.

Clearly articulate and graphically represent the tasks to be supported. Task analysis is the foundation for the design and development of EPSS. Determine whether the tasks are straightforward and procedural or complex and abstract ones that require cognitive analysis, synthesis, and the manipulation of information employing complex, branched, and interrelated processes. In the latter case, you are likely to have to construct new types of deliverables to represent the processes. Look to the expert systems field for guidance in this area.

Scott Johnson, a professor at University of Illinois at Champaign-Urbana makes considerable progress with this effort in his article, "Cognitive Analysis of Expert and Novice Troubleshooting Performance" (*Performance Improvement Quarterly*, Learning Systems Institute, Florida State University, Volume 1, Number 3, 1988).

Establish and define the performers' requirements for information and support. Continually put yourself in the performer's head and ask "What data, knowledge, or advice do I need to proceed?"

Locate and organize all information, resources, and support mechanisms currently in place to support the performer. For each of these mechanisms, identify where it is, what form it is in, how complete and accurate it is, and who owns it. Determine how helpful it *really* is to people.

Categorize the information required. See Table 4.2 on page 37, "The Seven Basic Types of Information Based on Information Mapping's Method."

Determine the best way to represent each information type. Figure 8.5 is a sample of effective screen structures for each type of Info-Map™ (Barry Raybould, "Building an Electronic Performance Support System: Comparing Alternative Development Platforms," *Proceedings, Eighth Conference on Interactive Instruction Delivery.* Society for Applied Learning Technology: Orlando, Florida, February 1990).

Indicate the modes of presentation that would most quickly result in understanding by various users for each piece of information. Individual pieces of information may, in fact, be represented in more than one mode. Modes include text, fixed or animated graphics (including manipulable images, full-motion video, audio, or still images), and logic (including step charts, flow charts, formulas or scientific notation, and computer programs). See page 37 for further detail on this.

Identify all the software and other tools that performers need, independent of the information, to act on or utilize the data, knowledge, or information presented.

Develop techniques for representing and mapping relationships among and between information type, mode, and task. This representation will likely be complex for all but the most straightforward tasks to be supported. It involves creating relational links for a large, multi-level complex of cross-referenced tasks. The problems in mapping relational information are discussed in detail below.

Consider using computer-assisted software engineering (CASE) tools for representing information and relationships among and between information. There is more discussion about CASE tools below.

Limit investment and risk by conducting frequent and rigorous reviews of analysis and deliverables to date. Be sure that represen-

---

Deliverable: Development Phase

```
[pbww7.20
Headers and Footers
~W use insert include attach add inject alter correct modify
~W transform replace shift edit revise set update
~H 20.6
```

In Word, you can easily insert **headers** or **footers** into your documents. Headers and footers can be static throughout the document or they can be set up so that even-numbered pages have one header and odd-numbered pages have a different one. Because the first page of many documents is handled differently than succeeding pages, you can set up a header and footer that is different for the first page.

The following topics provide information about working with headers and footers:

```
\HOverview of Headers and Footers\H~L7.20.1
\HHeader/Footer Pane and Icon Bar\H~L7.20.2
\HFields in Headers and Footers\H~L7.20.3
\HInserting a Header or Footer\H~L7.20.4
\HCreating a Different Header or Footer for the First
Page\H~L7.20.5
\HEditing a Header or Footer\H~L7.20.6
\HPositioning Headers and Footers\H~L7.20.7
\HAlternating Headers and Footers for Odd and Even Pages\H~L7.20.8
\HAdding Date of Printing, Page Numbers, or Time of
Printing\H~L7.20.9
\HFormatting Page Numbers in the Header or Footer\H~L7.20.10
\HRestoring a Link with the Previous Header or Footer\H~L7.20.11
\HExiting from the Header/Footer Page\H~L7.20.12

[pcww7.20.1
Overview of Headers and Footers
~W describe define explain tell
~H 20.6
```

A header is text or graphics that appears at the top of every page. A footer appears at the bottom of every page. Footers are different from footnotes.

Figure 8.1 illustrates a hypertext deliverable from Ziff Technologies' Word for Windows EPSS (see the case study). The particular type of hypertext was developed by embedding format commands, destinations, and matches in word processed files. The developer must detail:

Courtesy Ziff Technologies

• *Specific hypertext* options (or buttons available to the user by differentiating the word(s) from other word(s) in the text. In this example, the words between the \H marks (\Hxxx xxx xxxxx xxx\H) appear on the screen display in the color red and underlined.

Deliverable: Development Phase (Continued)

• *Destinations for the links.* (i.e., the location of the related information) so, when activated by the user, the appropriate information appears. In this example, ~L is followed by the page number to be invoked when the link is activated.

• *Related information or resources.* In this example, ~H precedes the destination link that will display a menu of related topics, Examples, or Advisor components of the EPSS.

• *Search synonyms.* When users employ the key word query-based search, the system locates synonyms, as well as exact matches. Developers must identify those synonyms and indicate them with a ~W within the text file.

---

tatives of all groups and constituencies that will have an opinion or can block progress actively participate in reviews. Be certain that their management or other sponsors make it clear that the reviews and active participation are a priority.

Prototype, prototype, prototype—including how you represent information and relationships.

Evaluate results with a particular eye toward business impact and improved performance. Tie the evaluation results back to the original basis for justifying EPSS development. See Chapter Five for a discussion of justification.

MISCELLANEOUS ISSUES IN INFORMATION RETRIEVAL DESIGN

Retrieval Techniques

The determination of how users will be able to access, retrieve, and integrate multimedia information is complex and is a discipline in and of itself. The power-simplicity tradeoffs associated with various techniques are significant. Figure 8.6 illustrates the relative power of different retrieval techniques. As an EPSS grows larger in size and scope, it becomes increasingly difficult for users to find the information they need quickly. Providing users with a variety of retrieval techniques *and* alternative access points becomes critical for productivity. Creating mechanisms for browsing or for query-based retrievals—and assuring user orientation during the process—will be one of the major design and development activities of the EPSS project.

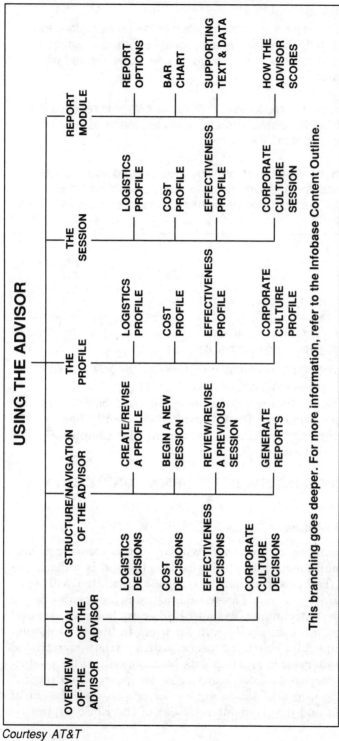

Figure 8.2 is a graphic display of the infobase structure that supports the Advisor functions in the AT&T Training Delivery Consultant (see the case study). These tree structures are a deliverable for use during the design process and are also part of a paper reference to the EPSS so that users can view the framework of the software product if they wish. This tree structure also reflects the fundamental structure of the Advisor component itself (i.e., sessions) and the Advisor outputs (e.g., Corporate Culture Profile, Bar Chart).

Courtesy AT&T

```
A SuperCard Script
on idle
  global howLong, startTime, defaultDrive
  if howLong is not empty then
    If the secs - startTime > howLong then
      repeat while the number of current wds > 1
        close currentWindow(1)
      end repeat
      put the secs into startTime
      visual effect iris close
      if defaultDrive is empty then put getDriveName (the long
      name of  this stack) into defaultDrive
      put defaultDrive & ":Context Information System:CIS Logo"
      into whereGo
      if fileExists (whereGo) then go stack whereGo
      send openStack to this stack
    end if
  end if
  pass idle
end idle
```

Figure 8.3 is a script written in the SuperCard (Silicon Beach Software) extension language. Such scripts are the deliverables that represent the implementation of a detailed design. Note that this is really a programming statement that describes the dynamics of what happens when certain user-initiated or system-initiated behavior occurs. This sample should generate a healthy appreciation for the level of detail required—and the skills that both developers and reviewers of deliverables must possess. The seduction of the "card"-based development tools' simple interface hides the reality of underlying development complexity.
Courtesy Steelcase Inc.

Converting Information

Be sure to avoid the trap of thinking in terms of "converting" information or material from a current analog form into electronic form. On-line information should be organized *differently* than information designed for paper representation. Further, integrating reference information with other EPSS components and linking it in hypermedia form is very different from a simple indexing or cross-referencing task (see my article "Issues in Computer-Based Reference," *CBT Directions*, March 1991). Bielawski and Lewand affirm the point. "One note of caution is that developers should not adopt the original organization structure of a document or a set of graphics if it will limit possibilities of creating a nonlinear approach to the linking of related information. Here lies a question of balance: developers should not feel obliged to generate a new informational structure based on hypermedia if an existing structure can simply be enhanced

241

INSTRUCTIONS TO EPSS TESTERS
Project name/number: _____
Project manager: _____
Tester's name: _____
Date testing should begin: _____
Anticipated completion date: _____

Comments: The project manager should sit down with the tester for
the first hour of testing to point out project-specific "catches."
- -
TO THE TESTER

The following passes should be done separately. Never combine
them; doing so will cause you to miss problems.

During each pass, used the attached testing sheets to identify
problems. Mark the sheets with the number of the window on which
the problem/problems occurred and give a brief description of the
problem. It is essential that you keep track of the screens by
number--you will never be able to remember where problems were
later if you don't keep track as you go along.

Look at the WordStar script as you go through these passes.

PASS 1: TEMPLATE PASS

_____ 1. Start with the first window in the lesson. Look at the
   window and check it for:

 - colors (are they consistent with the template?)
 - appropriate template window (is a question screen used for
   a question, a concept screen for a concept, etc.?)

 - correct border on text boxes

 - correct coordinates (placement on screen) for text boxes

 - text in correct place in box (not too close to box edge,
   centered, or whatever course calls for)

_____ 2. Repeat step 1 for every window in the lesson.

_____ 3. Repeat steps 1 and 2 for each lesson in the
      course.

Figure 8.4 is a sample of detailed instructions to the EPSS evaluator. It
represents a subset of the elements to be reviewed and tested in detail.

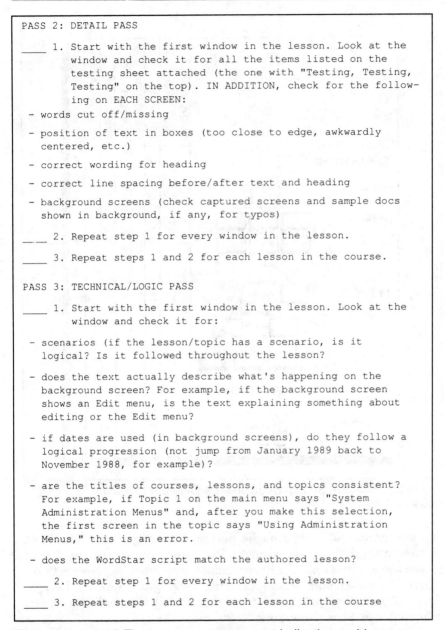

PASS 2: DETAIL PASS

_____ 1. Start with the first window in the lesson. Look at the window and check it for all the items listed on the testing sheet attached (the one with "Testing, Testing, Testing" on the top). IN ADDITION, check for the following on EACH SCREEN:

- words cut off/missing

- position of text in boxes (too close to edge, awkwardly centered, etc.)

- correct wording for heading

- correct line spacing before/after text and heading

- background screens (check captured screens and sample docs shown in background, if any, for typos)

_____ 2. Repeat step 1 for every window in the lesson.

_____ 3. Repeat steps 1 and 2 for each lesson in the course.

PASS 3: TECHNICAL/LOGIC PASS

_____ 1. Start with the first window in the lesson. Look at the window and check it for:

- scenarios (if the lesson/topic has a scenario, is it logical? Is it followed throughout the lesson?

- does the text actually describe what's happening on the background screen? For example, if the background screen shows an Edit menu, is the text explaining something about editing or the Edit menu?

- if dates are used (in background screens), do they follow a logical progression (not jump from January 1989 back to November 1988, for example)?

- are the titles of courses, lessons, and topics consistent? For example, if Topic 1 on the main menu says "System Administration Menus" and, after you make this selection, the first screen in the topic says "Using Administration Menus," this is an error.

- does the WordStar script match the authored lesson?

_____ 2. Repeat step 1 for every window in the lesson.

_____ 3. Repeat steps 1 and 2 for each lesson in the course

Figure 8.4 (cont'd) The tester creates a report indicating problem areas and needs. Once revisions are made, those areas are reevaluated. Reproduced with permission of Comware, Inc., Cincinnati, Ohio.

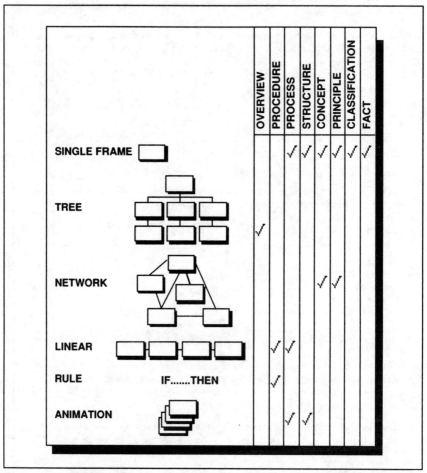

	OVERVIEW	PROCEDURE	PROCESS	STRUCTURE	CONCEPT	PRINCIPLE	CLASSIFICATION	FACT
SINGLE FRAME			√	√	√	√	√	√
TREE	√							
NETWORK					√	√		
LINEAR		√	√					
RULE		√						
ANIMATION			√	√				

Figure 8.5. Effective Screen Structures for Different Info-Maps™
Courtesy Barry Raybould

by incorporation of a hypermedia design. Similarly, they should not be hamstrung by original sequential or hierarchical structures that reduce the effectiveness of a hypermedia-based mode of presentation." (Larry Bielawski and Robert Lewand, *Intelligent Systems Design, Integrating Expert Systems, Hypermedia, and Database Technologies,* John Wiley & Sons: New York, 1990, page 138).

The Problems of Mapping Relational Information

There is a set of significant, yet unanswered questions about how to define, represent, and relate multiple types of multimedia information. Questions include:

• How do you map complex, interrelated, multimedia information?

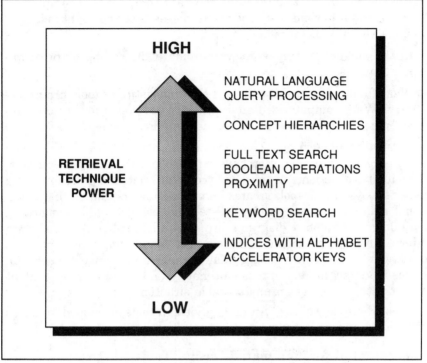

Figure 8.6. Relative Power of Different Retrieval Techniques
Courtesy Barry Raybould

- How can hypermedia structures that include any and all organizational schemes ranging from linear and hierarchical through relational and network be represented for both design and easy maintenance?

- What about the relationships between information and user condition or context within software or task performance? How do you represent the relationships to assure clarity and completeness?

- How can we store and represent this information so it can be structured for review and verification by nontechnical domain or subject matter experts?

- How do we store this information in a form amenable to the inevitable editing, revision, and updating that accompany the review and update processes? Can we structure both the information and its representation to permit rapid update by nontechnical personnel?

- Can this design and representation process be accomplished manually, or are powerful electronic tools required?

245

- How do we minimize stress, the constant companion of complexity, as we reach beyond our capacity to define and represent relationships verbally or on paper?

- In the longer term, how do we automate the coding or programming process?

- What functions, capabilities, and characteristics of tools are necessary? What computerized environments developed for systems development appear promising for use in EPSS design?

Answers to such questions are not simple, and few in the fields of training and documentation have experience with these problem sets. Even limited experience in developing complex relational programs using hypertext systems or tools creates immediate understanding that traditional manual (or even automated) techniques such as flow charting, outlining, and webbed diagrams are painfully inadequate. And once others must review or change programs, the design representations quickly fall of their own weight. Maintenance and change of such programs is largely limited to those intimately familiar with their content and structure. Clearly an unacceptable situation!

So where do we look? Automated design tools developed for other disciplines appear promising.

The Potential for Automated Design Tools

Clearly, automated computer design tools are available. Computer-aided design (CAD) tools for creating multidimensional, manipulable, and flexible representations of designs of physical objects or structures exist and have been widely implemented. Because they are representing familiar physical structures, users can easily relate to them. Real payoff is associated with their use before designs are committed to production. Users can extend their existing paradigms and easily understand how and when to use these tools.

Similar automated design tools have been developed for modeling abstract processes and information. These computer-assisted software engineering, or CASE, tools are growing in popularity and installed base. CASE tools provide the ways and means to represent information and processes in both hierarchical and relational form by using automated diagraming software. They provide the ability to create and quickly maintain "maps" of "entities," "processes," and "data" and the links among and between them. In the terminology of trainers and writers, these are "audiences," "procedures and processes," and "content."

Problems in Using CASE Tools for EPSS

Limited Implementation success to date among systems developers. Implementation and utilization of CASE tools within the systems development community has been only modestly successful to date because users must reframe their thinking and adopt new paradigms associated with information engineering (for a description of information engineering, see James Martin, *Information Engineering, Books I and II,* Prentice-Hall: Englewood Cliffs, New Jersey, 1990). Paradigm shifts do not come easily. And the use of CASE tools requires system developers to make a major shift from focusing on *processes or transactions* to focusing on *modeling data.* Developers must employ the extended relational analysis (the concept is described in Richard L. Synoradzki, "Basic Data Modeling," *Information Center,* September 1988) or information engineering process, rather than conventional process analysis techniques. This is a hard shift to make.

These points are related to EPSS development in that developers from conventional disciplines such as instructional systems design (ISD) have typically focused on *task analysis* and have largely considered *content analysis* as a way of simply listing and hierarchically organizing the information associated with task performance. Developers have rarely, if ever, been involved in the kind of relational analysis of information associated with hypermedia and context-sensitive linking.

Language within CASE tools does not directly relate to commonly used language in training, documentation, and artificial intelligence. Translations must be made—and people are resistant to such translations.

CASE tools are structured largely to generate applications software in the Cobol programming language. Cobol or other languages are not necessarily the appropriate environments within which to construct EPSS. Specialized versions of CASE tools would be necessary to produce advisors, hypermedia infobases, etc.

We lack sufficient clarity about our needs to jump into the CASE tool process without significantly more knowledge, skill, and thought.

CASE tools have a steep learning curve associated with their methodologies.

CASE tools are relatively expensive and require workstations to utilize them.

THE BUSINESS OF COSTS AND TIME ESTIMATING

Given the range, breadth, depth, media, number and types of components, individualization capabilities, hardware and software platforms, and nature and scope of content and tasks that EPSS can be developed to support, it's virtually impossible to give time and cost estimating guidelines. In *Making CBT Happen,* I summarized thirty-seven variables that contribute and interrelate in the time and cost estimating process for CBT alone. Once other types of components such as advisory systems and hyper-reference are brought into play, the estimating process is further complicated.

Table 8.2 is a partial list of factors that should be considered in time and cost estimating, and Figure 8.7 shows graphically how they affect time and expense.

It is important to remember, however, that an electronic performance support system is different than the sum of its parts. For example, when CBT is integrated with hyper-reference, there is far less development of tutorials in the traditional sense of the word. The CBT component then may be more or less time-consuming to develop depending on the number and nature of the interactions involved. Manage expectations around the learning curve and the lack of direct parallels while we are learning what goes into EPSS time and cost estimating.

Frankly, we've been developing information systems for twenty-five years, and the time and cost estimating associated with that development appears to get worse, rather than better. I'll leave this topic on that optimistic note...

IMPLEMENTATION ISSUES

There are important implementation issues to consider. Elegant design and development are irrelevant when implementation planning is inadequate. Poorly implemented performance support systems may either never be used or fall into disuse. Effective sales people know that no products sell themselves—and that even products with high payoff to the user are neglected when inadequately introduced into environments where people are under pressure and lack the luxury of time to explore new software or products.

What are the issues?

Implementation Planning. Implementation planning must be adequate to generate and sustain momentum around the EPSS and its use. The nature and depth of the plans required will vary based on product complexity, the characteristics and skills of the target user population, technological support requirements, amount of effort required to change behavior and to learn how to use the EPSS, relative advantage to the users, computer experience, and local management commitment to and sponsorship of the EPSS. Other factors include the political impact of the EPSS (in other words, what effect it will have on power and control of individuals or groups previously working without its availability). Politics should not be underestimated. Really good products can be killed from either political attack or lack of political sponsorship. See the chapter on sponsorship and critical success factors for a more detailed discussion of required sponsorship and potential sources and types of resistance to EPSS implementation.

Training on EPSS Use and the Use of EPSS in Training Programs. Whether users must be trained on the EPSS and its use is related to its design, ease of use, content, relationship to other systems, technological requirements, and the computer experience and skills of the target user populations. In my experience to date, it is desirable to conduct orientation or training experiences on the EPSS itself so that individuals are *proficient* in its use and understand what's in it and how it benefits them personally.

Some organizations develop CBT programs to train on EPSS use. If self-directed learning is the desired training mode *and* use of the EPSS is strategic or has considerable payoff, then you will have to institutionalize (i.e., require and monitor) requirements for users to complete the CBT course(s). Without this institutionalization, good intentions go down the drain when competitive demands on time surface. And they always do.

Other organizations introduce EPSS in seminars or group contexts. Much depends on user geographic location, human resource available for EPSS training and introduction, and organization culture. The confidence of the target user population and their experience with computers is also a factor.

Remember, also, that the availability of EPSS can dramatically change the way training is conducted. If people can get what they need on the job when they need it, the requirements to fill people up with information in advance decrease or are eliminated. As is illustrated in the Dow Chemical case study, the possibility of changing the nature of the training experience itself emerges. So consider how things might be different with EPSS availability—and reorient your training experiences accordingly.

Administrative Procedures and Processes. There must, of course, be appropriate administrative procedures and controls in place prior to and after initial implementation. The specific procedures required are a function of the nature of the EPSS, the technological delivery environment, and organizational philosophy around the EPSS use (i.e., *must* people use it for certain activities or is its use *discretionary?).*

For example, at Aetna Life & Casualty, there is a performance support tool around the Aetna Management Process (AMP). The PC-based tool works people through the process, steps, and deliverable development for evaluating business alternatives or alternative ways of doing work in the company. AMP is very similar to the total quality process. The sponsor of the process and the EPSS is the company

Table 8.2

THE VARIABLES IN TIME AND COST ESTIMATING

Design Variables
- Number of components
- Types of components
- Complexity of components (e.g., complex simulations in the interactive learning component vs. limited tutorial structures; rule-based expert systems vs. simple decision-tree structures)
- Interrelationships (i.e., links) among and between components
- Scope of the infobase, including breadth and depth
- Number of information views required to tailor information to specific categories of users (e.g., by location, job title, etc.)
- Media required, type and complexity
- Links to and from applications or productivity software
- Requirements to build task-specific software for calculations, analysis, variable manipulation, etc.
- Whether standard user interfaces will be employed (e.g., Microsoft Windows or Macintosh) or unique user interfaces must be constructed
- Design specification standards
- Reusability and extensibility of modular/granular design structures, including information (i.e., object-oriented)
- User tracking requirements
- Reporting requirements
- User customization options
- Requirements for accessing or outputting data into software or deliverables (e.g., constructed elements)
- Availability and quality of source materials
- Stability of content

Technical Variables
- Available development tools for hardware/software platform
- Match between development tools and design requirements
- Nature of the tools (i.e., object-oriented or other structure)
- Tool stability
- Tool complexity
- Tool flexibility
- Number of tools that must be learned and supported
- Requirements for integration of tools
- Delivery platform capabilities and limitations (e.g., non-graphics terminals limit use of graphics)
- Availability of automated design tools, such as CASE

Human Variables
- Knowledge, skill, and experience of development team
- Number of team members involved
- Quality of team relationships: ability and willingness to communicate synergistically

Table 8.2 (Continued)

THE VARIABLES IN TIME AND COST ESTIMATING

- Degree of management sponsorship
- Commitment and available time of non-team members involved in the project
- Percentage of team members' time dedicated to the project
- Staff turnover in team and client organization
- Staff motivation
- Number of projects team has worked on together before
- Political factors
- Management pressure
- User expectations
- Role clarity

Other Variables

- Project development methodology (i.e., structured, tightly controlled)
- Availability of standards, templates, agreed-on conventions

president. It's his intent that *all* proposals and cost benefit analysis be performed within the context of this tool. He expects that the deliverables to successive levels of management are direct products of the system. In other words, he wants the AMP EPSS to influence the *way people work*. Naturally, the kind of sponsorship, communications, consequence management, and controls associated with that goal is *very* different than the user-controlled utilization of the *Word for Windows* EPSS discussed in the case studies. For example, if middle managers accepted presentations that were not a product of the AMP EPSS, people would quickly get the message that its use is discretionary.

On the other hand, if one of the intended outcomes of the *Word for Windows* EPSS were to reduce calls to the help desk, it would be very important that help desk staff work people through how to use the installed EPSS, rather than answer the request directly. In other words, the message the help desk must communicate is that users should first attempt to solve their problems or answer their questions themselves. Monitoring activity must be suitable to the objectives.

Understanding, anticipating, and managing *resistance* to EPSS are important for successful implementation. Resistance is discussed in detail in Chapter Five.

Involving Appropriate Others. When implementing EPSS, it's important to understand whether and how other organizational units can provide assistance in implementation. Actively involve appropriate individuals and groups in implementation planning. Depending

EPSS Development Time and Cost: A Profile

PROJECT COMPLEXITY ↑ / **TIME & EXPENSE** →

- Fewer than three components, including hypertext
- Decision-tree structure advisors
- Linked components
- Standard user interface
- Limited, agreed-on content/process
- Available, quality source materials
- Strong sponsorship
- Expertise in one or two departments
- Known hardware/software platforms
- Text with only limited, static graphics
- Experienced developers, skilled in tool use
- Available EPSS models that match the need

- Three or more integrated components
- Several media
- Complex or voluminous content
- Content and subject/task experts available
- Experienced developers, familiar with tools
- Stable development tools/platform
- Some available EPSS or component models
- Motivated team members who work well together, even when multiple departments/functions involved
- Strong sponsorship

- Six or more components
- All components integrated and cross-referenced
- Complex, voluminous content
- Multimedia, including sophisticated, animated graphics, video, sound
- Complex expert systems
- Links to software
- User interface must be constructed
- Voluminous content with multiple types of user access required
- Content must be developed while constructing EPSS
- Data exchange with software or databases
- Multiple sponsors with mixed or limited commitment
- Numerous departments involved
- Turf battles
- Lack of experience with hardware or software platforms
- Development tools new to market with limited installed base/user experience
- Initial EPSS project by inexperienced developers
- No available EPSS models for the type of application being developed
- High political risk

Figure 8.7 shows the variables that contribute to time and cost. While no formulas can be provided, since an individual variable (such as inadequate sponsorship) can cause even a simple project to be expensive, this model shows how complexity interacts with time and expense. Use it as a jumping-off point to estimate time and cost in development.

on the EPSS nature, scope, and technological platforms for delivery, you may need to involve one or all of the following functions:

- Training

- Systems

- Systems training

- Information center

- Help desk

- Union representatives

- Documentation or technical publications

- Expert systems development

- Special interest groups (e.g., customer groups).

Of course, there may be others who should be included, even though not listed above.

Evaluating Utilization, Effectiveness, and Impact. This is a hard area to be specific about, because the nature and amount of effort expended on tracking use, effectiveness, and business impact will, again, vary widely based on the situation, the EPSS itself, the organizational culture, and the urgency of statistically demonstrating use and results.

In my experience, tracking results is important. Utilization level is less important than impact, but some effort to systematically evaluate use, reaction, and impact will be important at early stages of EPSS design and sponsorship. This is true even when there is an enthusiastic leap of faith made about the concept or the particular product. Consider the following in determining the nature, depth, and duration of your monitoring activity.

- What results would be important to sponsors? To users? To staff groups?

- Why?

- What indicators would be both necessary and sufficient to either maintain their commitment or overcome resistance?

- Is emotional reaction of users of interest? (i.e., do they *like* it?)

- What numbers should be tracked or generated? What use will they be? Who will want to see them?

- How long should tracking and reporting go on? Should it be intermittent?

- What degree of formality or statistical precision will be necessary within the culture?

- Will this vary based on the criticalness of the EPSS in supporting business functions or in relation to the support or resistance of those involved?

- Who would benefit from knowing about the results?

- Is it important to track utilization of all components of the EPSS? Why? Is it useful to track utilization to determine whether such functionality should be built into future EPSSs?

- What mechanisms must be built to get feedback about required changes, content, problems with clarity, bugs? Consider users, functional groups, business experts, customers, and so on.

- Should focus groups be conducted with users? Who should know the results?

- Should various tracking mechanisms available within development software (e.g., authoring systems, expert system shells) be used? If so, for how long? If so, what should be tracked?

In the Innovis DesignCenter case study, there are reports from independent market researchers about the satisfaction and utilization of the DesignCenter EPSS. You may recall being more directly impressed with such clear and positive results than you were with simple anecdotal results. If so, there's a message in your experience: keep people's attention on the benefits and impact. If you don't, someone else will get the attention, sponsorship, and resources for their activity—even when yours might be more important.

CHAPTER 9

Technology

Nobody has printed any
roadmaps for navigating the
uncharted territory of tool
selection and use, but we know
the general topography from
the reports of people who have
been there.

I have said a great deal about the human and political aspects of EPSS in this book, but technology is fundamental to the concept. Both hardware and software technologies are, after all, permitting us to define, develop, and implement electronic performance support systems. For over a decade, many have labored in the fields of interactive training, on-line reference, and expert systems. And developments have been substantial. But until a critical mass of technological alternatives that could be *integrated* emerged, EPSS was hardly even a fantasy.

In fact, elements of what we have discussed have been successfully developed in more limited technological environments. The ability to create expanded help, context-sensitive reference, and interactive training programs that could be accessed from mainframe-based applications software has existed for several years. And hypertext tools, authoring systems, and expert system shells have been combined (to varying degrees) to create development platforms that resulted in quite powerful EPSSs. Some hardware environments, such as the Macintosh series of computers, also support multimedia representation of information without substantial additional investment. The graphical user interface and the very nature of graphical machines spurred development of the EPSS concepts. The appearance of development environments such as *HyperCard* and *SuperCard* have resulted in an explosion of creative activity.

To date, most of the more creative applications have been developed on the Macintosh platform because of the availability of rich development software, the common graphical user interface, multitasking, and multimedia capabilities. These attributes and tools generated the creative mind-set and the means to implement the visions. I fully expect equally creative work to emerge in *Unix*, OS/2, and MS-DOS machines—especially in graphical user interface environments.

As was demonstrated by the developers of the AT&T Training Consultant (see the AT&T Case Study), even a limited technological environment such as an MS-DOS computer without windowing capability can be sufficient for certain types of EPSS applications. In this chapter, however, we will be focusing on the environments necessary to support more robust EPSS designs and implementations.

Longer term, we can expect that computer workstations will replace personal computers. And these multimedia machines will be networked and behave as virtual machines, responding to almost any input mode, including voice. They will permit any type of output and display. And this rich functionality will be available in increasingly portable environments. For now, however, we will discuss the technological issues associated with 386-based (and higher) machines operating in windowed environments or Macintosh II family of machines or workstations, such as Sun and Hewlett-Packard. *Unix*-based machines are currently lagging behind in interface and multimedia capabilities, but it won't be long before capability exists there.

This discussion of technology is *not* intended to cover specific products, except by way of example of a type of tool or to illustrate a capability. No endorsement of mentioned products is intended. Because the rate of change in the software marketplace, it's possible that new and better tools will appear before the ink dries on this page. And vendors will appear, disappear, merge, and purge on an ongoing basis.

The objectives of this chapter are, however, to:

- *describe minimal hardware and operating system environments* within which powerful and robust EPSS can be developed,

- describe the *types of development tools* necessary to construct EPSS components and features,

- briefly describe the *relationships between development tools and design*, and

- to surface some considerations and guidelines related to *software selection*.

BUILDING AN EPSS DEVELOPMENT PLATFORM

It's important to understand that because of the range of components, functionality, and types of information and support within an EPSS, you will have to *build or construct* a development platform that:

- can develop and/or execute in your hardware, operating system, software, and data communications environment

- permits construction of the functionality, record-keeping, data exchange, and media you require

- permits integration of that functionality (e.g., hypertext linked to rule-based systems) with other components or functions via links, a front end, or other means

- is affordable

- can be used by the development staff you have available or who can be hired or contracted with.

While many of the development tools that are available today are interesting and powerful, and some even multi-function, there is likely no individual tool that will meet all of your needs. Of course, the product marketplace changes daily—and it is not unreasonable to believe that integrated platforms developed with EPSS production capability in mind are not far into the future. But none are evident today.

257

There are many tools and technologies available to build performance support systems. They include:

Infobase Development Tools

- computer-based reference systems
- hypertext systems
- electronic documentation systems
- text management and retrieval systems.

Interactive Training Development Tools

- CBT (computer-based training) authoring systems
- concurrent authoring systems.

Advisory System Development Tools

- knowledge processors
- rule-based expert system shells
- case-based expert systems
- procedure-based expert system shells
- object and frame-based expert system tools.

General Purpose Tools

- graphics editors
- word processing tools
- flowcharting software
- database management systems.

Special-Purpose Tools

- animation software.

Programming Environments

- scripting and extension languages
- programming languages
- object-oriented languages
- "card"-based development tools such as *HyperCard* and *SuperCard*.

It's important to note that tools initially perceived to be associated with a given EPSS component might be appropriately used to develop another component. For example, if the advisor component of your EPSS is suited to a decision-tree structure, a hypertext development tool would be more appropriate to use than an expert system shell. Often, a hypertext system can be used to represent the knowledge or information that would normally be contained in an authoring system for the CBT component. By organizing the information in a hypertext mode and using the CBT authoring tool to construct interactions or track user performance, you can reuse the reference information within the infobase. Remember not to fixate on the use of a tool based on *what it is called or how it is marketed.* Creative evaluation may result in broader application and use. It is far more desirable to *limit*, rather than to increase the number of platforms employed in EPSS development. Limiting the need to learn, support, and license numerous tools has many benefits. On the other hand, be certain you have *all* of the tools you need. The most important outcome is employee performance, and development complexity may not be the thing that should be traded off.

The appropriateness and applicability of a given development tool are a function of what you want to build and the hardware and operating system platform you are building for. Within a given category of tool, capability, functionality, ease of use, and support vary widely. And these development systems vary considerably in how they handle such key design issues as presenting graphics, finding information, handling complex information, and providing "hyperprogramming" capabilities to develop custom navigation and displays.

There are a number of critical questions that must be answered and issues that must be discussed *before* you can construct an EPSS development platform. The issues are related to *EPSS design considerations, technological considerations,* and *managerial considerations.* Since these issues and the answers to the questions vary based on each EPSS development situation, no single definitive set of selection criteria are appropriate. Be certain that knowledgeable people are involved in the tool evaluation and selection process. If key factors are not considered, you may find your EPSS design is a function of the limits and structures of the tools you select, rather than what is required.

TECHNOLOGY CONSIDERATIONS

Tools: Features, Function, and Requirements

Platform requirements

- What hardware/operating system platform(s) will you develop on?

- What hardware/operating system platform(s) will your EPSS be implemented in?

- What common user interface does the tool support? If none, how acceptable or compatible is the tool interface?

- Are there software standards within your organization that limit consideration of other tools (e.g., for expert system shells, authoring systems, etc.)?

- How will any custom interface be developed?

- Can the alternative development tools be integrated with your planned EPSS common user interface?

- How compatible are the development tools with existing platforms, communications, software, operating systems, and so on?

Technical Integration

- Can the various tools under consideration be technically integrated within the EPSS? What effort or technological support is required for integration?

- What data exchange capabilities do the tools support?

Relationship to Design Requirements

- How well do the attributes or structures of the alternative development tools match your EPSS design requirements (i.e., are they amenable to your design or will considerable effort be required to accomplish your desired outcome?)? What, if any, critical needs will not be addressed by the tool(s)?

- Are there products available that provide preconstructed *shells* and functionality which can be populated with your information, data and processes? If so, can these be customized to accommodate the number of steps in your processes, etc.?

Product Integrity and Capability

- How mature and stable is the product? What experience exists among users in relation to bugs, documentation, support, and ability of the products to perform as promised? How reliable is the product under various software and performance conditions?

- What future product capabilities are planned? Do they matter for your application? How far along is development? What confidence do you have in their delivery?

- What is required for in-house installation and support (e.g., technical expertise, systems programming, software, lead times)?

- How many organizations use the product?

Maintenance

- What is involved in maintaining or changing information, structure, or design? What are the costs of updating the system?

Scalability
- Can you expand the content of a prototype system to a full-scale system without running into limitations of database size, storage requirements, or maintenance problems?

Design

Functionality Requirements
- What functionality is required to support user needs (see discussion of components and power in Chapter Four)?
- What is the nature of the EPSS infobase? Size? Types of information? Modes in which information must be represented? How does the tool match the requirements?
- Will you be using a standard interface convention, such as Macintosh or Microsoft Windows, Open Look, or OS/2, or will you be constructing the interface?
- Do you need hyperprogramming?

Information Search and Retrieval
- How do you want users to find information? What alternative information search and retrieval mechanisms are desired? Query-based retrieval? Prowsing-based retrieval (e.g., hypertext, hierarchical outlines or tree structures, manually constructed indices, database retrieval)?
- How complex is it for users to learn the search techniques?
- How do the tools match the requirements?

Advisory Support
- How will you handle complex information and processes such as analysis and decision making? Will expert systems be required? If so, is rule-based, case-based or decision tree table support best?
- How do the tools match the requirements?

Media Support
- Do you need graphics or other media to represent information or processes?
- Can you use available external graphics files or media?

Customization Potential
- Will you want to identify specific information, activities, levels of detail, and so on to accommodate identified user populations so that access is limited to specific user profiles such as location, security level, job title, task, and so on?

- Will users be able to customize their view or version of the EPSS? By what means?

- Will users be able to add, change, or delete information from the EPSS?

- How well do the tools match the requirements?

Structured Learning Experiences and Assessments

- Will structured interactive tutorials (CBT) be needed? If so, what instructional strategies are required?

- Will the tutorials link to applications software to execute concurrently? Must links be context-sensitive?

- Will the tutorials link to the reference base or infobase? Must links be context-sensitive?

- Are performance assessments or tests required? If so, what type? Will reports be necessary? Are they for users only, or must reports be developed for others?

User Tracking

- Must user activity within any or all components be tracked? What activity? What reports or information are necessary?

- If the EPSS links to applications software, must user activity within the software itself be tracked? What will be done with the tracking information (e.g., used as input to expert system, to invoke structured learning experiences, and so on)?

- Will users be able to print any or all information from screens, infobase, tutorials, advisor recommendations, etc.?

- Will users be able to cut and paste information or output from the EPSS for use in other electronic or printed documents?

- Will users be able to provide electronic notes for personal use? To developers?

MANAGEMENT CONSIDERATIONS

The Development Community

- Who will be using the development tools to design and construct the EPSS? What design and computer skills do they possess?

- Will the people doing maintenance or information updates and changes be the same or different from developers? If different, what skills do they have in relation to the required activity?

- How much structure will developers need for component development? How can sufficient structure be built using methodology and tools?

- How difficult will the tools be to learn and use by the anticipated developer population? How long will it take to learn to minimally use the tools? To possess sufficient depth to develop and execute adequate design? How long does it take to become sufficiently proficient on the tools to support the particular design anticipated?

- What are the attitudes, skills, and experience of your anticipated developers? Are they motivated to learn if their current skills and knowledge are less than required by the development tools?

- Is a sophisticated programmer required to generate the functionality and design? Is such expertise available?

- What other organizations are using this tool? What is their experience with the tool? Vendor?

Available Training and Support

- What type of training and support are available for development tools? From the vendor? From other sources, including within your organization?

- What is the nature of the training and support? Are computer-based resources available? Telephone support? How responsive is the vendor?

- Where is the training offered? Vendor site? Your site? Public training programs?

- Is training and support available from third party consultants?

Costs

- What are the costs for purchasing the tools? Is pricing based on the number of installed copies? Utilization? Are volume discounts available?

- Are there different costs for development versus run-time or delivery versions of the tools? Are site licenses available? What about pricing for network versions of the system?

- Are royalty payments to the development tool publisher required if EPSS products are sold or distributed outside of the developer organization?

- Are upgrades included in purchase or licensing costs? If not, what costs are involved in upgrades?

- Is the system available for a test or evaluation period? What are the costs?

- Are there any installation expenses?

- Are training and support included in the purchase/lease price? What additional costs can be anticipated?

- How much do service contracts cost? Would a multiple-site installation affect costs?

Vendor Capabilities

- How experienced is the vendor with EPSS, including the integration of their tool with other tools?

- How financially stable and viable are the tool vendors? What track record do they have in the marketplace?

- Do user groups exist for various development tools? What do they do? Will involvement be helpful?

- What other consulting or support services does the vendor offer?

Consultants

- What consultants are available with skills/resources for development using the tools?

- Where are they located?

- What costs are associated with development (including time, travel, and living expenses)?

OTHER APPROACHES TO EVALUATION

Larry Bielawski and Robert Lewand in their book *Intelligent Systems Design: Integrating Expert Systems, Hypermedia, and Database Technologies* (John Wiley & Sons: New York, 1990), devote considerable attention to understanding and selecting alternative development tools. Their approach to tool selection focuses on four environments.

- The applications environment, or what you are building

- The development environment, or technological considerations

- The user environment, or the user interface

- The run-time environment, or the delivery environment.

They develop several tool selection criteria for each of the environments, and I refer you to page 101 of their book for a summary table. It provides yet another perspective on the topic. In Chapters

Nine and Ten of their book, they review a number of PC-based and Macintosh-based intelligent systems development tools using their guidelines. Be sure you update the information, since many of these tools are dynamic—and the information is based on early 1990 releases. It also represents the particular reviewer perspectives.

Of course, there is an industry focused exclusively on software review. It's likely that your organization subscribes to services that offer detailed, ongoing evaluation of available tools. Several references in the bibliography of this book, including the PDR summary, include extensive software reviews.

To assist those identifying and evaluating EPSS development tools, Barry Raybould of Ariel Performance Systems, Inc. in Mountain View, California (Telephone [415] 694-7880) has developed an EPSS on a diskette to assist in the process: The *International Guide to Performance Support System Authoring Systems*™ This PC-based software product, which runs on a 286+ AT-class machine contains:

- a hypertext information base of vendor-supplied information on EPSS hypertext, expert system, and CBT authoring system tools for PC, Macintosh, U*nix*, and mainframe machines

- an advisor that works users through establishing criteria for tool selection; the advisor then compares user requirements to the available products and develops short and long lists for consideration; users can access the product hypertext infobase for more information

- limited tutorials about the concepts and features of the types of tools.

This interactive guide can assist in product identification and provide yet another perspective on the tool selection process. In addition, it is a means of acquainting yourself with the EPSS concept in action. It's an imaginative effort.

FUTURE ISSUES

We are rapidly learning that many of the development tools, such as hypertext platforms, were never designed to deal with the huge volumes of information stored in manuals and reference sources in our business and government organizations. These tools that permit cross-referencing require manual connections to be made among and between chunks of information. Tools like H*yperCard* by Apple Computer and *Toolbook* by Asymetrix, for example, do not include the means by which to map connections.

Developing techniques for mapping huge amounts of cross-referenced information (for both controlled development and easy maintenance) will soon become a priority. In Chapter Eight, we briefly discussed the potential for the application of computer-assisted software engineering (CASE) tools in the EPSS design and development process. Because EPSS is a new concept—and because information systems management is working hard to successfully use CASE tools in the traditional systems development process, little attention has been paid to this application of CASE tools to date.

It will be necessary *sooner*, rather than later, to address this issue. The types of cross-referencing activities we are experiencing in the early use of hypertext will soon be unacceptable, and we will need to seek more powerful electronic design environments to manage this process. CASE tools are the ones available now. Other types of tools, yet to be conceived of, are also a possibility. Keep yourself informed on these subjects.

Once one gets beyond initial EPSS advocacy and pilot EPSS design and implementation, it will quickly become clear that many of the structures, such as Advisory components and Infobases, can or should be reused across EPSS applications. Object-oriented databases and programming languages offer the potential for creating EPSS components that stand alone and function—and yet can be reused and extended across applications. The grand vision of an encyclopedia of functional components that can be mixed and matched and configured like electronic *Lego* blocks is before us. Object-oriented programming (OOP) concepts are relatively new—and the development of object oriented development environments is likely to be the foundation of the next generation of EPSS development tools. Again, keep an ear to the ground on this technological area.

TRADEOFFS

There are, of course, *always* tradeoffs involved in tool selection. One of the best T-shirt slogans I've ever seen sums up those tradeoffs. It read: "I'm not perfect, but parts of me are *excellent!*" As with people, your relationship to a software tool may involve taking the bad with the good.

The tradeoffs basically fall into three categories:

Power vs. Simplicity. The easier things are to use, the less you can typically do with them. Complex tasks require complex design, that is, design is typically tightly coupled with technical complexity.

Structure vs. Freedom. The more structure the tool imposes in terms of menus, prestructured sequence, design capabilities and limits, interface, etc., the less creative you can be with it.

Productivity vs. Creativity. Tools that have built-in templates and other mechanisms for productivity typically have accompanying reductions in creative possibilities. The more creativity the tool permits, typically the more difficult it is to use—and the more the development environment looks like programming (e.g., extension languages are programming languages, even if the commands look like normal language). Creativity usually involves complex logic.

Of course, these tradeoffs are not one-for-one. And, as more and more functionality and flexibility are built into tools, optimization can increase. But rarely do you get mileage and acceleration in a single model. And remember, the more flexibility, the more developers will *play* to make things work. There's good and bad news in those options. And beauty is in the eye of the beholder as it relates to available time, money, performance pressures, and so on.

And because there are likely to be numerous *types* of tools in the EPSS development platform, the evaluation and selection tasks must consider interrelationships among and between software, as well as evaluation of an individual tool's capabilities.

MAKE THE USER EXPERIENCE YOUR PRIORITY

It's imperative that priorities be clearly established so that confusion and uncertainty don't result in anxiety that limits positive action. The unconditionally highest priority must be that the EPSS users can get what they want when they want it without undue logistical or technological complexity. This can be accomplished with relatively simple and straightforward technology. There are some excellent examples using hypertext systems—or even the hypertext system in Microsoft Windows alone. In this world, sometimes less is more. An ounce of elegant design is worth more than a king's ransom in technological tools.

A clean, consistent interface and well organized, integrated accessible information and support go much further than technical pyrotechnics. After all, user support, rather than developer amusement and challenge, is the *raison d'etre* of electronic performance support.

NETTING IT OUT

In summary, software can be enabling or limiting. It is important to evaluate all the technological tools we discussed—and more—integrating them based on needs and technological compatibility. Involve appropriate technical resources (read "people") if your own technical knowledge or confidence is not sufficient for adequate analysis and decision making. Having the right combination of tools for the tasks at hand makes a big difference in both output and quality. In short, it makes life a lot easier.

Note: The work and publications of Barry Raybould of Ariel Performance Systems, Inc., Mountain View, California, and Gerry

Puterbaugh of AT&T Paradyne were important influences on this chapter. I want to extend my thanks for their development of these ideas and their contributions to the field. References to their work are in the bibliography at the end of the book.

CHAPTER

Strategy

When you adopt electronic
performance support systems,
you will have a strategy—
whether you know it or not.
Recognize what you are doing
and control it.

A *strategy* is the science and art of employing the political and economic forces of a group to afford the maximum movement toward a goal. Webster adds that it's "a careful plan or a method." I agree. At the next lower level, *tactics* are "the art or skill of employing available means to accomplish an end." Typically tactics are smaller-scale actions serving a larger purpose.

In my consulting work, I see a broad range of strategies and tactics surrounding EPSS. Some strategies are conscious, deliberate, and well planned. Others are random and reactive. Some support carefully thought-through objectives for using EPSS to address performance needs. Others don't relate to the business per se but support a goal of "using the computer for its own sake." Frankly, using the computer for its own sake seems to me irresponsible, irrelevant, or both. Using it to address real unmet business needs is a necessary condition for success in most organizations. But regardless of your goal, strategy is the key.

Whether it's conscious or unconscious, planned or reactive, every organization has a strategy. Successful organizations, vendors, or advocates for a particular activity clearly and consciously articulate objectives, formulate a general approach to getting there, and develop specific tactical plans to move themselves toward the goal. Managers monitor conditions and goals as they implement strategies and tactics, making changes when appropriate.

The degree to which strategy development is more or less important and formal is a function of how you view EPSS. If you see it as an activity that is another alternative to add to the array of approaches to employee development, only moderate strategy development is necessary. You begin with an *activity* view and migrate toward a *major change* view as you develop success. If you view EPSS as a fundamental change in the way you accomplish performance in your organization, an early in-depth strategy is necessary.

In my opinion, we are embarking on an *age* during which our efforts will be focused on reorganizing the knowledge bases within our organizations. This effort is analogous to the reorganization of business information into strategic databases that began two decades ago. The database evolution is still going on after twenty years of effort and still employs legions of analysts and programmers. Strategic implementation of EPSS is likely to require similar time frames and resources.

Currently, much activity around electronic performance support is in the area of developing pilots that are essentially a "proof of concept" or in solving an individual problem (such as sales support). There are also individual large-scale efforts to integrate EPSS with major software systems development. Such activity is important. But once the concept is demonstrated, evaluated, and proven, an overall organizational EPSS strategy must be developed and appropriate sponsorship obtained. After all, if the effects of EPSS are so substantial, strategic implementation of EPSS to support mission-critical objectives can be an enormous marketplace and performance advantage.

I'll summarize the general components of an effective EPSS strategy, and then I'll go one step further by describing one for you to use as a departure point in thinking through your own. A successful EPSS strategy should contain

- clear, achievable results or outcomes in the business, educational, technological, political, or psychological arenas (e.g, solving business problems, creating technological architecture, building commitment levels)

- alternative general approaches to achieving these results or outcomes (e.g., educating, developing commitment levels, creating a technological architecture) and the determination of whether the strategy will be to "start small" and build incrementally or "start big" and address a broad range of development in a consistent and in-depth manner

- identification of key sponsors (see the chapter on sponsorship) whose political, logistical, or economic support is necessary to legitimize and institutionalize the activities throughout the organization

- specific tactical plans for activities to achieve strategic goals (e.g, conducting an in-house EPSS conference to establish a broad base of understanding of the concept and its implementation; identifying three priority business problems that EPSS can solve better than current practice or traditional training; funding an EPSS pilot project)

- clear definition of roles, players, and responsibilities (of sponsors, facilitators, "doers," managers, vendors, and consultants)

- identification of possible resistance sources in the organization; development of strategies to manage that resistance (see the chapter on justification and resistance)

- monitoring and evaluating activities.

To see how these elements fit into a plan, examine Tables 10.1 and 10.2. One is a set of goals, objectives, and action steps, together with advice for implementing them. The other is a sample three- to five-year strategic plan for an organization that already believes electronic performance support systems will pay off. This comprehensive plan was developed from the perspective of a staff person functionally responsible for implementing EPSS as a concept. If it had been written by a line manager whose concern was solving a particular business problem and for whom the rest of the organization's needs were irrelevant, the plan would be different. A plan, of course, must fit the objective of the person or group who develops it.

For an organization unsure of how actively or whether to pursue EPSS, a simpler plan would be more appropriate. You can limit your strategy simply by selecting elements from Table 10.2. Learn what constitutes a strategy, build one appropriate to your organization, and get necessary sponsorship to make it work. Then, determine whether and when you should go to the next step.

Use the components of the comprehensive strategy in Table 10.2 as a laundry list of ideas for your more limited strategy. Or think up entirely different things. Remember, the strategy must fit the nature and magnitude of the goals—and defining specific goals is where you start. The strategy must also fit the organizational culture to be successfully implemented and integrated into the business operations. These are necessary conditions for success.

Table 10.1

GOALS, OBJECTIVES, AND ACTION STEPS FOR IMPLEMENTING ELECTRONIC PERFORMANCE SUPPORT SYSTEMS (EPSS)

GOALS

Goal. Refocus attention from activities, such as training and expert systems development, to performance conditions, requirements, and outcomes. Reframe thinking from historical frameworks and paradigms and solutions (e.g., training, documentation) to a broader perspective.

Goal. Assure consistent employee performance. Accelerate employee performance and performance development.

Goal. Redefine the means by which employees are trained and supported during job performance based on new technological alternatives. To incorporate the best of the traditional alternatives and minimize or eliminate their relative weaknesses.

Guidance for Setting Goals: Define goals in terms of needs and outcomes, *not* project or product.

Table 10.1 (Continued)

GOALS, OBJECTIVES, AND ACTION STEPS FOR IMPLEMENTING ELECTRONIC PERFORMANCE SUPPORT SYSTEMS (EPSS)

TWO DISTINCT APPROACHES

START SMALL. Acquire a full range of EPSS development capabilities, but limit investment until value has been concretely demonstrated and development and implementation skills have been acquired and demonstrated.

or

START BIG. Develop substantial in-house EPSS development capabilities quickly and proceed with widespread, high dependency applications with aggressive timetables.

Guidance for Determining Approach to Objectives: Think Big. Whether you choose "Start Small" or "Start Big," design the whole picture first, then look at how you want to proceed so each component you develop fits.

Objective. Find the right problem

Action Step. Identify high impact applications for EPSS concepts and systems and support those jobs or tasks with commercially available or custom-developed EPSS solutions. Clearly articulate the business and performance problems. Involve others and seek necessary political support to effectively surface situations that have not been successfully addressed due to lack of effective alternatives.

Action Step. Identify problems that are:

• Likely to succeed

• Important to your organization

• Solvable by new technology

• Difficult or impossible to solve using existing, conventional methods

• Capable of leveraging your existing investments in technology, people, and skills.

Action Step. Educate, involve and work collaboratively with all appropriate organizational units currently involved in traditional aspects of training and performance support (e.g., training, documentation, systems development) to gain widespread commitment to the resultant vision and strategy.

Objective. Narrow the list

Action Step. Rigorously justify the recommendations through development of a business case which includes efficiency, effectiveness, and value-added outcomes. Include management sponsorship potential in the equation.

Table 10.1 (Continued)

GOALS, OBJECTIVES, AND ACTION STEPS FOR IMPLEMENTING ELECTRONIC PERFORMANCE SUPPORT SYSTEMS (EPSS)

Objective. Identify, organize, and secure resources

Action Step. Develop an understanding of the technological, organizational, political, logistical, and human resource requirements associated with EPSS development and implementation.

Action Step. Redefine the desired organizational and staff structure necessary to effectively and efficiently develop EPSS. Anticipate which individuals and groups need or want to be involved, based on who would use the EPSS, who must provide input or approve the system or its content, and who must sponsor its development and implementation. To accomplish this redefinition, ask:

- who would use the EPSS
- what data or knowledge they need
- where that data or knowledge is now
- what form it must be in
- what electronic tools, systems, or data EPSS users will need in addition to the infobase content
- what technology is required for development and implementation
- who controls, funds, or has input to the above
- who decides what is implemented.

Action Step. Recommend a short and longer term technological architecture for EPSS development and implementation, including hardware and software and multimedia alternatives. To integrate recommendations with the overall technological strategy and direction of the organization.

Guidance for Specifying Architecture: Again, apply the "Think Big, Work Small" approach. When you look at the entire architecture, you can look at each piece and identify numerous alternatives. If you only have one alternative, you probably don't know enough to proceed. You will find all kinds of technical, business, economic, and political issues surfacing. Be prepared for them. Of course, all alternatives should be evaluated in relation to requirements.

Objective. Win management sponsorship

Action Step. Recommend a strategy, including approach and timeframes, for design, development, and implementation suitable to the business requirements, organization culture, technological environment, and available financial resources.

Table 10.1 (Continued)

GOALS, OBJECTIVES, AND ACTION STEPS FOR IMPLEMENTING ELECTRONIC PERFORMANCE SUPPORT SYSTEMS (EPSS)

Action Step. Develop and maintain strong and widespread senior management sponsorship for the EPSS strategy in the initiation stage. Identify and develop equivalent support among those who must sponsor and sustain the effort over time.

Guidance for Gaining Sponsorship: Remember, consider exploiting external connections and use external resources to validate your ideas and recommendations. External sources include vendors, customers, competitors, and consultants. Remember, initiating and sustaining sponsors are usually different people.

Objective. Set and manage expectations—and deliver on them

Action Step. Create realistic expectations about process, requirements, resources, schedules, and economic commitments through education and communication.

Develop and deliver EPSS prototypes and initial products and systems.

Implement EPSS products and institutionalize their use.

Guidance in Managing Expectations: Creating realistic expectations does *not* mean you should fail to communicate the big picture. It means managing expectations about what you can do toward achieving the big picture within a given time frame.

Objective. Monitor, evaluate, and communicate. Pontificate, too.

Action Step. Evaluate the effectiveness, impact, and acceptability of EPSS. Incorporate findings in future strategy, development, communications, and implementation efforts.

Action Step. Assure that all required individuals and groups are fully aware of the results and the reasons for them.

Guidance for Communication: Don't underestimate the *communication* required. People will *think* they understand what you mean, and they won't. Keep going back until you are sure that the concepts and operational implications are clear. Communicate with presentations, circulating articles, vendor presentations, and so on. You can never communicate too much, or even enough, for that matter.

Table 10.2
STRATEGY AND TACTICS IN SUPPORT OF GOALS AND OBJECTIVES

STRATEGY. Identify and evaluate potential application areas and recommend scope, nature, and content of EPSS development.

Benchmark and network with other companies, competitors, and industry leaders and consultants. You'll learn a lot and develop fuel for the fires of internal commitment building and design.

> **Tactics.** Identify business problems, pain points, unacceptable costs or conditions, competitive problems, or other indicators of needs. Review management reports, task force or study group activities and reports, quality team efforts, turnover problems, error conditions, HELP desk or support group activities and problems, overhead and cost indicators such as scrappage, yield, etc.
>
> Identify externally-developed generic and custom-developed EPSSs to stimulate ideas and evaluation. Demonstrate them for your organization. Assist others in generalizing from their structure, problem category, etc.
>
> Work collaboratively with others within and outside the organization throughout the process.
>
> Prioritize needs in relation to potential for EPSS to be successfully designed and implemented to address them.

STRATEGY. Develop a broad base of knowledge and understanding of EPSS concepts and design, interactive technologies, development requirements, and commercially available tools. Make sure you have options at every stage.

> **Tactics.** Retain external consultants with specific knowledge in EPSS for one-on-one or group educational activities. Concentrate on reframing the problems from training or documentation to performance problems, EPSS design concepts and execution, technological alternatives, strategy components, development process, marketplace issues, appropriate applications, and so on. Use software tool vendors as resources.
>
> Exploit the work being done by others in your organization. Take advantage of their research, experience, and so forth. Be sure you understand hidden agendas when people communicate their opinions. Recognize that people who've spent time and money on technology or other types of programs will fight hard to convince you they have chosen the *right* solution.
>
> Attend public conferences, meetings, and trade shows, workshops, and seminars. Specifically attend the Electronic Performance Support System Conference (sponsored by Weingarten Publications, Inc.). As appropriate, attend meetings devoted to components of EPSS (e.g. artificial intelligence, CBT, hypermedia). Network and benchmark. Record the outcomes of the benchmarking and networking activities. Keep accurate records so you exploit the information.
>
> Participate in local groups or professional association programs whose membership, agenda, or focus relates to EPSS or its components.

Table 10.2 (Continued)
STRATEGY AND TACTICS IN SUPPORT OF GOALS AND OBJECTIVES

Purchase or borrow commercially available or custom-developed programs for review and evaluation to increase understanding of applications, effective and ineffective design, instructional strategies, and learner perspectives when using EPSS. Whenever possible, evaluate programs developed in, or intended for, your industry. Sources: consultants, technology tools vendors, peers in other companies, commercial product vendors, custom-development vendors.

Read:

- *Electronic Performance Support Systems* by Gloria Gery (Weingarten Publications, Boston, 1991)
- *Making CBT Happen* by Gloria Gery (Weingarten Publications, Boston, 1987)
- *Intelligent Systems Design: Integrating Expert Systems, Hypermedia, and Database Technologies* by Larry Bielawski and Robert Lewand (John Wiley & Sons, New York,1991)
- *Mapping Hypertext* by Robert Horn (The Lexington Institute, Lexington, MA, 1989)
- *Information Engineering—Introduction, Book I, Book II*, James Martin, Prentice-Hall, Englewood Cliffs, NJ, 1989
- *CBT Directions* (magazine from Weingarten Publications, Boston, MA)
- *Performance Improvement Quarterly* (a publication of the National Society for Performance and Instruction, Washington, DC)
- Other media or technology publications and newsletters.

As appropriate development tools are identified, bring them in-house for pilot evaluation.

Attend and become moderately active in the software user groups or attend the national users' group meetings. Maintain communication with internal staff who are piloting or evaluating development tools.

Make a presentation on internal EPSS activities at a major regional or national conference.

Use vendors to educate yourself.

STRATEGY. Assume responsibility for educating constituents to a common understanding of EPSS.

Build general knowledge, understanding, and commitment to EPSS among staff and line management within the organization. This will be an ongoing activity. Things will change quickly, so you must maintain organizational knowledge and enthusiasm.

Generate common definitions of terms and concepts. Create a language for EPSS that is both understood and used.

Identify key EPSS sponsors within the training and line management organizations and target activities toward building their commitment and solving their performance problems.

Table 10.2 (Continued)
STRATEGY AND TACTICS IN SUPPORT OF GOALS AND OBJECTIVES

Develop and maintain knowledge about and communication of internal results among departmental and divisional training management.

Tactics. Develop among targeted sponsors specific understanding of the training issues and problems. Identify driving and restraining forces associated with use of EPSS. "Qualify" targets based on need, potential for commitment building, available resources, and technological delivery possibilities. Target activities toward areas and people of high success probability.

Structure educational and commitment-building activities toward targeted units. Provide formal and informal learning opportunities for training and line management personnel with training needs where EPSS might apply. Don't underestimate what is required. Do not assume that people who say they are qualified to do things like developing hypertext *are* qualified. They may not be. Activities include:

- Conducting internal meetings or symposia or briefings focused on EPSS
- Developing an internal library of related books and journals accessible to interested people on a loan basis
- Circulating information, articles, case studies, handouts from conferences, conference information, seminars etc. as appropriate (target distribution based on organization level, function, and need)
- Conducting periodic demonstrations of software development tools, and generic or custom EPSS products for both general and targeted audiences
- Developing an internal library of commercially available EPSS products for evaluation or use
- Scheduling periodic seminars and workshops addressing management, design, technical, and other issues (e.g., authoring system skill workshop, EPSS design seminar)
- Providing broad access to external consultants hired for general discussions, specific problem-solving activities, education, or "motivation" to internal developers
- Conducting one-on-one meetings and demonstrations with targeted potential trainers or line managers with EPSS potential. Place priority on the most likely "buyers" and those most likely to solve business problems not currently being addressed by conventional training alternatives
- Developing an internal EPSS users' group or task force for ongoing relationship development, education, and communication by internal EPSS users
- Developing ad hoc study groups or teams for specific EPSS activities (e.g., recommendation of technological architecture, evaluation of development tools, courses, etc.)
- Actively using vendors and other companies to assist in your education and demonstration efforts

Table 10.2 (Continued)
STRATEGY AND TACTICS IN SUPPORT OF GOALS AND OBJECTIVES

- Reporting monthly on activities, results, issues, and problems to sponsors, advocates, and appropriate others. Determine the appropriate people to report to. Consider individuals and groups who must understand what you are doing throughout the organization. Find the appropriate mode for communicating.

STRATEGY. Gain experience with EPSS development. Use experienced custom developers to assure successful pilot courseware development. Actively participate in development effort to bring knowledge and skill in-house.

Tactics. Establish criteria for pilot EPSS projects. Identify high payoff EPSS applications.

Establish a specific and controlled development process to assure timely and high-quality EPSS development.

Fund the development from centralized funds, but assure investments and sponsor commitment within targeted organization (possibly shared funding). External funding sources should also be considered (e.g., vendors).

Establish criteria for external vendor selection.

Jointly evaluate vendors and proposals with client organization.

Jointly manage EPSS development, including standards development, and project activities, with client organization.

Retain external consultants as appropriate to educate, maintain control, and participate in design.

Evaluate resulting EPSS, including critical evaluation of the EPSS development process, learning effectiveness, and learner reactions.

STRATEGY. Identify organizational, administrative, reward system, and policy issues that must be addressed for effective EPSS implementation.

Tactics. Identify policies, practices, monitoring and measurements, and reward systems that need study regarding EPSS (e.g., rewarding trainers for activity using *student days* or body counts, requiring learners to take formal *courses* to demonstrate learning, equating courses with certification, record keeping). Determine whether they are positive, negative, or neutral in relation to EPSS use in this organization.

Assess the specific organizational culture in relation to EPSS (e.g., does the culture place a high value on live instruction; does the culture support or resist efforts to apply computer technology to problems; is the culture able and willing to make a paradigm leap to EPSS or is it more likely to accept only incremental change, and so on). Consider external customer cultures and expectations if the EPSS is likely to be directly seen or used by customers (e.g., in sales support systems using laptop computers, field engineering use of computers in troubleshooting, or customers assuming responsibilities previously performed by your organization).

Table 10.2 (Continued)
STRATEGY AND TACTICS IN SUPPORT OF GOALS AND OBJECTIVES

Evaluate the impact of the above on EPSS sponsorship, design, development, and implementation. Consider various sponsors, change agents, and target groups.

Develop recommendations on organization and administration. Obtain management sponsorship for any required new or changed policies and practices.

STRATEGY. Evaluate and recommend an EPSS architecture that is compatible with the organization's existing hardware and software architecture. Identify and evaluate any short-term issues or limitations that affect EPSS development and implementation. Establish the architecture with options to accommodate technical, political, and economic alternatives.

Tactics. Obtain formal and informal documents regarding internal information systems hardware and software architecture and future plans.

Evaluate alternative EPSS technological development and delivery alternatives. Articulate tradeoffs.

Capitalize on research and work done by external and internal organizations, including targeted groups within the organization. Use external consultant resources as necessary. Involve internal information systems, training, documentation, expert systems groups, and line managers in the study, and evaluate. Benchmark with other organizations.

Recommend short- and long-term EPSS development and delivery architecture, including hardware, and design, authoring, programming, and delivery software.

Gain appropriate management sponsorship for the recommendation, including those who are able and willing to enforce the policy.

Maintain awareness of what vendors are communicating to other units within the organization. To the extent it is possible, limit their access to other units to avoid confusion, proliferation of incompatible tools, and duplication of expense. Become as familiar as possible with all available technological alternatives and their relationship to both your technology and your requirements. Be alert to others continually suggesting tools they use, know, or have heard about and you will need to be able to discuss them intelligently in terms of their viability and desirability for your situation.

Monitor internal and external technological activity, including evaluation of tools and recommendation of new tools as they emerge.

CHAPTER

Philosophy and Politics

Electronic perfomance support
raises a host of tough
questions, but there's a world
of excitement in the answers.

Innovation and change have consequences, both anticipated and unanticipated. In seeking to address current problems or needs, we often create new ones. And, as you know, sometimes we find out that in the long run, the cure is worse than the disease. What do electronic performance support systems portend? Over time, as full-blown EPSSs emerge, significant changes will take place in our organizations. It would be hopelessly naive to think this concept could alter two centuries of workplace history without creating serious philosophical questions. We may well find ourselves without answers, but we owe it to ourselves to start thinking about the issues now, before we are forced to.

TOUGH QUESTIONS

What will employee training and development look like when the employees have access to information, coaching, examples, and advice at the moment of need? Will training as we know it exist at all? Will training be shorter, different, focus on different things? Will it be more task-based? How will we track it? Does it matter?

Will we care whether people actually *know* things—or will we only care that they can *do* things while they are being electronically supported?

Will people have incentives to strive for mastery, expertise, levels of recognition? If so, how will we define these things? Will the things they strive for be different? Will motivation deteriorate? If motivation deteriorates as a result of EPSS, what can we do about it?

Will we want to certify people's competence? If so, how? If so, why? If so, on what? If not, why not?

Will functional areas in training, documentation, help desks, and so on remain in their current form? Will they merge? Will they exist at all? Or will the structures, templates, and means be available for line managers to construct EPSSs and other interactive programs independent of of these traditional functions?

What implications will EPSS have for trends in *empowerment, flatter organizations, self-managed teams, and customer-focused organizations?* Will EPSS be the means by which these noble goals are accomplished, or will it have a negative impact?

How will employees feel when much of their interaction and support occurs via computer?

What implications are there for group or team work? How can EPSS be integrated into group process? Should it?

What implications does EPSS have for the way we currently assign, monitor, and evaluate work and compensate people for it?

Will people still have defined job descriptions with assigned salary levels? Or will there simply be a wage, since employees at various levels of skill and experience will be able to perform similar work with similar performance outcomes?

What kind of individual, group, and organizational incentive systems will be appropriate? Will we need or be able to differentiate among and between employees in terms of task performance? Will interpersonal skills, style, and charisma be the key points of differentiation?

Will customers prefer to assume the work previously performed by company employees or agents? If they can assume tasks or get information via EPSS, is this a good or bad thing? Will we charge for the EPSS as we now do for service or information or time?

What implications does EPSS have for *where* work is performed? Will it extend the global reach of organizations? Will Third-World development accelerate? What implications are there for the American economy? Will EPSS accelerate outsourcing professional and technical jobs to be performed in India, Barbados, and Brazil much as data entry activities are now performed? What are the economic implications?

Will various types of *offices* disappear? Will the *virtual office* come into its own with people working out of their cars? Out of their homes? On their boats?

Who will support and resist this concept, and why? Will unions and other employee-focused groups view this as positive or negative? Enabling or restricting? Expanding or eliminating jobs? Will trainers, documentation specialists, and other staff professionals lead or resist the charge?

Where will leadership come from? Is this going to be driven by systems professionals or line managers who live with the performance development issues? Training? Documentation? Senior management?

What will happen to the vendors of authoring systems, on-line reference systems, hypertext tools, and expert system shells? Will they merge? Permit integration of their products with other products? Where will the *glue* that holds different types of software together come from? Or will new integrated software development platforms emerge? From what quarter?

LIMITED ANSWERS

Of course, there are no answers right now. In fact, most of these questions have not yet been raised. I predict, however, that the answers or approaches will be hashed out in hotel bars in various Level

One convention cities all over the world. The discussions will inevitably move from bars to conference rooms and, ultimately, to board rooms. The issues around organization, reward systems, employee development strategies, and work itself will continue to be discussed, fueled anew by the implications of electronic performance support systems.

INNOVATIVE THINKERS, APPLY HERE

If you've ever stood in line for one of the more thrilling rides at a modern theme park, you've had the opportunity to read warning signs. Those with heart conditions and back problems, pregnant women, and so on are advised not to get on the ride. I wish we could post similar signs for those waiting to get on the EPSS development ride.

This ride is not for the faint of heart or those who need absolute certainty about what to do, how to do it, and what will happen *before* they begin. It is also not for provincial thinkers who are *deeply committed* to points of view, disciplines, or ways of doing things that are grounded in the past. Those who hate dealing with politics need not apply. And those with the naive belief that you can develop sophisticated and powerful systems without getting deeply involved in technological questions and software should get out of line right away. Nobody is going to think any less of you if you find a nice bench to sit down on.

Those who don't see any *need* to do things differently should bear in mind this is not the ride they just left. They might still be humming "It's a Small World" and thinking about slow boats and singing dolls. EPSS is more like "Back to the Future," and riders must be prepared for high-tech thrills, chills, and time warps. Yes, you get knocked around, but it's unbelievably exhilarating, and you won't *want* to go back to the singing dolls. I speak from experience on both rides!

Those who seek an emotional charge and who can tolerate periods of considerable dizziness and disorientation, will love this ride. It's important, as we walk the fine line between exhilaration and terror together, that we understand there are safety precautions that make the ride thrilling and safe at the same time. These are not mutually exclusive conditions, so it's necessary to heed the advice and instructions of those who've been there, while recognizing that their experience, while valid, is still very limited.

Those among us who are able and willing to think beyond action plans and development tools will need to surface these political, organizational, and philosophical issues relatively quickly to begin the necessary dialogs. Sooner or later, these questions—and those we have yet to even think of—come along with the introduction of major innovation and change. I encourage you to be among those who lead the charge in creating the visions that will so dramatically affect work itself and have the potential for such impact on human performance, self-esteem, individual satisfaction, and organizational life.

Enjoy the ride!

Bibliography

Ambron, Sueann and Hooper, Kristina. *Interactive Multimedia: Visions of Multimedia for Developers, Educators, and Information Providers.* Microsoft Press: Bellevue, Washington, 1990.

Apple Computer. *Human Interface Guidelines: The Apple Desktop Interface.* Addison-Wesley Publishing: Reading, Massachusetts, 1987.

Barrett, Edward. *Text, ConText and HyperText, Writing with and for the Computer.* MIT Press: Cambridge, Massachusetts, 1988.

Bielawski, Larry and Lewand, Robert. *Intelligent Systems Design, Integrating Expert Systems, Hypermedia, and Database Technologies.* John Wiley & Sons: New York, 1990.

Brooks, Frederick P. *The Mythical Man-Month: Essays on Software Engineering.* Addison-Wesley Publishing: Reading, Massachusetts, 1979.

Clark, Ruth Colvin. *Developing Technical Training.* Addison-Wesley Publishing: Reading, Massachusetts, 1989.

Davis, Stanley M. *Future Perfect.* Addison-Wesley Publishing: Reading, Massachusetts, 1987.

Dervin, B. "Information as a User Construct: The Relevance of Perceived Information Needs to Synthesis." In Ward, S.S. and Reed, L.J. (Eds.) *Knowledge Structure and Use: Implications for Synthesis and Interpretation.* Temple University Press: Philadelphia, 1983.

Diamondstone, Jan. "The Workplace as Upstairs, Downstairs," *CBT Directions,* April 1991.

Dick, Walter and Carey, Lou. *Systematic Design of Instruction.* Third Edition. Scott Foresman, Little, Brown Higher Education: Glenview, Illinois, 1990.

Engelbart, D.C. "A Conceptual Framework for the Augmentation of Man's Intellect." In Howerton, P.D. and Weeks, D.C. (Eds.) *Vistas in Information Handling, Vol. 1.* Spartan Books: Washington, DC, 1963.

Frenzel, Lou. *Crash Course in Artificial Intelligence and Expert Systems.* Howard Sams Publishing (Division of Macmillan): Indianapolis, Indiana, 1986.

Frenzel, Lou. *Understanding Expert Systems.* Howard W. Sams (Division of Macmillan): Indianapolis, Indiana, 1987.

Gery, Gloria J. "Closing the Gap," *Authorware Magazine,* January 1990.

Gery, Gloria J. "Computer-Based Reference: Explorations and Issues," *CBT Directions,* March 1991.

Gery, Gloria J. "Electronic Performance Support Systems," *CBT Directions*, June 1989.

Gery, Gloria J. *Electronic Performance Support Systems*. Weingarten Publications: Boston, 1991.

Gery, Gloria J. *Making CBT Happen*. Weingarten Publications: Boston, 1987.

Gery, Gloria J. "The Quest for Performance Support Systems," *CBT Directions*, July 1989.

Gery, Gloria J. "Training vs. Performance Support: Inadequate Training is Now Insufficient," *Performance Improvement Quarterly* (National Society for Performance & Instruction) Volume 3, 1989.

Harless, J.H. "Guiding Performance with Job Aids," In *Introduction to Performance Technology*. National Society for Performance and Instruction: Washington DC, 1986.

Harmon, P. and King, D. *Expert Systems*. John Wiley & Sons: New York, 1985.

Harmon, P. and King, D. *Expert Systems, Artificial Intelligence and Business*. John Wiley & Sons: New York, 1988.

Harmon, P and Pepper, J. "Toward an Integrated Maintenance Advisor," *Hypertext '89 Proceedings*. Association for Computing Machinery: New York, 1989.

Horn, Robert. *Mapping Hypertext*. The Lexington Institute: Lexington, Massachusetts, 1989.

Horton, William. *Designing and Writing Online Documentation, Help Files to Hypertext*. John Wiley & Sons: New York, 1990.

IntelliCorp. "How to Get Started in Knowledge Systems. IntelliCorp's Guide to Getting Off On the Right Foot," IntelliCorp Software & Services: Mountain View, California ([415] 965-5500).

Johnson, Scott. "Cognitive Analysis of Expert and Novice Troubleshooting Performance," *Performance Improvement Quarterly* (National Society for Performance & Instruction) 1(3), 1988.

Jonassen, David. *Hypertext*. Educational Technology Publications: Hillsdale, New Jersey, 1988.

Jonassen, David. *The Technology of Text*. Educational Technology Publications: Englewood Cliffs, New Jersey, 1985.

Kolodner, Janet L. "Improving Human Decision Making through Case-Based Decision Aiding," *AI Magazine*, Summer 1991.

Kearsley, Greg. *On-Line Help Systems, Design and Implementation.* Ablex Publishing Corp: Norwood, New Jersey, 1988.

Kuhn, Thomas S. *The Structure of Scientific Revolutions*, Second Edition. University of Chicago Press: Chicago, 1970.

Learning Systems Institute (Florida State University), in cooperation with the National Society for Performance & Instruction. *Performance Improvement Quarterly Special Issue on Emerging Information Technologies*, Volume 2, Number 3, 1989.

Lemons, Larry. "PSS Design: Getting Past that First Step," *CBT Directions*, February 1991.

Linton, Frank. "A Coach for Application Software," *CBT Directions*, March 1990.

Martin, James. *An End User's Guide to Data Base.* Prentice-Hall, Inc.: Englewood Cliffs, New Jersey, 1981.

Martin, James. *Information Engineering, Book I: Introduction.* Prentice-Hall, Inc.: Englewood Cliffs, New Jersey, 1990.

Martin, James. *Information Engineering, Book II: Planning and Analysis.* Prentice-Hall, Inc.: Englewood Cliffs, New Jersey, 1990.

Moscicki, John. "Just in Time Training," *Co-Action Magazine* (Authorware, Inc., Minneapolis, Minnesota) Autumn 1988.

National Society for Performance and Instruction. *Introduction to Performance Technology.* Washington, DC, 1986. (ISBN-9616690-0-4.).

Neilsen, Jakob. "The Art of Navigating through Hypertext," *Communications of the ACM*, vol. 33, March 1990.

Neilsen, Jakob. *Hypertext & Hypermedia.* Academic Press, Inc.: San Diego, California, 1990.

Nelson, T.H. *Dream Machines.* The Distributors: South Bend, Indiana, 1974.

Owens, George. "Building a Business Case," *CBT Directions*, February 1989.

PDR Information Services. *No Hype, Just Media: An Independent Evaluation of PC Hypermedia Software.* (2901 Tasman Drive, Suite 215, Santa Clara, California 95054).

Puterbaugh, Gerry. "CBT and Performance Support," *CBT Directions*, June 1990.

Puterbaugh, Gerry and Raybould, Barry. "PSS Development Platforms." Presentation at the Ninth Annual Computer-Based Training Conference, San Antonio, Texas, April 1991 (Weingarten Publications).

Raybould, Barry. "Building an Electronic Performance Support System: Comparing Alternative Development Platforms," *Proceedings, Eighth Conference on Interactive Instruction Delivery.* Society for Applied Learning Technology: Warrenton, Virginia, 1990.

Raybould, Barry. "Choosing the Right Hypertext Product for Performance Support," *CBT Directions*, July 1990.

Raybould, Barry. *International Guide to Performance Support Authoring Tools.* (Ariel Performance Systems, Inc., 100 View Street, Suite 114, Mountain View, California 94041 [415] 694-7880). (This is an IBM-compatible electronic performance support tool for development software selection. It includes an expert system, hypertext product description, and database.)

Raybould, Barry. "Solving Human Performance Problems with Computers. A Case Study: Building an Electronic Performance Support System," *Performance & Instruction* (National Society for Performance & Instruction), November/December 1990.

Romiszowski, A.J. *Developing Auto-Instructional Materials.* Nichols Publishing: New York, 1986.

Rossett, Alison. "Electronic Job Aids," *Data Training*, June 1991.

Rossett, Alison and Gautier-Downes, J.H. *A Handbook of Job Aids.* Pfeiffer Associates: San Diego, California, 1991.

Schneiderman, Ben. *Designing the User Interface, Strategies for Effective Human-Computer Interaction.* Addison-Wesley Publishing: Reading, Massachusetts, 1987.

Schneiderman, Ben and Kearsley, Greg. *Hypertext Hands On.* Addison-Wesley Publishing: Reading, Massachusetts, 1988.

Synoradzki, Richard L. "Basic Data Modeling," *Information Center,* September 1988.

Tufte, Edward R. *The Visual Display of Quantitative Information.* Graphics Press: Cheshire, Connecticut, 1983 (P.O. Box 430, Cheshire, Connecticut 06410 [203] 272-9187).

Winograd, T. and Flores, F. *Understanding Computers and Cognition: A New Foundation for Design.* Ablex Publishing Corp: Northwood, New Jersey, 1986.

Zuboff, Shoshana. *In The Age of the Smart Machine: The Future of Work and Power.* Basic Books: New York, 1988.

Index

About the Author

Gloria J. Gery is an independent consultant specializing in business learning and electronic performance support in large, complex organizations. She is consulting editor of *CBT Directions* magazine and the author of *Making CBT Happen,* widely regarded as the best practical book on the implementation of computer-based training systems in business. She has written dozens of articles for the trade press on computer-based training and electronic performance support systems and has given hundreds of presentations, both in the U.S. and abroad. Her corporate experience includes three years at Corning Glass Works and twelve years at Aetna Life & Casualty in Hartford, where she was director of information systems education. Her many consulting clients are predominantly Fortune 500 organizations. She lives with her husband Bob (also a consultant) in Tolland, Massachusetts.

Gloria J. Gery can be reached at

Gery Associates
108 South Trail
Tolland MA 01034-9403
(413) 258-4693